20/07

WILLIAM CALCRAFT

Other Books by Geoffrey Abbott

Ghosts of the Tower of London

Great Escapes from the Tower of London

Beefeaters of the Tower of London

Tortures of the Tower of London

The Tower of London As It Was

Lords of the Scaffold

Rack, Rope and Red-Hot Pincers

The Book of Execution

Family of Death

Mysteries of the Tower of London

Who's Who of British Beheadings

Crowning Disasters

Regalia, Robbers and Royal Corpses

Dedicated to my good friends Alan and Eve Fiddes
who, when roped in for advice,
urged me not to hang about
but to stick my neck out,
and write this book!

CONTENTS

List of Illustrations	viii
Foreword	x
Acknowledgements	xii
Chapter One: The Early Days	1
Chapter Two: The Scaffold and the Drop	11
Chapter Three: The Child Killer and the Body Snatchers	16
Chapter Four: A Murderous Valet, a Vengeful Couple	33
Chapter Five: Calcraft is Charged with Neglect	52
Chapter Six: Panic on the Scaffold	69
Chapter Seven: Poisoners and Pirates get Short Shrift	90
Chapter Eight: A 'First Class' Murderer - and Others	106
Chapter Nine: The Strain Starts to Tell	119
Chapter Ten: Calcraft's Last Executions	134
Appendix One: Confessions of the Body Snatchers	153
Appendix Two: Last Messages of the Three Fenians	160
Appendix Three: Broadsheets of Calcraft's Victims	163
Appendix Four: Other Executioners and their Idiosyncrasies	186
Select Bibliography	188
Index	190

LIST OF ILLUSTRATIONS

Section 1
1a: William Calcraft: the "classic" picture
1b: William Calcraft: a rare mid-19th century photo
2a: Calcraft wielding the whip
2b: Calcraft's short-drop noose
3a: A typical deathmask
3b: Dissection in Surgeons' Hall
Newgate Prison – much associated with William Calcraft
4a: Newgate Prison
4b: Old Gateway, c.1750
4c: Multiple hangings at Newgate Gallows, c.1783
5a: Newgate Prison: the scaffold inside the prison
5b: Newgate Prison: Outside this door, public executions were held
Other prisons associated with William Calcraft
6a: Derby: Vernon Street Gaol
6b: Wandsworth: whipping post
6c: Horsemonger Lane Gaol
7a: A broadsheet from the Greenacre trial
7b: John Head, *alias* Thomas Williams; John Bishop
On board the convict ship "Success"
8a: Convict imprisoned in the Black Hole
8b: Punishment by cat-o'-nine-tails
8c: The compulsory salt bath, the victims scrubbed with salt water

Section 2
9a: Daniel Good and Jane in the stable
9b: Daniel Good in the Condemned Cell
10: China statues of the Mannings
11a: The Mannings, drawn in court by Robert Cruikshank
11b: The execution of the Mannings
12: The 'Five Pirates' from *The Illustrated Police News*
Franz Muller and the world's first murder on a train
13a: Broadsheet recording the execution & confession of Franz Muller
13b: Franz Muller
13c: 'Murder on the Railway Train' broadside
14a: The executed Fenians
14b: Drop Table
15a: 1917 Home Office Drop Diagram
15b: William Marwood – Hangman
16a: Muriel Brooke: Great granddaughter of William Calcraft
16b: Thomas Henry Calcraft: Great grandson of William Calcraft

FOREWORD

Many famous executioners have had accounts of their lives published, Albert Pierrepoint, Sid Dernley, James Berry, John Ellis and others, but our great-grandfather William Calcraft surely has claim to be included among those who bestrode the boards of the scaffold, if only because he holds the record of serving longer than any other English executioner - no less than forty-five years, from 1829-1874. Moreover he was the last executioner to carry out a hanging in public in England, that of Michael Barrett in 1868, the last one to carry out a multiple hanging in public, five pirates in 1864, and the last public hanging in Glasgow, Dr Pritchard in 1865.

Nor was that all; he hanged the first man to commit murder on a railway train in this country, Franz Muller in 1864, and was the first to carry out an execution in private in England (i e behind prison walls), that of Thomas Wells in 1868. He was also the last hangman to be a salaried employee, his scaffold successors being engaged only when they were actually required.

William may have had the longest reign, but he used the shortest rope, three feet or less in length, the vast majority of his victims thereby dying slowly by strangulation, but he can hardly be blamed for employing this horrific method of execution, for it was actually endorsed by some medical authorities of the day, who asserted that the very pressure of the rope on the great blood vessels in the neck would, if not actually result in instant death, at least cause the victim to lose consciousness from the build-up of pressure on the brain; 'effusion and concentration of tumours in the brain pan would prevent feelings of torment' was the way they phrased it. The famous diarist Samuel Pepys, in his entry for February 1662, wrote 'All the doctors conclude that there is no pain at all in hanging, for that it do stop all sense and motion in an instant.'

The short drop, then, painful or not, was taken for granted by society in general for most of our ancestor's career. At that time in the 19th century living conditions among the masses

Foreword   xi

were harsh, violent crime widespread, life expectancy comparatively short; hygiene was almost non-existent, illness, disease and epidemics were rife. Teeth were extracted without analgesic (in 1845, the dental records of one London hospital reveal that no fewer than 5,143 teeth were drawn in that manner – ouch!) and hospital operations were carried out without anaesthetics, these benefits not being introduced until much later; patients requiring invasive surgery or amputation were held down by four burly hospital porters while the surgeon wielded his instruments as quickly as he could. Only about fifty percent of the patients survived the ordeal, and of those who did, one out of every three were doomed to die later from blood-poisoning, gangrene or tetanus, antiseptics not being discovered until the late 1860s. Suffering, from one cause or another, was just a way of life.

Understandably then, there was little or no consideration given by those responsible in the government of the day to the possibility of easing or preventing the apparent agonies endured by the victim on the scaffold - and anyway it was morally assumed that he, or she, deserved it! And apart from anything else, the prolonged and gruesome spectacle unfolding on the scaffold provided many thousands of spectators with free and frequent public entertainment!

Not that William, in playing the leading role, was in any way a hero in the eyes of the public - far from it. Throughout the ages, executioners were reviled and abused - unjustly, for without the hangman, what was the point of having laws decreeing capital punishment, then praising the police, the judges and juries for their application of that law, but castigating the hangman for carrying it out? And although 19th century England was far from perfect, our great grandfather was the man who undertook that unsavoury task on behalf of the people. A man of his times, a servant of the State, he was there simply to hang convicted criminals in the regulation manner, not to introduce innovative and humanitarian measures.........!

Muriel Brooke (nee Calcraft)   *Thomas Henry Calcraft*
Great granddaughter   *Great grandson*

ACKNOWLEDGEMENTS

Thanks are hereby tendered to the many librarians and curators in whose departments I spent so much time combing through micro-fiches, local newspaper archives and other records for the merest mention of Calcraft involvement; to Dominic Whiston for his indefatigable efforts in researching little-publicised executions which had taken place in and around his home county; and to the Derby Local Studies Library, the *Times, Telegraph, Derbyshire Advertiser, Derby & Chesterfield Reporter, Derby Gazette, Derby Mercury* and the *Lancaster Gazette*.

My sincere gratitude is also extended to some of William Calcraft's direct descendants, namely his great grandsons Thomas Henry Calcraft and Geoffrey Calcraft, his great granddaughter Muriel Brooke and to his great great grand-daughters, Norma Fern, Elaine Hinchliffe and Anne Baines, whose personal contributions have proved invaluable.

Acknowledgements are due to Lancashire County Council for permission to reproduce the illustration of Calcraft's noose, to Mr. Paul Rose for the Fenian illustrations from his definitive book on the subject, *The Manchester Martyrs,* published in 1970 by Lawrence & Wishart, and to all others who, directly or indirectly, assisted in making this book an informative and, hopefully, a worthwhile supplement to the judicial history of executioners.

Whilst every effort has been made to trace copyright to all material in this book, the author apologises if he has inadvertently failed to credit any ownership of the same.

Photographic work by Chris Holmes, Kendal and Dominic Whiston, Castle Donington, Derbyshire.

CHAPTER ONE

THE EARLY DAYS

William Calcraft was born in 1800, reportedly in the little village of Baddow, near Chelmsford, though he was later to claim that Barnet, north London, was his birthplace. His parents were poor, their financial circumstances further exacerbated by their having twelve children, of whom William was the eldest. He was a bright lad and attended the local free Sunday School regularly, where he learned to write with flair if not altogether grammatically, as subsequent letters to prison governors requiring his services showed.

He grew up to be a tall strong youth, and first tried his hand at being a cobbler, but life permanently spent bending over the last with a mouth full of tacks quickly lost its appeal, and he obtained a job as watchman at Reid's Brewery, Liquorpond Street (now Clerkenwell Road, EC1). By some means he learnt of a vacancy as butler to a gentleman in Greenwich, the gentleman in question perhaps being one of the firm's customers. But he soon became disillusioned with domestic service and, leaving his employer, returned to London. Urgently in need of a job, he realised that a lucrative market existed in catering for the hungry hordes gathered around the scaffold at the frequent executions which took place in the capital, the crowds waiting sometimes for hours for the show to start, and so he became a hawker of such delicacies as pies and sweetmeats. And in supplying the audience, he also became acquainted with the entertainers – the executioners who, at that time, were James Foxton or Foxen and his assistant, Thomas Cheshire.

The characteristic attitude adopted by, or inherent in, the hangmen of the day, was explicitly revealed during an interview with Cheshire in 1828, immediately prior to a multiple execution he was due to carry out;

'While the wretched convicts were ruminating, in the dark

and cold solitude of their cells, on the few minutes left to them of mortality, Tom was amusing the turnkeys, in a room near the drop, in the details of a few of the incidents which have marked his eventful life, till the gaol keeper entered the room and showed a new halter to the orator. He (Cheshire) examined it with a scrutinizing eye and, untwisting a part of it, applied it to his nose, for no doubt the smell of a well-twisted rope is as pleasant to Tom's olfactory nerves as the sweet south wind breathing over a bed of violets. Twice and thrice was the rope sniffed at and when, at last, he held it at arms' length, he broke into criticism "Vy, master, it smells of junk and hasn't been twisted as a halter should be; now here's one" – taking one from his deep pocket – "summat like; it cost me eighteen pence. I've tried all them there ropes with my own weight, at a three-foot or three-foot-two drop, and they'll bear any chuck."

Tom was asked how many of his fellow creatures he had relieved of their worldly cares; he replied "Vy, I've knocked off somewhere about five hundred and fifty, and never had an haccident, because I always carry a good rope. These three" – referring to the unfortunate sufferers about to be consigned to his merciless hands – "makes three more, and then I've another at Oxford and three more a' Wensday at Newgate." He completed his statement with a loud laugh.

Old Tom later inspected the dreadful machine on which he was about to operate. He was asked whether he approved the plan of it. "I call it a foolish thing" he enjoined "It's like going up a church steeple to get to the top of it." It was intimated to him, for Tom always had a good eye for business, that one of the culprits had a good watch in his pocket. "Then it belongs to me, and as soon as he's off, I'll bone it; I don't much mind their clothes, and if their friends wants 'em, they shall have 'em for a fair price."

'Tom now thrust his legs nearly into the ashes in the fireplace' the interview continued 'and, rubbing his hands, which seemed not to have come into contact with soap for the last year, with an expression of the highest satisfaction at his exploits, he entered into a long narrative of some of the principal executions at which he had attended. "I did the business for Mester Fontliroy in style, (Henry Fauntleroy, hanged for forgery, 30 November 1824 – author), everybody said I did it well; and it was a good job, for I got above £3 for his clothes. I tucked up Thistlewood and all them chaps (Arthur Thistlewood, together with Brunt, Ings,

Davison, and Tidd, conspired to overthrow the government, were found guilty of treason and imprisoned in the Tower, then hanged and decapitated in public at Newgate – author); I held all their heads in this here hand" he laughed again "There was a lot on 'em – they never complain after me!"

In this heartless way did *Mister* Thomas Cheshire', so he designates himself, proceed, till it was announced that the prisoners had finished their last devotions in the chapel, and then he hurried out to pinion them, with an alacrity which showed that his horrible mode of life was to him a real pleasure!' Such was the way of life and inhumane attitude of the 19th century executioner!

Despite the pitiless attitude shown by Cheshire and others he had watched perform on the scaffold, Calcraft must have felt that he had the necessary aptitude for such an occupation, and so, probably while listening to Foxton and Cheshire in 1828 discussing the latest scaffold gossip, he heard of the need for someone to assist the Lincoln hangman to execute two criminals. At such a golden opportunity to mount a scaffold rather than ply his confections at the foot of it, he wasted no time in volunteering, and was accepted, although probably did little more than stand by and help with the pinioning when told to do so.

By then he had been married for three years and was only too aware of the need to get a settled job and earn a regular wage; this he put into so many words when, later in life, he was interviewed for a book on his life and recollections (subsequently published in 1880). He said "Trade was bad with me – in fact I could not get anything to do. Being in no way particular what I turned my hand to to earn money, as long as it was honestly come by, one day in December 1828, when I watched four men being hanged, I saw Foxton come out from below the gallows. He appeared to be weak and faint. Poor chap! He wasn't up to his business that day and was evidently a good deal flurried, or may be he was a bit frightened, for there was a mob on that morning, and no mistake. I stood a few yards from him and heard him call for the beer-man, who did not appear to take much notice, so I went up to him and said 'If you want a draught of porter or ale, say the word and you shall soon have it.'

'Can you get me some?' said he; 'Certainly I can.' I replied, and proceeded to oblige. When I returned, he drained off the largest portion, then handed me the remainder, which I refused. 'Ah!' he said 'Too proud, I suppose, to drink with a hangman!'

'I ain't proud at all' I answered 'I will drink with you, and so here's to better luck for both of us.' Foxton said 'I s'pose you can do with a little?' 'With what?' I asked. 'With a little better luck.' he rejoined.

Calcraft went on to describe how he had told the hangman that he wasn't afraid of hard work and would even take to his line of business when he gave it up. At that, he said, Foxton expressed his surprise, warning him that 'It's a miserable calling, a wretched despicable occupation.' But, said Calcraft, that didn't deter him, and he told his new friend that he would take to it if he got the chance. 'Well' said Foxton 'You'll soon have the chance as far as I'm concerned, for I tell you I'm sick of it and mean to turn it in shortly.' On hearing that, Calcraft recalled, he had urged Foxton to put in a good word for him, to which the hangman had said 'Well, you are a rum 'un, wanting to take up my line of business, but since you seem so anxious, I will pass my word to speak for you if ever an opportunity occurs, so give me your name and address.'

Calcraft said that he gave the hangman one of his business cards, Foxton then exclaiming 'Oh, in the shoe-making line, are you?', to which he had replied 'I'm in any line so that it brings something to support myself and my wife' Foxton looked at him; 'What will your old woman say? Does she know you want to take my place?' Calcraft said he remembered laughing as he said 'How can she? I didn't know myself half an hour ago – never dreamed of such a thing!' And when he did arrive home he said to his wife Louisa 'Well, missus, I've had a bit of a game this morning' and then went up and told her all that had occurred. 'Law, never!' she ejaculated 'You, turn hangman! How came you to think of such a thing? Oh, it is not a nice business, to say the least of it!' To which I had replied 'Well, I hope not.' And that part of the interview ended by Calcraft saying 'We were, however, both mistaken."

Some time later Foxton gave notice that he intended to retire in the near future, and the vacancy was consequently advertised. So many crimes carried the death sentence early in that century that there was a continued need for executioners; during the years 1825 – 1831, for instance, there were 410 public executions, the rate running at approximately 70 a year, so it was essential that as far as possible there was always a full complement of executioners.

The obvious choice was the deputy hangman Thomas

Cheshire, who had held that position since about 1808, but 'Old Cheesy' was nearly seventy years of age and also nearing retirement, so the authorities decided to bring in a younger man. The terms of employment were simple and straightforward; to despatch those who had been condemned to death by the courts. No stipulation was given of the need to do this in a caring or humane way; it was accepted and indeed endorsed by society in general that criminals did not deserve it. And anyway, it was considered that the more callous and brutal the execution, the more it deterred other potential criminals.

William discussed the opportunity with his wife, and on her saying that he ought not to go back on his word, he promptly submitted his application, penning the following letter to the Honourable Court of Aldermen for the City of London on 28 March 1829;

'Gentlemen; having been informed that the office of executioner will soon be vacant, I beg very humbly to offer myself as a candidate. I am twenty-nine years of age, strong and robust, and have had some experience in the office. I am familiar with the mode of operation, having had, some months ago, been engaged on an emergency to execute two men at Lincoln. I did so, and as the two culprits passed off without a struggle, the execution was performed to the entire satisfaction of the Sheriff of the County.'

Of the many applicants, two were finally considered for the post, Calcraft and a man named Smith, an ex-soldier who had been a member of many a firing squad. But the Committee for City Gaols, taking into account Calcraft's previous hands-on experience at Lincoln, together with a recommendation by his ally Foxton, expressed their preference for expertise in hemp rather than lead, and decided in his favour.

Initially William spent some time learning the ropes – in more ways than one! – as deputy to Foxton, and shortly after the death of the latter on 14 February 1829, Calcraft became the Number One, it being recorded in reference 563b of the minutes for the period July 1826-August 1829; 'William Calcraft of No. 8 Mount Pleasant East Road, City Road, London was, on 4 April 1829, officially sworn in by the Gaol Committee of the Court of Aldermen as the Executioner for the City of London and Middlesex, taking the oath "to hang or behead or otherwise destroy all felons and enemies of our Lord the King, and of his subjects duly sentenced according to the law, and that I will do the like, unto father, mother, sister or brother and all other kindred whatsoever, without favour or hindrance, irrespective of sex or age; so help me God."'

The salary for this was one guinea a week, the appointment also requiring him to carry out the same duties for the County of Surrey at Horsemonger Lane Gaol, with an annual retainer of five guineas plus one guinea for each hanging. Nor was that the limit of his judicial territory. By 1832 the two hundred and twenty crimes which carried the death sentence had been reduced to fifteen, the penalty for many offences being downgraded to that of transportation to the penal colonies in Australia. As a result of this reduction in the number of executions, most towns wasted little time in making their own hangmen redundant, relying instead on London to provide the necessary official. So Calcraft had a peripatetic way of life, carrying out executions across the country, his 'parish' ranging from Aberdeen to Worcester, Bristol to Carlisle, Chatham to Liverpool, receiving £10 for each hanging, half that sum in the unlikely event of a reprieve.

Prior to the advent of the railways, people rarely ventured far from their own towns and villages, and so communities had their own, local, time, this sometimes varying by twenty minutes or more from that adopted by even neighbouring towns; standardisation was simply not necessary. So rather than risk turning up late for an execution, and also as required by the rules then in force, Calcraft invariably arrived at the gaol the day before, this also giving him the opportunity to inspect the gallows and the doomed criminals, and he continued this practice even after the railway companies had introduced timetables of arrivals and departures, such schedules thereby bringing about 'railway time', the synchronisation of time throughout the country. It also ensured that the hangman, having to spend the night in the gaol, was more or less sober for his next day's task!

On one occasion however, despite reaching his destination in plenty of time, he nearly missed carrying out an execution, for on his arrival he was 'kidnapped' by practical jokers and confined to a house in the town. Meanwhile the sheriff was on the verge of having a heart attack for, in the absence of a hangman, the execution, as laid down by law, would have to be performed by him! Fortunately Calcraft managed to escape later and report to the prison governor, no doubt to be welcomed with open arms.

His job description also included flogging juvenile culprits, usually at Newgate prison (now, appropriately enough, the site of the Old Bailey Central Criminal Court), for which he received 10/- per week and 2/6 for each flogging, plus an allowance for birch rods and cat-o-nine-tails. The former consisted of a number of willows, about four feet in length, plaited together and fastened at one end with strong cord; the latter, a long-handled whip having nine thongs, these being of very hard cord about one-sixteenth of an inch in diameter, each knotted every four inches along their length. Wielding the cat-o-nine-tails was hardly a job for a weakling, sentences of between twenty-four and thirty-six lashes frequently being handed down by the Bench for offences under the *Vagrancy Act* of 1824, which included punishing 'those actions of the vagabond who persistently gathers alms, who begs in public places, neglects to maintain his family, is guilty of sleeping out, destroys works of art in museums, or is guilty of blackmailing'.

This, together with other Acts such as the *Knackers Act* of 1786 against anyone slaughtering horses or cattle without a licence, and the *Treason Act* of 1872 against persons aiming or discharging firearms at the sovereign, gave the judiciary plenty of scope to bring in guilty verdicts, thereby increasing Calcraft's income and muscular development. The application of such fearful instruments to the female anatomy was forbidden under the *Whipping of Female Offenders Abolition Act* of 1820, and when whipping in public was eventually abolished, Calcraft carried out the punishment within the confines of prisons, although this task was later taken over by prison warders.

He admitted that he was somewhat apprehensive on the first occasion he had to administer a flogging; when questioned later in his career, he said "When I arrived at the flogging yard I felt a little nervous, being afraid I may make some mistake; four young ruffians had to undergo the punishment. The mode of operation had already been explained to me by the prison officials, and I got through the task in a way which seemed to be altogether satisfactory to those who were present during the infliction of the punishment, which I have always maintained is both salutary and efficacious when administered judiciously to young ruffians who, as a rule, dread the lash more than a lengthened term of imprisonment.

"I soon found out" he continued "that it was very rare indeed for a (court) sessions to pass over without a batch of juvenile delinquents having to be flogged. But the days are altered since then, and now other modes of punishment are substituted in lieu of flogging. I am free to confess that I did not like the lash at first, but in a very short time I got used to it, and looked upon flogging as part of my duty."

His not ungenerous income was supplemented by other, more traditional perquisites. He was entitled to the clothes worn by his victim on the scaffold, sometimes selling them for display in Mme Tussaud's Baker Street Galleries and similar exhibitions; he also sold small lengths of the ropes he had used, as souvenirs or for allegedly curative purposes, charging 5/- an inch or more, depending on the notoriety of the victim, malicious rumours asserting that on occasions the total length of rope sold following a hanging exceeded the length of the Strand! Literally a case of 'money for old rope'!

However since his main income depended on the frequency or otherwise of executions, he augmented it by continuing his earlier trade of shoe-making, and then settled down with his wife Louisa, whom he adored, in their house in Devizes Street near the Rosemary Branch, Islington, not far from the common and the church, a rural area which, until about 1835, was dominated by two windmills. When going to an execution he would leave home early in the morning or after dark, carrying a small canvas bag containing his 'tackle', ropes, straps, restraining belt and white cap; walking in somewhat of a shambling manner, he would look straight ahead and ignore passers-by.

When not travelling all over the country to despatch felons on provincial scaffolds, he might be found fishing in the New River which flowed nearby, or discussing the finer points of rabbit-rearing with fellow enthusiasts over a tankard of ale in the 'Tiger' alehouse, a tavern where he frequently enjoyed a game or two of skittles. Very much an animal lover, not only did he also breed pigeons but even had a pony which followed him around like a dog – a pet much appreciated by his children, 'all morally brought up and well-schooled' – and also by his grandchildren.

These surprisingly gentle aspects of his character were endorsed by the well-known 19th century London journalist James Greenwood, who delved into the seamier side of the City's life for the many articles he wrote for the newspapers and magazines of the day. In one such he recounts how he unwittingly made the acquaintance of the executioner in an Islington public house (probably the Tiger Tavern) while engaged in conversation with a small group of customers. With the critical eye of a newsman he identified his drinking companions as a builder, a plasterer, a shoemaker and a greengrocer. However the profession of another member of their little coterie, a tall, quiet, heavily built man with grey whiskers and a beard, defeated him. Describing his thought processes in his article, he continued 'He was respectably dressed and his hands were evidently unacquainted with hard work. Was he a tax-collector? The softness of his speech at once forbade that assumption. Was he a house-agent, a commercial traveller, a canvasser for a coal company? The shyness of his mien refuted the guesses as fast as they were born. What could be gathered from his conversation? Nothing – nothing, at least, to give an inkling of his profession. His talk was political, modest and of a liberal-conservative tendency.'

After a while the stranger left and the conversation continued, the shoemaker exclaiming how good-hearted their recent companion was, and the greengrocer agreed, Greenwood quoting him as saying "I wish I had his brown pony! He's a beauty if you like! A nice thing for Epping Forest on a Sunday arternoon, gentlemen! If I had his pony and garden, I think I could retire comfortable!" The general discussion went on, praising the man's additional skills as a gardener, the pedigree of the goat he owned and the fine quality of the rabbits he bred. At last the shoemaker almost inadvertently relieved Greenwood's continuing frustration, by mentioning that their friend lived nearby and often called in and had a chat over a drink or two; and the name eventually came out – Calcraft the hangman!

The others in the company went on to point out that their drinking companion never gave any sign of taking any pleasure from his profession; indeed on one occasion he was most upset at having to hang a man with whom he used to drink in that very tavern!

So by all accounts Calcraft was more of a 'softie' than an executioner – at least when not on the scaffold. Neighbours would see him pass their doors en route to collect his weekly wages at Newgate Prison, one of his infants accompanying him, clinging to his hand. On Sundays he and Louisa attended local church services and, as the journalist's drinking companions had mentioned, when time and the weather permitted, the hangman would spend hours tending his garden and was so proud of his horticultural prowess that whenever his duties took him to the Session House (the Courts) in the Old Bailey, he would take some of his blooms to the landlady of the nearby inn, and sometimes even wore a rose in his buttonhole when on the scaffold, the flower brightening up the funereal black suit and odd-shaped black hat he usually wore when on duty.

And it was the way he performed those very duties which, unjustly or deservedly, resulted in the hostility and abhorrence directed at him throughout his career.

CHAPTER TWO

THE SCAFFOLD AND THE DROP

Over the centuries the actual method of hanging changed considerably. In the early days of executions a rope would be slung over the branch of a tree and pulled tight, lifting the victim off the ground and causing death by strangulation; later, the gallows, a wooden post with an extended arm, was used instead, thereby permitting executions to take place within towns and cities lacking trees, or at least those with suitable branches. The victim had to mount a ladder propped against the gallows, it being turned to throw him off after he had been noosed, but as only one felon could be hanged at a time, a new method was introduced, one which facilitated the despatch of several felons simultaneously. Conveyed from gaol in a cart, the vehicle would halt beneath the gallows, the doomed passengers then being noosed; a slap to the horse's flank would cause it and the cart to depart rapidly, leaving the numerous victims dangling in the empty air ('swinging in unison, like suits in a wardrobe' commented one observer).

To increase production – or rather, destruction – at Tyburn, London's principal execution site, near the junction of what is now Edgware Road and Oxford Street, three posts were joined by crossbars, each capable of accommodating eight felons at once, twenty-four at a stroke, or slap. This innovation met with much disapproval from the vast crowds of onlookers, drastically reducing, as it did, the entertainment they had come to enjoy.

The next major development came about in the 18th century, the vehicle and steed being replaced by a platform incorporating a 'drop', a small raised square of wood on which the noosed victim stood. The drop was supported by beams of wood to which ropes were attached, and at the crucial moment the hangman would pull the ropes, thereby removing the props, and the drop would fall until level with the surrounding boards, allowing the victim to swing, his or her feet usually, but not always, clear of the platform, then to die by slow strangulation. The first occasion on which this contraption was employed was on 5 May 1760 at Tyburn, Earl Ferrers, found guilty of murder, having the privilege of being the guinea-pig. Alas, the rope was as short as ever, the length of fall, about twelve inches, insufficient to sever the spinal cord, and the noble lord took an unconscionable time to expire.

Early in the following century the system became minimally improved. The design of the scaffold used at the Northampton County Gaol for the execution of James Thurtell in 1828, and widely adopted, was described by the authorities, not without some civic pride, as 'consisting of boards, raised seven feet above the ground, and dovetailed into each other so as to close every crevice. This platform is about thirty feet in length and fifteen feet in width, approached by a short flight of steps which leads directly from the door of the prison. Above this platform is a crossbeam to which the fatal cord would be affixed.'

Gone were the underlying support beams, the report describing how 'the New Drop consisted of a single falling flap (flush with the scaffold) supported by bolts (sliding lengths of wood), and upon this the felon was to stand. The bolts were fixed in such a manner as to be removed in an instant, and as instantaneously the victim of his own crime would be launched into eternity. The boards and all machinery, being painted black, presented a very gloomy appearance.'

This then was the *modus operandi* in force in 1829 when Calcraft took office, on one occasion spectators describing how 'he went beneath the gallows and withdrew the bolt'. And it was during his reign on the scaffold that a further modification took place; the 'double leaf', twin-trapdoor system was introduced, each flap being hinged to the side of the hole in the scaffold boards, the victim having to stand with the soles of his feet bridging the join. The flaps were held in place by a wooden support running on a wheel which rested in an iron groove, the pull of the rope attached to the support withdrawing it and so allowing the trapdoors to fall.

But tragically, little or no notice was paid to the fact that death still came mainly by strangulation and not by severance of the spinal column, Calcraft seeing no need to increase the length of his ropes. These he bought himself, those not sold as souvenirs being constantly reused, thereby risking one snapping, with the possibility of horrific results.

Among the other items of equipment he used was a white cap, a hood, which, on arrival on the scaffold, he pulled down over the criminal's head, it then being held in place by the noose lest his or her rapid descent caused it to rise and so reveal the felon's distorted features to the crowd.

It was also customary to secure the victim's hands either behind or in front, the latter position occasionally resulting in the victim raising them in a vain attempt to remove the hood or even grasp the rope above. To obviate this, Calcraft, not entirely bereft of initiative, used his cobblers' expertise to devise a harness consisting of a leather waist belt incorporating straps and buckles which secured victims' elbows to their sides and their wrists together in front of them. He was later reported to say proudly "It's my own invention. The old pinions used to hurt the old fellows so. This waist strap answers (fits) every person and is not in the least uncomfortable'. One would have thought that an uncomfortable belt would have been the least of a condemned person's worries at that particular time!

When the situation demanded, he would employ even more initiative; to speed his victims' demise he would cling on to their backs or pull their legs, not necessarily for humanitarian reasons, but simply because his job was to ensure that they died. On witnessing this, the novelist William Makepeace Thackeray (1811-1863) later described to a friend how the hangman 'came up from his black hole (after releasing the drop) and, seizing the prisoner's legs, pulled on them until he was quite dead – strangled!' In 1866 the authorities ordered that black curtains be fitted along the scaffold rails, not to provide the felons with some Christian privacy in their final moments on earth, but to conceal their convulsive death throes from the more sensitive of the spectators!

It was in that year, 1866, on giving evidence before the members of a Royal Commission, that a former sheriff of London described Calcraft's detached attitude on the scaffold 'as that of one hanging a dog'. But in mitigation it should be remembered that by then Calcraft had been hangman for nearly forty years and doubtless went through the scaffold routine like an automaton; it might even be said that only by 'switching off' his emotions in that way, whether deliberately or subconsciously, could he have continued at all, in such a life-taking profession. He even once admitted that he rarely recalled just who he had executed, saying "as soon as I've done it, it goes from me like a puff of 'baccy smoke".

He was not entirely without a sense of humour however; once, evidently in reply to the inevitable questions regarding his profession, he said that he never put anyone to death – he simply made all the preliminary arrangements in accordance with the law, and allowed the criminal to kill himself by falling! It was also reported that once, on entering a tavern where he was well-known, one man exclaimed "When I come to London, the hangman is always the first person I see!" To which Calcraft retorted with a smile "And you may be sure that he will also be the last!"

That he went about his business efficiently if not actually humanely, was evidenced by an article published in the *St James' Gazette* of 31 August 1892, written by David C Murray who had been present in an official capacity at the execution of murderer Thomas Alvarez Hughes at Liverpool on 11 September 1863.

He wrote 'I shall never forget the spidery, black-painted galleries and staircases, and the white-washed walls of the corridors. I shall never forget the living man who stood trembling and almost unconscious in the very gulf of cowardice and horror. I shall never forget the face of the wretched young chaplain who, like myself, found himself face-to-face with his first encounter with sudden death, and who, poor soul, had over-primed himself with stimulant. I shall never forget, either, that ghoul of a Calcraft, with his disreputable grey hair, his disreputable undertaker's suit of black, and a million dirty pinpricks which marked every pore of the skin of his face.

'Calcraft took the business businesslike' Murray continued 'and pinioned the man in his cell, with a terror-stricken half-dozen of us looking on, as calmly, to all appearances, as if he had been a tailor fitting on a suit. The chaplain read the Burial Service, or such parts of it as are reserved for such occasions, in a thick and indistinct voice. A bell clanged every half-minute or thereabouts, and it seemed to me as if it had always been ringing, and would always ring.

'I have the dimmest notion – indeed, to speak the truth, I have no notion at all – as to how the procession formed, and how we found ourselves at the foot of the gallows. The doomed man gabbled a prayer under his breath at a galloping speed, the words tumbling over one another "Lord Jesus, have mercy on me and receive my spirit." The hapless chaplain read the service. Calcraft bustled ahead. The bell boomed. Hughes came to the foot of the scaffold, and I counted mechanically nineteen black steps, freshly tarred and sticky. "I can't get up" said the murderer. A genial warder clapped him on the shoulder, for all the world as if there had been no mischief (nothing unusual) in the business. Judging by look and accent, the one man might have invited the other to mount the stairs of a restaurant. "You'll get up" said the warder. He got up, and they hanged him.'

The eyewitness's account went on 'Where everything was strange and dreamlike, the oddest thing of all was to see Calcraft take the pinioned, fin-like hand of the prisoner, and shake it, when he had drawn the white cap over the face and arranged the rope. He then came creaking in new boots down the sticky steps of the gallows, pulled a rope, and the man was dead in a second. The white cap fitted close to his face, and the thin white linen took on a momentary stain of purple, as if a bag of blackberries had been bruised, and had suddenly exuded the juice of the fruit. It sagged away a moment later, and assumed its natural hue.

'I learned from the evening paper, and from the journals of next morning, that the prisoner met his fate with equanimity, and recited a prayer as he approached the scaffold. I think that in that report I bottomed the depths of human stupidity, if such a thing is possible. I had never seen a man afraid before; and, when I found time to think about it, I prayed that I might never see that shameful and awful sight again.'

During William Calcraft's long career he despatched many hundreds of victims, men and women (including a nine-year-old boy sentenced to death by the courts for arson), most of them only listed at the time by name and date, tabloids of the day neglecting to identify the hangman concerned. Particulars of others have vanished along with the ancient records, but some of the more vividly detailed accounts still extant have been deemed worthy of inclusion, and will also serve as a lasting memorial to all those who suffered the ultimate agonies of the infamous Short Drop.

CHAPTER THREE

CALCRAFT MAKES HIS DEBUT

If Calcraft thought he was going to have a little time in which to purchase the various items of his 'tackle' and perhaps even have a dry run or two, practising by using a sandbag on the scaffold, he was in for a shock, for on the 13th April, only nine days after being sworn in, he was faced with his first execution; he was going solo! Nor was this to be the despatch of a meek little felon who, resigned to his fate, would go quietly – very far from it! In fact Calcraft's baptism of fire could hardly have been more of an ordeal, for his victim was a woman who, moreover, would cause him more trouble than any number of male victims.

Esther Hibner was not a pleasant person; indeed on hearing the details of her appalling crimes, she was dubbed the 'Evil Monster' by the Londoners. In the guise of a 'do-gooder' she cajoled workhouse keepers, those who gave food and shelter of sorts to unwanted and abandoned children, to allow her to employ some of the young girls in their care to work in her house. Once under her control she wasted no time in treating them with extreme brutality, her cruelty finally being exposed when the corpse of one of them was discovered. The child had obviously been frequently and severely beaten, her scarred and undernourished body covered in filth and sores.

Esther Hibner's trial was a mere formality and she was sentenced to death. It then became apparent that although she could hand out punishment, she could not take it herself, for while in the condemned cell she tried in vain to commit suicide. On the fateful day itself she refused to put her clothes on, the warders then having to dress her in a black skirt over her nightgown, a spectator later describing how 'with the sallowness of her complexion, this contributed to give her a most unearthly

Calcraft Makes his Debut   17

appearance.' And when the Ordinary (the prison chaplain) and officials arrived to conduct her to the gallows, the woman resisted so violently that she had perforce to be strapped in a straitjacket, then half-carried up the scaffold steps, to the deafening chorus of jeers and cheers by the waiting multitude.

This, then, was the scene which faced Calcraft on his debut as hangman, but despite his lack of experience he rose to the occasion with surprising confidence, buoyed up no doubt by the encouragement he received from the vast crowd as he quickly noosed the murderess; "Good old Calcraft!" they shouted as he operated the drop "Three cheers for the hangman!" Surely one of the very few times an executioner had been so acclaimed, an occasion to which, in years to come, Calcraft would no doubt look back on with nostalgia!

> That year was celebrated in the sporting world as being the first in which the University Boat Race took place at Henley – Oxford won! And 1829 not only heralded the arrival of a new hangman but also a revolution in transport, which came about with the introduction by a Mr George Shillibeer, of omnibuses pulled by three horses, each bus carrying twenty people from Paddington to Bank, for a fare of one shilling. As the most probable route was via Edgware Road, Oxford Street, Holborn and Newgate Street, no doubt the vehicles travelling in both directions were overcrowded with morbidly excited passengers on execution days! And the passing of Sir Robert Peels' Metropolitan Police Act having come into effect, Calcraft would doubtless have welcomed 'peelers' or 'bobbies' patrolling the streets of the capital; the resultant increases in arrests and charges, especially for murder, would lead to more executions, his finances benefiting similarly. In June some of the officers doubtless lined the Bethnal Green road to control the crowds gathering to watch the hangman who, in accordance with a court order, administered seventy lashes to a journeyman silk weaver; many spectators were evidently disappointed, for reports described the whipping as being only lightly inflicted!

Later that year the scene shifted to Carmarthen, Wales, when Calcraft was ordered to hang David Evans, a young man found guilty of killing his sweetheart. On the scaffold it immediately became evident that the hangman's earlier honeymoon with the public was definitely at an end, for on operating the drop, the rope snapped and the victim fell to the boards, unhurt but not unnaturally in a severe state of shock. No cheers greeted Calcraft this time; "Shame! Let him go!" demanded the crowd, and the victim, staggering to his feet, gasped "I claim my liberty – you've hanged me once and you have no power or authority to hang me again!"

Nor was that all; as the crowd surged forward, crushing up against the scaffold, the gallows were seen to sway dangerously, threatening to collapse on those gathered below, and it was then found that the carpenter responsible had failed to secure the crossbeams sufficiently. Evans, now distraught, was heard to shout "It is against the law to hang me a second time!" But Calcraft, determined to impose his authority as executioner on the situation, said firmly "You are greatly mistaken. There is no such law as that, to let a man go if there is an accident and he is not properly hanged." And he clinched the argument by averring "My warrant and my order are to hang you by the neck until you are dead. So up you go, and hang you must, until you are dead." And with the assistance of two warders – and risking attack by the now infuriated crowd – he proceeded to despatch Evans into the next world.

When 31 December 1829 arrived, four men who were definitely not available for the guest-lists of those intending to celebrate the arrival of the New Year, were ex-Customs House clerk Thomas Maynard, Stephen Stanford, William Leslie and William Newitt.

Maynard had yielded to temptation and, in the words of the judge 'had forged certain documents to his pecuniary advantage'. In accordance with the law, sentence of death was passed on him, a judgement which also conferred on him a record he would doubtless have preferred not to have achieved, for he was the last person to be hanged for that particular crime. As for the three colleagues lined up with him on the trapdoor; they were certainly not the last felons to be executed for the crimes they had committed, Standford and Leslie having been found guilty of burglary, while Newitt had no defence to the charge of sheep-stealing.

Their demise at the hands of Calcraft was far from rapid and painfree, it being reported that 'all struggled very much after the trap had opened'.

The year that followed was one of drama and tragedy. On 4th June 1830 King George IV died and was succeeded by his brother, the Duke of Clarence, who became William IV. The

Liverpool Member of Parliament William Huskisson attended the opening of the Liverpool to Manchester railway and was fatally injured after being struck by Stephenson's Rocket. But it was not all bad news; the passing of the Beer Act that year removed restrictions on the sale of that refreshing commodity, a decree doubtless appreciated by Calcraft and his friends in the Tiger Tavern!

In 1831 the redistribution of parliamentary seats brought about by the passing of the Reform Bill led to riots breaking out all over the country, town halls, municipal buildings and prisons being attacked and the convicts released. Which meant of course that Calcraft was more or less fully employed. One of his victims was a certain George Hearson who, apparently oblivious to his fate, did a dance on the Nottingham scaffold, waving and calling to his friends in the crowd. Calcraft wasted little time, his short length of rope ensuring that while his victim's verbal salutations ceased abruptly, his gyrations didn't.

It was also in that year that a national scandal of horrific proportions finally erupted. With the advances in medicine and the need for invasive surgery over recent decades, schools of surgery had been established in the big cities to train students, but the major obstruction to this was the shortage of specimens on which they could get the practice they needed in order to qualify as surgeons. There were no computer models, no plastic skeletons in those days; all that was legally available was a body or two a year, those of executed criminals delivered direct from the gallows. This lack of corpses brought about intense rivalry between the surgeons owning the schools, some of them taking desperate measures to retain their students – and the fees they paid – by raiding local cemeteries themselves, together with some of their pupils, and exhuming recently buried bodies. But inevitably the criminal classes saw this as a new and very profitable career; why risk capture and death as a pickpocket or burglar when, after an hour or so's digging in a deserted graveyard, one could reap a harvest of a dozen or more corpses and sell them at exorbitant prices to surgeons?

Despite all the efforts by communities to protect their dead, ranging from sealed iron coffins to nightly patrols, thousands of corpses were dug up and sold to the surgeons, matters not coming to a head (!) until the arrest of murderers Burke and Hare in Scotland. Hare turned King's Evidence and Burke was hanged in Edinburgh by Williams, the Scottish hangman, in front of a vast crowd. Burke and Hare were not grave robbers, but the very fact that they sold their victims' bodies ignited widespread fury among the Scots.

Nationwide communications being primitive compared to those of today, little notice of the case was taken further south, cemetery-plundering continuing unhindered, until on 5 November 1831 three men, John Bishop, his brother-in-law Thomas Williams (previously known as Thomas Head) and James May attempted to sell the body of a young boy, Carlo Ferrari, first to surgical staff at Guy's Hospital and then to Mr Grainger's Anatomical Theatre in Webb Street, off Tower Bridge Road, Borough. Meeting with no success, they approached Mr William Hill, the dissection room porter of King's College, London, May stating that the corpse 'was very fresh and was a male subject about fourteen years of age.' Bishop offered it for twelve guineas but eventually settled for nine. Although having dealt with them before, the porter first demanded to see the body before paying up, and Williams left, returning with a large hamper containing the corpse wrapped in a sack.

Mr Partridge, the lecturer of anatomy, inspected the cadaver and, observing the serious injuries which had been inflicted on it; that it did not seem to have been removed from a coffin, since the left arm was bent and the fingers clenched, and that the teeth had been removed (in order to be sold separately to dentists who would then instal them in the mouths of their more affluent patients), he played for time by appearing willing to close the deal but saying that he had only a £50 note on him so would have to get change; leaving the room he immediately notified the police.

On their arrival the men were arrested and taken into custody in Bow Street Police Station. Further enquiries elicited the fact that May had indeed approached Mr Thomas Mills, a dentist who practised at 39 Bridge House Place, Newington Causeway, that very morning and attempted to sell him twelve human teeth for a shilling each. The offer had been refused because of the pieces of flesh and fragments of jawbone still adhering to the molars, signs that they had been wrenched out of the victim's jaw with extreme force. A search of their house revealed two chisels, a bradawl and a file, together with bloodstained clothing buried in the garden. When shown the bradawl May replied "That is the instrument with which I punched the teeth out."

Although apparently in the same category of murderers as Burke and Hare, John Bishop confessed that in twelve years of moonlighting – or rather, non-moonlighting – he had in fact been a body snatcher and had dug up and sold between five hundred and a thousand bodies, large and small, the latter at so much an inch, from London cemeteries. Williams was likewise a well-known member of the grave-robbing gang.

News of the ghastly details of the crime had spread like wildfire throughout the City and at their trial in the Old Bailey on 1 December before Chief Justice Tindal, Mr Justice Littledale and Mr Baron Vaughan, and watched by a packed public gallery, the spectators also including members of the aristocracy and graced by His Royal Highness the Duke of Sussex, the prisoners were charged with murder. May was respited for lack of evidence but was sentenced to be transported for life. Bishop and Williams were found guilty, the verdict being greeted by vociferous cheering by those crowding in the street outside; so loud in fact, that the officers of the court had to close the windows so that those present would be able to hear the judge's next words. On hearing him deliver the death sentence, Bishop remained unmoved, but Williams snarled "We are murdered men!" and uttered dire threats to the witnesses, vowing that they would suffer for giving false evidence.

The day before their execution, 4 December, both condemned men made full confessions before the under sheriff, including admissions that they had also murdered a woman and a boy of eleven (see Appendix 1). The confessions were printed in the *Weekly Dispatch*, more than fifty thousand copies of which were sold the next day.

By one o'clock on the morning of 5 December 1831 a great crowd had assembled in front of the Newgate scaffold and it became obvious that hangman William Calcraft was going to have the audience of his life, for by daybreak the number had swelled to 30,000, and two hundred special constables had been sworn in by the Lord Mayor in an attempt to maintain some sort of order. Seats in the surrounding balconies had been hired out, prices starting at one guinea and rising tenfold depending on their proximity to the scaffold. The *Observer* newspaper, evidently scandalised, commented that 'not only in the crowd were numbers of the fair sex, but the windows were chiefly filled by them. On the roofs of the houses, persons of both sexes had placed themselves in situations of such danger as to excite fears for their safety, many having no other safeguard than a hold of the chimney pots to prevent themselves from rolling down the sloping roofs'. And the reporter of the *Times* described how 'the pressure in the immediate neighbourhood of the scaffold was tremendous in spite of the barriers and many persons who were exhausted with fatigue as early as 7 o'clock rescued themselves with difficulty from the throng and were heard to exclaim as they passed the outskirts of the mob "Thank God, I have got away!" Many of those who quitted the scene with torn clothes and faces streaming with perspiration had been on the spot for hours.'

By mistake three chains had been suspended from the gallows crossbeam, to which the ropes would be attached, but as May had been respited, one chain was removed by an official, to the accompaniment of raucous abuse from those who suddenly realised that they were to be deprived of one third of their entertainment.

In the prison Bishop was escorted from his cell and slowly entered the Press Room, his eyes downcast, apparently oblivious to his fate, but on seeing the gathered assembly of sheriffs and other officials, he gave a shuddering groan. On being ordered, he obediently stretched his arms out to have his wrists tied together, turning to allow his arms to be similarly bound.

Williams was next to appear. The felon's air of insolent confidence had long since vanished, to be replaced by one of absolute horror, and he trembled so violently that a warder had to grip his arms and hold them still, to allow the official to pinion them. As the cords tightened he exclaimed "Oh, I have deserved all this and more! Oh, I have deserved all I am about to suffer!" He was then allowed to sit on a bench in the prison's Soup Room clutching the Ordinary's hand, his grip tightening as the shouts reached a crescendo.

When Bishop was led out, the multitude hooted and yelled, the cacophony increasing as Calcraft pulled the hood down over his victim's head. Positioning the noose round the man's neck, he then attached it to the chain secured to the crossbeam.

Next it was his fellow felon's turn to face the mob, the savage baying of the crowd continuing as the hangman hooded and noosed Williams. With an ease borne of long practice, he then deftly operated the drop, both bodies falling in unison. Bishop died more or less instantly, but Williams was seen to writhe in the death throes for several minutes before his body finally hung limp and lifeless.

Calcraft Makes his Debut 23

At that the crowd broke through the barriers and a scene that almost defies the imagination ensued as they rushed towards the scaffold. A very heavy barrier had been secured to strong uprights set in the ground at the end of Giltspur Street in an endeavour to hold back the mob, but in vain, for under the overwhelming pressure it gave way, men and women falling and being trampled underfoot. The *Times* journalist was obviously caught up in the melee, describing how 'the screams of the females and the confusion that ensued were truly alarming; one female of very respectable appearance, with her husband, was most dreadfully injured by the barrier falling on their chests and by others of the crowd who fell upon them. A city constable was also caught under the barrier, which rested on his abdomen, and his cries were most deplorable. A cry of "Stand back! For God's sake, stand back!" was raised, but it was of no avail. At length some of the officers from the Compter prison came out and with the assistance of several other officers the individuals were rescued from their perilous situation and carried to St. Bartholomew's Hospital, wards being filled with those who had been crushed under the feet of the crowd.'

The gentry on the scaffold wasted no time in observing the time-honoured Newgate tradition whereby the sheriffs invited the under sheriffs, the Ordinary and other guests to join them for a hearty breakfast; accordingly they retreated from the scaffold and returned behind the prison walls. Calcraft, however, not being classed as one of the elite, had hastily sought refuge from the stampede elsewhere, but in accordance with the law, emerged an hour later and cut the bodies down.

At that time a statute passed in 1752 during the reign of George II was still in force, it stating 'That the body of every person convicted of murder shall, if such conviction and execution shall be in the County of Middlesex or within the City of London, or of the liberties thereof, be immediately conveyed by the sheriff or sheriffs, or their deputy or deputies, and his or other officer or officers, to the Hall of the Surgeons' Company, or such other place as the said company shall appoint for this purpose, and be delivered to such person as the said company shall depute or appoint, who shall give to the sheriff or sheriffs, his or their deputy or deputies, a receipt for the same; and the body so delivered to the said company of surgeons shall be dissected or anatomised by the said surgeons or such persons as they shall appoint for that purpose; and that in no case the body shall be suffered to be buried unless after such body shall have been dissected or anatomised.'

The due delivery of the two cadavers then took place, the scene which followed being described by a witness: 'A small cart drove up to the scaffold and the bodies were placed in it, covered with sacks. The cart then moved at a slow pace, followed by the sheriffs, the City Marshal and a large number of constables, to no. 33 Hosier Place, the house of Mr. Stone the surgeon, the vast crowd lining the route yelling and making discordant noises as they proceeded. At the house it was with great difficulty that the bodies were removed from the cart, the crowd appearing more than anxious to gain possession of them themselves. The bodies were placed on a table and in the presence of the sheriffs, in conformity with their duty, an incision was made in their chests. The bodies were later removed, Bishop's to King's College (!) and Williams' to the Theatre of Anatomy in Windmill Street, Haymarket, to be dissected. They were publicly exhibited on Tuesday and Wednesday at both places, when immense numbers of persons were admitted to see their remains'.

So William Calcraft, albeit indirectly, was a major player in an event which had such important consequences, for due to the widespread publicity surrounding the despatch of a self-confessed body snatcher such as Bishop, Parliament passed the *Anatomy Act* in the following year, which enabled surgeons to obtain a sufficient number of unclaimed dead bodies legally under licence from workhouses and similar institutions, for the purpose of teaching anatomy. This enactment rendered thousands of grave robbers immediately redundant, they perforce having to retrain as burglars, pickpockets or the like, and thereby still qualify as potential candidates for Calcraft's short drop at some future date.

Later that month however, when the hangman had to execute John Holloway, guilty of murdering his wife, he made a rash mistake in trying to do someone a favour, and almost lost his job into the bargain. It should be remembered that many superstitions existed, in this country and on the Continent, regarding the therapeutic value of items associated with those who had been hanged; for instance in earlier centuries a cure was reputedly effected by a substance called Usnea, a type of moss which grew, not on tree trunks, but on the skull of a criminal who had been hanged in chains, this being scraped off and, in liquid form, was highly recommended as a treatment, in particular for those suffering from nervous diseases. It was classed as an official drug, its curative properties were described in detail in the first edition of the *Encyclopaedia Britannica*, and it was available, probably on prescription, from apothecaries. Another certain panacea was that of stroking the affected part of the skin with a used piece of hangman's rope (a belief from which Calcraft at times benefited financially!), but failing that, stroking it with a dead man's hand would suffice.

And so the hangman was hardly surprised when he was approached by a man who, all his life, had suffered from a painful wen, a cyst, on his neck, and who asked him whether he would somehow arrange for his victim's hand to touch the cyst. Whether Calcraft wished solely to do the man a good turn, or perceived some pecuniary reward, is not known, but he agreed.

Having duly executed Holloway, he waited until all the struggles had ceased, then beckoned the man up on to the scaffold and, lifting one of the corpse's limp hands, rubbed it on the man's neck. On seeing that, the crowd, superstitious or not, went wild, causing the sheriffs to step in quickly and terminate the 'curative' performance, Calcraft later receiving a severe reprimand over his outrageous behaviour.

Some time later the hangman was detailed to despatch Eliza Ross, a woman who had been found guilty of selling a body to surgeons. Although the authorities couldn't find the corpse, her son said she had; the court believed him, so they hanged her – or rather William Calcraft did.

Despite being described as a body-snatcher by the local newspapers of the day, it was hardly likely that the lady was indeed an active member of the resurrectionists; digging deep holes in a cemetery in the middle of the night, breaking open one end of the coffins, then hauling the corpses out by their necks, called for rather more brute strength than that possessed by most women. But members of the fairer sex were employed in less operational roles by some of the many gangs of body snatchers operating in London; in order to protect the 'silent tenants' of the graveyards, carefully concealed spring guns were positioned, aimed at newly occupied graves and operated by tripwires attached to the triggers. Female confederates, under the guise of being grieving wives or relatives, would dress in black and visit the cemetery, there to kneel, sobbing, by adjacent graves, meanwhile noting the siting of the wires for the benefit of their male counterparts later that night. The wires would then be cut, the body removed, and the wires reconnected, for should any trace of their visit be left, that particular cemetery would have been a no-go area for months to come.

Women were also employed to watch out for funeral processions and on seeing one, to follow the cortege at a discreet distance, make note of the cemetery and the actual plot in which the body was buried, then report back to HQ, probably the Flower Pot Inn in Bishopsgate or the Bell Tavern, Smithfield, both notorious meeting places for the sack-em-up men.

Eliza, however, was not charged with participating in such unsocial activities, but of murdering, then selling the body to one of the surgical schools, as in the case of Bishop and Williams, above. She was a well-known character around the Red Lion Court, a locality near Fleet Street, named after an inn of the same name, where she lived with Edward Cook, himself an ex-body snatcher. A veritable virago, possessing a temper with a short fuse, she made a living selling old clothes and animal skins, usually those removed from unwilling local pets, and occasionally took in lodgers. One of them, an old woman named Catherine Walsh, was the mother of Anne Buton, a neighbour who had moved away to a house in Playhouse Yard, once the site of the Blackfriars Playhouse, in which William Shakespeare had a financial share.

In August Eliza and Edward also left Red Lion Court and went to live in Goodman's Yard, a road off the Minories, near the Tower of London. They took Mrs Walsh with them and sometime later Anne visited the house, only to find her mother absent. Eliza said that she herself had been out, and on returning she had found that Mrs Walsh had apparently left the house and gone; where, she did not know.

Not unnaturally the daughter was concerned that her mother might have come to some harm and as the weeks and months went by she searched the streets, enquired in local taverns and contacted the hospitals, all with negative results. Fully aware of Eliza Ross's far from salubrious reputation, Anne then feared the worst. The police were called in and, clothes sold to Eliza's market customers being identified as having belonged to Mrs Walsh, Eliza and her eleven-year old son Ned were taken to the nearest police office.

When questioned, little could be elicited from the suspect,

who flatly denied any knowledge of what had happened to her lodger. Young Ned however was an honest lad and reluctantly, bit by bit, the awful truth was cajoled from him. Late in the evening of the day on which the old lady had moved in, he said, he had seen her lie on the bed, watched his mother suffocate her by holding her hand over the woman's nose and mouth until she was dead, then saw the body carried downstairs. Even worse was to come, the boy relating how, in the cellar, he found a large sack, from the open end of which protruded the head of their late lodger, the face swollen and contorted. And that night the sack had gone.

Hospital and surgical school porters were questioned regarding the identities of corpses purchased from body snatchers but none was positively identified as being that of Caroline Walsh. It was eventually surmised however that the cadaver could have been packed, together with others, in barrels labelled as pork, fish, apples, or anything similarly innocuous, and despatched to Liverpool, Manchester or Edinburgh, there being a regular trade in supplying bodies to surgical schools in those and other major cities.

So although Elizabeth Ross vehemently denied the charge of murder, and despite there being no body, Ned's testimony was accepted as valid, reliable and admissible by the Old Bailey judge. The jury brought in a verdict of guilty, and Elizabeth Ross was sentenced to death. So on 9 January 1832 William Calcraft once again had the distasteful task of hanging a woman although, aware of the shocking details of her crime, no doubt he had little compunction in doing so. Living up to her reputation, on the scaffold she loudly demanded justice, declaring her innocence and berating those witnesses who had testified against her, including her own son. The hangman wasted little time in dropping the noose over her head, the contact of the rough fibrous rope on her throat stilling her outburst; tightening, it also stilled her writhing body – eventually.

Ironically, if Catherine Walsh had died of natural causes and been buried, and Eliza had exhumed her body and sold it, she would not have been committing a crime, for other than a statute dating back to the reign of James I which made it a felony to steal a body for the purpose of witchcraft, at that time there was none against taking a corpse for dissection; there was no legal property in a body; no-one owned it! Equally, no-one owned Eliza's, except the law governing those of murderers; accordingly, after being cut down by Calcraft, hers was handed over for dissection by the surgeons.

Because of the appalling living conditions of the poorer classes, the shortage of clean drinking water and the primitive methods of sewage disposal, diseases of the most virulent kind were never far from the inhabitants of London and this was never more evident than in 1831, when a cholera epidemic spread through Rotherhithe and Limehouse. There are no reports of Calcraft contracting the disease nor, surprising, did he succumb to the affliction endemic in the prisons he had to visit, that of gaol fever (typhus), which was brought about by the foul and fetid conditions therein. Even the court officials, being in contact with prisoners on trial, were liable to be infected, and the presiding judge usually held a few flowers beneath his nose in a vain attempt to dispel the suspect odours, the practice thereby becoming the origin of the traditional presentation of a nosegay to a judge arriving at court which has continued down the centuries.

But the year also brought many thrilling events, not least the opening of the new London Bridge, the old, outdated and totally inadequate one having been demolished. Medical science also brought many benefits to those in pain, with the discovery of chloroform – though Calcraft's victims did not qualify as deserving cases!

The hangman continued to despatch his victims throughout that year and those following, the judicial system being considerably improved in 1834 by the establishing of the Central Criminal Court. In October of that year, those manning London's Fire Brigades, the hook-and-ladder men, had their work cut out in fighting the fire which eventually destroyed the Houses of Parliament, the number of spectators at the conflagration vastly exceeding any of Calcraft's executions. And the perils of crossing London's roads were increased when Joseph Aloysius Hansom, introduced the fast horse-drawn 'hansom' cab.

1835 saw the opening of Mme Tussaud's Waxworks Museum, which attracted thousands of visitors and where, in the years to come, many lifelike effigies of Calcraft's victims would be displayed. In 1836 some visitors arrived via the first steam trains to operate in the City, travelling along the four mile track from Deptford, but the 'iron horse' was hardly likely to render its living equivalent redundant for a long time to come, for it was estimated that no fewer than 3,300 stage coaches and 700 mail coaches were in use throughout the country; gardeners, Calcraft among them, were no doubt appreciative of the ordure their motive power thus provided!

One of the effigies to be exhibited in Mme. Tussaud's Waxworks was that of James Greenacre, whose appalling crime shocked and horrified Londoners in 1836. It all started on the morning of 28 December when a workman, relaying some loose paving stones near the Pineapple Gate in the Edgware Road, raised one, only to find a sack buried beneath it, and his reactions can well be imagined when on opening the bundle, he found that it contained the decapitated torso of a woman swathed in part of a child's blue dress! And even more public revulsion was expressed when, on 6 January, a human head was found blocking lock-gates in the Regent's Canal at Stepney, eight miles away; dislodged by means of a boat-hook and brought to the towpath, it was found to have suffered severe injuries; one eye had been gouged out, the jawbone fractured and an ear badly lacerated. It was subsequently subjected to forensic tests, these establishing that as suspected, it had been severed from the Edgware Road torso.

Despite intensive enquiries, no further progress was made by the police, and it was not until 2 February that the news of another macabre discovery made the headlines of the London newspapers, their journalists avidly reporting in gruesome detail how a man named Page had found a pair of legs in a hedge near Coldharbour Lane in Camberwell, on the other side of the Thames! The limbs were taken to Paddington where the other remains had been stored, a grisly jigsaw proving that all the body-parts were those of the same person – but who was that person?

Lacking the benefits of television news and crime programmes, the corpse remained unidentified until, nearly a month later, a Mr. William Gay came forward to report that he had been unable to contact his sister, Hannah Brown, and was worried about her absence. He was told to prepare himself for a possible shock, then was shown the severed head, which had been preserved in spirits – it was indeed that of his sister!

Now having a direct lead, police investigations were intensified, and it was discovered that Hannah had been a washerwoman in the employ of one James Greenacre, a man of some standing in the community who, despite his self-opinionated attitude and radical views, had been a prominent politician in the Borough, and now owned a shop in the Old Kent Road, Southwark.

Upon going to his residence in Carpenter's Buildings, Camberwell, Greenacre was found to be packing his luggage preparatory to travelling to America on the following day, and when the suitcases were searched, part of a child's blue dress was found. A woman with him was also found to have in her possession some rings, a watch and a pair of earrings suspected to have belonged to Hannah Brown.

Greenacre was arrested and taken to the local police office and, faced with such damning evidence, he admitted his guilt. Despite his façade of prosperity he was in financial difficulties and, upon learning that his employee had savings amounting to some hundreds of pounds, had proposed marriage to her. Her death, he claimed, had been accidental; they had had a row and he had thrown a rolling pin at her. He panicked, he said, and tried to conceal the body by first dismembering, then disposing of it around London.

While held in the cells he attempted to commit suicide by tying his neckerchief and handkerchief together and formed a noose at one end, which he then placed around his neck. Bending one knee, he secured the other end to his foot, then straightened his leg and attempted to strangle himself, but the choking noises he made were heard by a policeman in the corridor who proceeded to cut him free. Although unconscious, he was resuscitated in the nick of time by Mr Girdwood, a surgeon; it was reported that, on regaining his senses, he exclaimed to that gentleman "I don't thank you for this – I had rather gone off!"

The callous crime was the sole topic of conversation among all walks of London society, so much so that, after having been tried on a charge of murder and sentenced to death, members of Parliament and the upper classes visited Newgate to see him in the condemned cell. And on the Sunday preceding his execution, people flocked to the prison, hoping to get a seat at the funeral service held in the chapel so that they could satisfy their gruesome curiosity and see the man soon to die, as he sat in the black-draped pew, his coffin resting on a nearby table.

On the morning of execution day, 2 May 1837, nearly 20,000 spectators packed the streets around Newgate Prison, many having arrived the night before in order to get favourable viewing positions around the scaffold positioned against the prison walls, in much the same way as those who attend Wimbledon and the Oval before important matches nowadays. Calcraft's refreshment-selling successors did a roaring trade with the roistering and merrymaking crowds, much ale being quaffed, many pies devoured; one culinary entrepreneur introduced 'Greenacre Tarts', pastries which proved to be particularly profitable confections!

Broadsheets and ballads, scurrilous or ribald, were usually peddled among execution *aficionados*, including so-called 'dying words' and confessions, complete with pictures of the man hanging from the gallows – usually the same picture each time! – and Greenacre's was no exception, his being included in Appendix 3.

As required, Calcraft had spent the night in the gaol, and just before eight o'clock he, together with the sheriffs, other City dignitaries and the Ordinary, the prison chaplain, together with the condemned man escorted by warders, came out through the gates and mounted the scaffold. At that the vast multitude surged forward in a frantic wave; "Hats off! Hats off!" came the shouts, not, as might have been assumed, as a mark of respect for the man about to be launched into the next world, but because the items of headgear referred to, obstructed the view of others. At the sight of the sea of upturned frenzied faces, Greenacre paled and, turning to Calcraft, beseeched "Don't leave me long with that pack of ghouls!" Nor was he, for the hangman swiftly drew the white hood down over the man's head and followed by positioning the noose around his victim's neck.

In his cell Greenacre had earlier attempted to hang himself, but Calcraft's rope was much, much more effective, for next moment the trapdoors opened and Greenacre dropped, his body jerking spasmodically for some minutes, though ceasing before the hangman thought it necessary to speed his victim's demise by pulling on the doomed man's legs.

That was not the end of the show as far as many of the spectators were concerned, for although the hangman and officials then vacated the scaffold, the macabre celebrations continued for nearly an hour, Calcraft eventually reappearing. Taking his jackknife from his pocket, the hangman severed the rope, allowing the corpse to drop to the ground below. From there it was carried back into the prison and buried in the graveyard, but not until a plaster cast had been made of the head, later to appear on display in the famous Chamber of Horrors.

32   William Calcraft

It was later reported that while in prison he had asked one of the sheriffs what had led to his arrest; when informed that it was because the face of his victim had been recognised, he exclaimed "God forbid me for my carelessness! I ought to have mutilated her features!" His features however would have needed no mutilation to avoid recognition, so distorted were they when Calcraft removed the white cap from *his* lifeless corpse.

Greenacre's execution was not the only attraction for Londoners that year, for not only was the National Gallery opened to the public, but an event of national importance occurred when Euston Station, the City's first railway terminus, commenced operations, a facility likely of benefit to the executioner for his train journeys to provincial scaffolds.

On 20 June the nation mourned the death of William IV, but then celebrated exuberantly the following year at the Coronation of Queen Victoria, Mr and Mrs Calcraft no doubt taking their eldest children to join the crowds lining the Mall to watch the regal procession. The hangman would also have been professionally interested in the abolition that year, 1838, of the pillory, wooden structures in which the victim was secured by neck and wrists, then to be the helpless target to the ridicule – and brickbats – of the spectators.

Should he have had an execution engagement up north around 26 February in the year following, he might have had a flutter on one of the horses running in the first-ever Aintree Grand National steeplechase, but one can hardly visualise him attending another momentous sporting occasion, at Henley, that town holding its first Regatta.

And because the hangman had to write to prison governors in order to arrange execution dates and times, he probably welcomed the introduction by Rowland Hill, in January 1840, of the Penny Post, though no doubt he added the cost to his claims for expenses incurred!

CHAPTER FOUR

A MURDEROUS VALET, A VENGEFUL COUPLE

In July 1840 the sculptors at Mme Tussaud's were once again busily engaged on an effigy of yet another of Calcraft's victims, a man named François Benjamin Couvoisier, a native of Geneva, who had been valet to Lord William Russell, an uncle of the Duke of Bedford. His Lordship, a widower aged 75, had lived at 14 Norfolk Street, near Park Lane in London, and on the 4 May, after spending the day at his club, had then returned home. Shortly after midnight, with the assistance of his valet, he had undressed and retired to bed.

The following morning the two women servants who lived in the house came downstairs, only to find the rooms on the first floor in disarray. Assuming the devastation to be the work of burglars they went to their master's bedroom to see whether he had been injured – to find him lying on the bed, his throat cut from ear to ear!

The police were called, and suspicion fell on Couvoisier when it was found that he had been stealing valuables from the house for some time, a search revealing rings and money hidden behind skirting boards in his room, and although he tried to throw the blame on the other servants, he appeared in court charged with murder. During his trial he secretly confessed his guilt to his counsel, Charles Phillips; this was not divulged at the time of course, but the evidence was so strong that he was found guilty and sentenced to death, the execution to take place on 6 July.

The day before his hanging, the Rev. Carver, Ordinary of Newgate Prison, held the customary funeral service in the chapel.

Although not due to start until 10.30 am, the approach roads were already packed with those who had sought and obtained tickets. The Lady Mayoress of London attended in state, also present being Lord Adolphus Fitzclarence, Lord Coventry, Lord Paget, several members of the House of Commons and even, it was reported, a few ladies.

Couvoisier, pale yet composed, and guarded by two turnkeys, sat on a bench before the pulpit, bowing his head whenever his dastardly crime was alluded to by the preacher, afterwards being conducted back to the condemned cell. That night he went to bed about eleven o'clock, the turnkeys reporting that the prisoner slept fairly soundly although sometimes he groaned and gnashed his teeth.

At half past six the holy sacrament was administered to him, following which Calcraft entered the cell. Extracting a rope from the black bag he carried, he tied his victim's wrists together in front of him, then pinioned the man's arms to his sides by securing the belt around his waist.

At eight o'clock the awful drama of the procedure was heightened by the sonorous tolling of the prison bell – which incidentally bore the inscription 'Ye people all who hear me ring, Be faithful to your God' and was exhibited in Mme Tussaud's Museum following the demolition of the prison in 1903 – and the grim procession moved off to where the inevitably vast crowd waited around the scaffold, some having been assembling there as previously as ten o'clock the night before. In that day's edition of the *Times* it was reported that 'among the crowd there was a considerable sprinkling of females and boys, and an extraordinary number of men servants were present, sent there, no doubt, by their masters to discourage any who might be planning a similar affair!'

When Couvoisier appeared, he was greeted by the inevitable torrent of abuse, but outwardly he appeared firm and collected as he mounted the steps, and while Calcraft was positioning him on the drop he moved his bound hands up and down slightly. The renowned novelist William Makepeace Thackeray, who was among the spectators, described how the condemned man 'turned his head here and there and looked about him for an instant, with a wild and imploring look. His mouth was contracted into a sort of pitiful smile. He went and placed himself under the beam. The tall, grave man in black (Calcraft) drew from his pocket a nightcap......I could look no more, but shut my eyes.'

The hangman pulled the cap over his victim's head, it being so tight fitting that the outline of the man's features was clearly discernable. The *Times* then reported what happened next. 'During this operation he lifted up his head and raised his hands to his breast. In a moment the hangman drew the fatal bolt, the drop fell, and in this attitude the murderer perished without any violent struggle. In two minutes after he had fallen, his legs were twice slightly convulsed but no further motion was observable excepting that his raised arms, gradually losing their vitality, sank down from their own lifeless weight.'

The body was allowed to remain suspended there for an hour before Calcraft returned to cut it down, warders then taking it back through the gates for burial within the prison walls, though not before a death mask was made for display in Mme Tussaud's Museum.

Among the spectators was Charles Dickens, who had sat up all night outside the prison. Appalled by the bestial behaviour of the crowd, he condemned them in a letter published in the *Daily News*, writing 'No sorrow, no salutary terror, no abhorrence, no seriousness; nothing but ribaldry, debauchery, levity, drunkenness, and flaunting vice in fifty other shapes. I should have deemed it impossible that I could have ever felt any large assemblage of my fellow-creatures to be so odious.' Thackeray echoed his sentiments, saying: "It seems to me that I have been abetting an act of frightful wickedness and violence, performed by a set of men against one of their fellows." Later in his life Dickens was to change his mind and support the death penalty – though only were it to be executed in private.

In January 1841 the London newspapers included graphic accounts of a hanging in which, unusually, William Calcraft was not involved. During the previous few weeks an American swimmer, Samuel Scott, had been entertaining the public by diving into the River Thames from scaffolding erected on the top of Waterloo Bridge, but on the 11th of that month things went horribly wrong. To amuse the vast crowd of spectators even further, he had taken hold of one of the many ropes attached to the temporary structure, formed it into a noose, and put it around his neck. What exactly happened next was unclear; whether the rope caught on some protruding piece of scaffolding or whether the swimmer slipped, the result was horrendous, for before his assistants could release him, Scott was dead.

On a lighter note, London's Royal Botanical Gardens opened later that year, an event which doubtless appealed to Calcraft's horticultural interests, but many plants must have died in the following autumn and winter, for severe weather wreaked havoc throughout the country. Nearly twenty inches of snow fell in Yorkshire, 15,000 skaters enjoyed themselves on the ice-covered Serpentine and 10,000 in St James Park. Even members of the Royal Family were tempted to take advantage of the wintry conditions, although it could have proved disastrous, as evidenced by a Court Circular which stated 'Her Majesty and Prince Albert fell through the ice at Frogmore on Tuesday last, he skating, and she following him around in her sledge. But they were extricated with only slight inconvenience from the cold water.'

However, exuberance was in short supply during the following year, when the government announced the introduction of Income Tax, the first ever in peace time; no less than 7d. in the pound for those earning more than £150 annually. One wonders whether this gave the hangman cause to worry over the amount of 'perks' he would have to declare! And the fact that in the same year, half farthings were minted, may have been some indication on the rising cost of living!

The regular execution-goers always attended Newgate in their thousands, even if they happened to sympathise with the condemned felon; there was always old Calcraft to have a go at. But the one type of crime for which they reserved their most virulent invective was one in which the murderer had not only killed but had also dismembered and mutilated his female victim. And so when Daniel Good appeared on the scaffold on 23 May 1842 the tirade of abuse reached new heights.

In April 1842 Good, a coachman employed by Mr Quelaz Shiel, a wealthy merchant in Putney, had disposed of a woman named Jane Jones, with whom he had been living, because he intended to marry another woman, Lydia Susannah Butcher. After slaying Jane Jones with an axe, he beheaded her and chopped off her arms and legs; her torso, which had been ripped open, was later found by police constable William Gardiner hidden beneath straw bales in the stables in which Good worked. In the fireplace of the adjoining harness room another police constable, Samuel Palmer, police number V6, discovered the badly burned remains of a head, other pieces of charred flesh and viscera having been thrown into the Thames. At the post mortem examination later, it was discovered that the flesh had been separated with a sharp instrument and the bones broken or sawed through with the bloodstained axe and saw found nearby. The tragic victim was also found to have been about five months pregnant.

Good subsequently fled from his house, No. 18 South Street, Manchester Square, and went to Tonbridge, Kent, where he got a job working as a bricklayer's assistant. However he was eventually recognised by Thomas Rose, a former policeman in Wandsworth, and taken to the local police station. There, he gave a false name, but on taking a comb out of his pocket and combing his hair back from his forehead – a nervous habit described in the police 'Wanted' notice as being that of the man they were seeking – he was promptly arrested and charged with murder.

At Good's trial on 13 May, His Royal Highness the Duke of Sussex took his seat on the judges' bench, and gasps of horror were heard when the ghastly details of the mutilation inflicted on the pregnant victim were read out. So overwhelming was the case against the accused that the jury took only half an hour of deliberation to return a verdict of Guilty. The prisoner vehemently protested his innocence, claiming that Jane Jones had cut her own throat and that on the following morning 'a man from whom I sometimes bought matches had called at the stables. I told him what had happened and he advised me to conceal the body. I said I would give him a sovereign if he would do it for me, to which he agreed. He cut off the head, then asked me to light a fire in the harness-room, but on my refusing to do so, he made a fire himself and then commenced burning part of the body.' Such obvious lies were rejected by the judge, who proceeded to sentence him to death.

On Sunday 22 May 1842, the day before the execution, the congregation attending Newgate Chapel to hear the 'condemned sermon' being read by the prison Ordinary included not only members of the public but also the Lady Mayoress and other ladies. The condemned man and his coffin were of course also present.

Early in the morning of the following day crowds started to gather outside Newgate, accompanied by the inevitable scenes of revelry and ribald debauchery. Business was brisk for the ballad hawkers; Daniel Good may have made a killing, but so did they, for no fewer than 1,650,000 copies of their broadsheets of the murderer's crime and execution were sold throughout London and the home counties, the verses appearing in Appendix 3.

In his cell Good, still persisting that he was not guilty, had broken down and was in tears, despite having been given a glass of port wine by the prison governor. Calcraft arrived and promptly took over. His victim was still wearing his traditional coachman's white cravat at his throat; this, the executioner immediately removed, then proceeded to pinion his victim's arms. And escorted by the officials, the murderer was led to where the scaffold – and the baying mob – waited.

It then became clear that killing and dismembering a woman was one thing, but facing lawful retribution oneself was quite another, for at the sight of the gallows Good flinched, his face pale and drawn, as Calcraft positioned him on the drop and proceeded to draw the white cap down over the man's head, followed by the official hempen cravat. The sound of muffled words came from beneath the thin material as the murderer sought to plead for mercy, but Calcraft was having none of it. Aware of the hostility of the crowd towards his victim, he brusquely advised the man to pray instead – and then pulled the lever.

Before being later taken away for dissection, the corpse 'was examined by several medical and scientific gentlemen, one of whom, Dr. Elliotson, took a plaster cast of the murderer's head for phrenological examination.'

In its write-up the next day, the *Morning Advertiser* described how Good 'struggled very little and appeared to die almost immediately. The only motion observed was about the hands which, the instant he fell, he raised up in the attitude of prayer, as far as the pinioning rope would allow them to go.' Rather than raising the hands in prayer, it is more likely that a victim would inevitably be endeavouring to slacken the noose around his or her throat, but whatever the reason, it availed the murderer naught; Jane Jones had been avenged.

For many months diggers and navvies had been busy beneath the River Thames under the supervision of Isambard Kingdom Brunel, until finally, in August 1842, the Thames Tunnel between Wapping on the north bank of the river to Rotherhithe on the opposite bank, was opened to the public, 60,000 pedestrians subsequently passing through it during four days. The nation however might well have suffered the loss of that great engineer,

A Murderous Valet, A Vengeful Couple   39

for some months later while entertaining some children by pretending to put a coin in his mouth and then producing it from his ear, he somehow managed to swallow it and fought for breath as it stuck in his throat. Medical aid was immediately sought, and as the record has it 'it was not until he was held in an inverted position and violently shaken, that the coin finally dislodged itself and he breathed satisfactorily once more.'

As well as the opening of the new Tunnel, another event which altered the London landscape was taking place above ground where, in Trafalgar Square, the seventeen-foot-high statue of Admiral Horatio Nelson was finally placed on the column which soared one hundred and seventy-seven feet above the pigeons!

The many country-wide railway journeys undertaken by Calcraft and those who commuted daily in and out of London at that time must have been extraordinarily uncomfortable, to the point of contracting not only colds, but severe back ailments, for the third-class carriages were open to the elements and their seats were bench-like, lacking any form of back support, and it was not until 1844 that the railway companies were forced to improve their rolling stock.

Not that all was doom and gloom in the Metropolis; in September of that year thousands of Londoners lined the banks of the Thames between the Houses of Parliament and Thames Bank, crowds gathered on the bridges, and scores of others chartered rivercraft to watch Barry the Clown, a member of the performing troupe of Astley's Circus, seated in a tub and being pulled along the river by a team of geese! Regrettably, when the same spectacle was attempted in the following year by a clown from Cooke's Equestrian Circus at the holiday resort of Yarmouth, the number of spectators congregated on the suspension bridge was so great that the structure collapsed into the river, more than a hundred onlookers, mostly children, being drowned.

On a brighter note, however, one wonders what sort of greetings the Calcrafts and others must have sent to their friends in years prior to 1844, for it was in that year that Xmas cards appeared for the first time in the shops, a novelty which became a 'must' ever afterwards.

In 1845 the 'Case of the Murderous Quaker' made the newspaper headlines and further enriched the broadsheet vendors; this was another in which William Calcraft was to be involved. The victim was a young lady, Sarah Hart, who lived in Salt Hill, Slough, in

Buckinghamshire, and who had had an affair with a married man, John Tawell. Claiming he was the father of her two children, she repeatedly wrote to him, asking for money. Rather than have his wife find out, he visited her on New Year's Day 1845 and murdered her by administering poison, prussic acid, in a drink.

Unfortunately for him, a neighbour heard Sarah's screams of agony and on investigating, saw a man dressed as a Quaker leaving the house. The police being sent for, they ascertained that a similarly clad man had left for London from Slough railway station. Wasting no time, they used the railway's newly installed 'galvanic telegraph' to inform the Metropolitan Police, the first time it had been so utilised, and on arriving at Paddington station the murderer was arrested and taken into custody by the police waiting on the platform.

Far from abiding by the Christian and humane precepts practised by Quakers, Tawell was a convicted criminal out on probation following release from a lengthy prison sentence served for defrauding a bank. At his trial a chemist who had a shop in Bishopsgate in the City stated that the accused, whom he recognised, had purchased that particular poison on 1 January. In his defence his counsel claimed that by eating the apples found in her room, Sarah had died from the cyanide in the pips; this was countered by the prosecuting lawyer who pointed out that this would only have been possible, had the pips been first crushed and distilled. And on 14 March 1845, after due deliberation, the jury found Tawell guilty, and he was sentenced to be executed at Aylesbury on 28th of that month.

On arrival Calcraft had somewhat different conditions to contend with, for there was no scaffold as such; instead executions took place on an iron balcony that projected from an upper floor of the County Hall. A beam jutted out from the wall immediately above the balcony, a hinged portion of the floor of which formed the drop. In front of the Hall a large area of rising ground extended for about three hundred yards, as far as the market house, this configuration thereby providing a natural amphitheatre for the thousands of spectators expected to attend.

And they certainly did, watching with horrified fascination as, together with the chaplain and other officials, Calcraft and his victim appeared in full view. The hangman deftly secured his rope to the beam, hooded and noosed the murderer, then operated the drop, the sound of the hinged section striking the wall reverberating across the square. Doubtless few could avert

A Murderous Valet, A Vengeful Couple   41

their eyes, much as they may have wanted to, for as reported in the *Times* on the following day: 'The length of drop Calcraft allowed him was so little that he struggled most violently. His whole frame was convulsed; he writhed horribly and his limbs rose and fell repeatedly, while he wrung his hands, his arms having been previously pinioned, and continued to wring his hands for several minutes, they being still clasped as though he had not left off praying. It was nearly ten minutes after the rope had been fixed before the convulsions which indicated his extreme sufferings ceased.' Whether those watching felt sympathy for the murderer or considered that he had got what he deserved, is a moot point.

Londoners found plenty to talk about in 1847. For the first time cabs were equipped with 'patent mile-indexes', meters, many of them plying for hire along New Oxford Street, that thoroughfare having been completed and opened to the public on 6 March. Later that year the riverboat Cricket, while en route between the Strand and London Bridge, burst its boilers, with tragic results, six passengers being killed outright and twelve others seriously injured; further tragedy occurring at a more hallowed spot, when a man committed suicide by throwing himself from the Whispering Gallery of St Paul's Cathedral.

Balloon ascents from the City's open spaces continued to attract so much attention that occasionally the police had to control the large numbers of spectators who gathered to watch. One such balloon, manned by Messrs Green and Gypson, took off from Vauxhall Gardens, the display of the fireworks suspended beneath its wicker basket lighting up the night sky as it rose to a height of 7000 feet, bringing exclamations of admiration from the spectators. However exclamations of a different nature issued from the daredevil aviators as without warning the all-important valve failed and the air started to escape from the envelope. Deflating rapidly, it descended at high speed, disaster only being averted by the close-knit netting covering the balloon which acted as a parachute, and the craft landed more or less safely a mile or so away from its launch pad, the occupants suffering little more than bruises.

Not only members of the public sometimes needed to be controlled – the same measures had to be taken in respect of those who controlled them, for at Christmas time that year, no fewer than twenty-two constables were dismissed for being drunk!

Calcraft continued to travel round the provinces from scaffold to scaffold, although on journeys necessitating a departure from Euston Station, no doubt he purchased some reading material from the bookstall established there by WH Smith in 1848, the first of its kind in the country. One also wonders whether his wife provided him with home-made cakes to eat en route, delicacies perhaps made with self-raising flour, that ingredient having been invented three years earlier by Henry Jones, a Bristol baker. And if wrapped up, perhaps the food parcel was secured by means of another now taken-for-granted accessory, the elastic band, devised by Stephen Perry of London in the same year.

Whichever main line station he departed from, however, there was one journey he later wished he had never had to undertake, which occurred in April 1849, when he had to hang Sarah Harriett Thomas. Sarah was an attractive seventeen-year-old maidservant who had the misfortune to be employed by a cruelly domineering mistress, a woman who never hesitated to thrash her for the slightest or even nonexistent fault. At length, driven beyond endurance by the beatings and lack of food, Sarah retaliated. Waiting until her tormentor was asleep in bed, she crept into the room and struck her over the head, killing her outright. The consequences were inevitable; the scaffold was the only possible penalty, the date of the execution being the 20 April.

Calcraft travelled to Bristol and there reported to the prison governor. Together they entered the condemned cell, to find a tragic scene, for the young girl was crying hysterically "I won't be hanged; take me home, oh, take me home!" Almost against his will, Calcraft proceeded to pinion the girl's wrists, this task requiring the assistance of warders in overcoming her frenzied resistance. Led into the yard, her frantic struggles increased at the sight of the crowds massed around the waiting gallows, and she had to be carried, screaming, up the steps. Calcraft realised that the only mercy he could possibly show her was to speed her demise, and he 'gave her time scarcely to appear before the multitude before he drew the bolt.' And although he very rarely divulged any of his innermost thoughts to the press of the day, he later confided to a reporter, saying "I never felt so much compunction as I did yesterday at Bristol, having to bring that young girl to the scaffold for the murder of her mistress. She was, in my opinion, one of the prettiest and most intellectual girls I have met with in any society."

A Murderous Valet, A Vengeful Couple   43

He did not have much time to get over that nerve-racking episode, for he had to carry out another hanging the very next day! His victim on that occasion was James Bloomfield Rush, a multiple killer guilty of the callous murders of Isaac Jermy, a barrister and Recorder of Norwich, and his son Jermy Jermy. Also wounded in the attack, which took place at the Jermy home, Stanfield Hall near Norwich on 28 November 1848, were the son's wife and one of the servants, Eliza Chestney.

The case evoked much public interest, including that of Queen Victoria herself, and started when Rush, a tenant farmer on the Jermy estate, became involved in an on-going property dispute with his landlord after Jermy had inherited the family estate some years earlier. Rush had backed another claimant, John Larner, who had actually managed to occupy Stanfield Hall until being forcibly ejected by the police and military.

Rush was also having considerable problems with his domestic circumstances. When his wife died he had employed a young woman, Emily Sandford, to look after his nine children, and although their relationship developed, she eventually having a child by him, he consistently refused to marry her. Nevertheless the affair continued, another baby being born in 1848.

As the months went by, Rush continued to press his claims against Isaac Jermy, even encouraging other tenants to turn against the landlord. Matters finally came to a head on 28 November when the Jermy family's evening meal was interrupted by an intruder clad in a long black cloak and wearing a wig, his face partially concealed by a red and black mask. After opening fire with the two pistols he carried, he then fled, leaving the two men dead. In the fusillade of shots the wife of young Mr Jermy was wounded so severely as she leant across her dying husband that she eventually had to have her arm amputated, and Eliza Chestney, the maid, received a bullet in the thigh. Despite their injuries both women identified the armed man as Rush.

Questioned by the police, Rush denied any involvement. Emily initially provided him with an alibi, but then had second thoughts and changed her testimony, stating that he had indeed left the house that night and on returning had urged her that, if questioned, she was to say that he had been out for no longer than ten minutes. A subsequent search of the premises revealed the cloak and a wig; the game was up.

Pending his trial, the convicted man was held in Norwich Prison and permitted to have his meals in a local hotel. With overbearing arrogance, he is reported to have sent a note to the landlord ordering that his evening meal should include 'Pig today – and plenty of plum sauce!'

In court, on 29 March 1849, Emily was the chief witness. Wearing black satin and a veil, between bouts of tears she repeated her damning evidence, refusing to retract it despite all Rush's bullying attempts to blacken her character and accusations of being a liar. Bitter at his past refusals to marry her – in an age when unmarried mothers were regarded as pariahs, social outcasts – she took her revenge and held to her story. The jury required a mere six minutes to reach a verdict of guilty; the judge sentenced Rush to death, the execution to take place on the 21 April 1849.

William Calcraft duly reported to the gaol, outside which the scaffold had been erected. Such was the outrage felt by the general public at the nature of the killings, the crowd was even larger than ever, their appetite to witness rightful retribution being exacted having been whetted by the editors of the local weekly newspapers, who printed news of the week-long trial on a daily basis instead, and the sales of the broadsheet proclaiming the murderer's alleged *'Sorrowful Lamentations'* (see Appendix 3) reached record levels, no fewer than two and a half million copies being sold around the country.

To a chorus of jeers Rush was escorted up the steps, there to be hooded by Calcraft, and even the hangman must have been taken somewhat aback by his victim's defiant audacity as, on positioning the hempen necktie round his victim's neck, he heard Rush prompt him almost mockingly through the thickness of the material that swathed his head, to "Put the noose a little higher – and take your time!" In response, Calcraft concurred with the first suggestion, but ignored the second one, despatching Rush with a minimum of delay, though some minutes elapsed before the murderer's body finally hung limp and motionless.

> After the execution Calcraft, worried about his family, must have hurried back to London, where the latest outbreak of cholera continued to rage, no fewer than 14,000 people eventually dying by the time the epidemic abated in October of that year. Of lesser interest at the time, but almost indispensable to the human race ever since, was the brainwave of a certain American gentleman named William Hunt; requiring to attach two pieces of material together, he invented the safety-pin!

A Murderous Valet, A Vengeful Couple

Kirkdale Gaol, Liverpool, had seen many murderers hanged, but surely none deserved that fate more than one John Gleeson Wilson; for once the melodramatic verses composed by the broadsheet ballad-bards of the day did not exaggerate the enormity of his crime (see Appendix 3).

In March 1849 Wilson murdered Mrs Henrichson, wife of a sea captain, who had been pregnant at the time; her two children, Henry George aged five, and John Alfred, three, together with Mary Parr, the maid, were also brutally slain. Captured and brought to trial, he was found guilty and sentenced to be hanged at Kirkdale Prison, Liverpool. On the night before his execution, hardly surprisingly, he was reluctant to go to bed until, as reported in the local newspaper 'he was quite overpowered with sleep and would have fallen off the chair had not the warder prevented him from doing so.' Eventually persuaded to lie down, he awoke at six o'clock and although refusing any breakfast, he later drank a cup of coffee and ate some bread and butter before being taken to the press-room, where he was pinioned by Calcraft.

By dawn on that day, 15 September, vast crowds had assembled outside the gaol, their numbers reinforced by the hundreds of spectators brought in by rail from the surrounding towns, cheap excursions having been laid on for the event. All was ready; the newspaper reporters had front row priority, Mme Tussaud's representative was in attendance 'in order to obtain the clothes of the wretch' and, waiting equally patiently, was Mr. Bully, a phrenologist, duly equipped with a container of clay with which to take a cast of the soon-to-be deceased's head.

A few minutes before 12 o'clock the iron gates leading to the scaffold were opened and the grim entourage appeared. Wilson, walking between two spiritual comforters, looked calmly at the sea of onlookers and allowed William Calcraft to position him on the drop. The hangman, only too aware that those surging round the scaffold were with difficulty being held back as they sought to wreak their revenge on the killer, wasted no time; with his usual alacrity he positioned the white cap and adjusted the noose, the shortness of the rope showing as little mercy for his victim as that shown by John Gleeson Wilson towards the helpless family, although it was subsequently reported that his sufferings were brief.

However the drama did not end there, for Calcraft proceeded to exacerbate the already inflamed mood of the crowd still further, by taking hold of the slowly rotating corpse and pulling the cap away from its distorted features. "Cover his face! Cover his face!" came the horrified cry; the hangman hastily complied, but no doubt had to give the reasons for his inexplicable lack of judgement to the sheriff afterwards.

Had the hangman only known, he was going to be involved in an even more sensational case before the end of that year, in which he would have to hang not one, but two victims, one of them being a woman! But before that, relatively minor executions had to be performed.

One of them was in Scotland and, such was the delicacy of one charge – that of rape – the trial was held in camera. The accused, James Robb, had imbibed too much at his local inn and then, succumbing, as they say, to desires of the flesh, broke into the cottage of elderly Mary Smith by clambering down the wide chimney, she having denied him entry via the front door. So brutal was the assault that the woman collapsed, the subsequent post mortem revealing that she had had a heart attack.

All the evidence pointing to his guilt, the police producing his soot-stained clothes, little mercy was shown him at the trial. John Murdoch, the Scottish executioner, being unavailable, Calcraft was summoned north, and on 16 October 1849 the executioner and his victim mounted the steps of the Aberdeen scaffold, one to walk down them again, his job completed, the other being left to rotate slowly in the chill autumn air.

A month after he had despatched James Robb, a crime was committed which created a furore in the country, involving as it did a married couple, Frederick and Maria Manning. This promised to be a scaffold spectacular indeed, and one in which Calcraft would play his usual leading part; a performance definitely not to be missed by the regular execution-attending clientele, for both husband and wife were to be hanged at the same time.

It all started when, with the cognizance of her husband, Maria, a reportedly attractive twenty-eight-year-old woman of Swiss descent, took a lover, Patrick O'Connor. He, a fifty-year-old moneylender, advised them to rent a public house in Shoreditch, but when the business failed, Maria accused O'Connor of cheating them and demanded compensation. On 8 August 1849 she invited him to visit them at their home at No. 3 Minerva

Place, Bermondsey, in order to discuss the situation; instead she shot him through the head. This however failed to kill him and so Frederick, who some time earlier had bought a crowbar, used it to batter their victim to death; after which the couple buried the body in the kitchen.

Whatever caused the subsequent rift in the relationship between the two murderers was not discovered, but Maria, unbeknownst to her husband, went to O'Connor's house and stole cash and valuables, including some railway stock, then travelled to Edinburgh. Meanwhile their victim's absence had been reported to the police and they, having ascertained O'Connor's last movements, searched the Bermondsey house. On noticing the fresh cement around some of the flagstones in the kitchen, they lifted them, to find a man's body, his legs doubled up and tied to his haunches. In an attempt to destroy all traces of the crime, quicklime had been poured over the corpse and identification was only established by the discovery of a set of false teeth. The bullet which had contributed to the man's death was also recovered.

Maria was arrested when she tried to sell the railway stock in Scotland, Frederick later being located in Jersey and similarly taken into custody. That there was little love lost between them was evidenced at the trial, Frederick blaming his wife for the murder, she denying all knowledge of the crime despite the shares found in her possession. When, after forty-five minutes the jury returned to bring in a verdict of guilty, Maria indignantly protested that she had loved O'Connor and if she had intended to kill anyone it would have been that man – pointing to her husband – who had made her life a hell on earth. On both being sentenced to death, Maria gave vent to a furious tirade against Judge Cresswell; he however ignored her outburst and ordered both prisoners to be taken down to the cells and from thence to Horsemonger Lane Gaol, the county gaol for Surrey, situated near the Elephant and Castle in Southwark, there to await execution.

At one time Mrs Manning had been a servant in the household of Lady Blantyre, whose mother, the Duchess of Sutherland, had been a close friend of Queen Victoria. From the condemned cell Maria wrote to Her Majesty, appealing for mercy but, her petition being in vain, she attempted to take her own life. She was guarded by three wardresses and one night, noticing that two of them were asleep and the third dozing, she tried to pierce her windpipe with her sharp pointed fingernails. The guard, waking up, realised what was happening and it took the efforts of all three wardresses to tear the woman's hands away from her throat and subdue her.

On Tuesday morning 13 November 1849, during their last few minutes before having to face the hangman, the doomed couple met in the prison chapel and it was reported that as they stood before the altar, Frederick expressed his wish that they should not part in animosity; she replied that she had none, and then kissed him. The Ordinary administered the last sacrament, after which Frederick said: "I think we shall meet in heaven."

Calcraft then appeared and, after securing Frederick Manning's arms, he proceeded to pinion Maria. It was a bitterly cold morning and the hangman tried, in his own way, to show some solicitude for his victim, urging her to allow the wardress to wrap her cloak around her, but Maria refused; instead she asked that her black silk handkerchief be tied about her eyes beneath the black veil she already wore. Thus blindfolded she was led by Mr Harris, the surgeon, in the sombre procession, the sonorous bell tolling the while, along the seemingly endless passageways and up the steep steps to where the gallows awaited.

Horsemonger Lane Gaol had a flat roof save for a few skylights, that architectural feature admirably permitting the erection of the scaffold thereon, thereby providing a perfect stage for the drama due to take place. Below and in front of the building the spectators, more than thirty thousand in number, filled every available hired space, balcony and roof-top, no fewer than five hundred police constables attending to maintain some semblance of order. To have some conception of the scenes that morning one only has to read this excerpt from a letter by Charles Dickens, which was printed in the *Times* on the following day.

He wrote 'I was a witness to the execution at Horsemonger-lane this morning. I went there with the intention of observing the crowd gathered to behold it and I had excellent opportunities of doing so, at intervals throughout the night, and continuously from daybreak, until after the spectacle was over. I believe that a sight so inconceivably awful as the wickedness and levity of the immense crowd could be imagined by no man, and could be presented in no heathen land under the sun. When I came upon the scene at midnight, the shrillness of the cries and howls that were raised from time to time, denoting that they came from a concourse of boys and girls already assembled in the best places, made my blood run cold.'

'When the day dawned' his letter continued 'thieves, low prostitutes, ruffians and vagabonds of every kind flocked on to the ground, with every variety of offensive and foul behaviour. Fightings, faintings, whistling, imitations of Punch, brutal jokes, tumultuous demonstrations of indecent delight when swooning women were dragged out of the crowd by the police, with their dresses disordered, gave a new zest to the general entertainment. When the sun rose brightly – as it did – it gilded thousands upon thousands of upturned faces, so inexpressibly odious in their brutal mirth or callousness, that a man had cause to feel ashamed of the shape he wore, and to shrink from himself, as fashioned in the image of the Devil...'

This was not just literary hyperbole, a reporter from the same paper describing 'the disorderly rabble smoking clay pipes and muzzy with beer, pickpockets plying their light-fingered art, little ragged boys climbing up posts, a ceaseless din of sounds and war of tongues...'

A gasp rose from countless throats as Maria emerged in full view on to the roof; she could have been mistaken for any respectable lady of the day out for a walk, for she wore her 'Sunday Best', an ankle-length black satin dress, its cuffs trimmed with white lace, black silk stockings and mauve-coloured gloves completing her ensemble. The *Times* reporter described the couple's last moments 'And when Frederick Manning ascended the steps leading to the drop his limbs tottered under him and he appeared scarcely able to move. Upon his wife approaching the scaffold, he turned round, his face towards the people, while Calcraft proceeded to draw over his head the white nightcap and adjust the fatal rope. The executioner then drew another nightcap over the female prisoner's head and, all the necessary preparations being now completed, the scaffold was cleared of all its occupants except the two wretched beings doomed to die.'

Total silence reigned as Calcraft swiftly drew the bolt, all eyes fixed on the two hooded and noosed figures silhouetted against the morning sky; the trap opened and the bodies dropped, oscillating slowly with the momentum of their fall, and dying almost immediately; or, as delicately phrased by the editor of the *Daily News* 'with far less muscular action than usual.' Dickens, with his enviable flair for painting word-pictures, wrote how 'the man was a limp, loose suit of clothes, as if he had gone out of them; the woman's fine shape, elaborately corseted and artfully dressed, was quite unchanged in its trim appearance as it slowly swung from side to side.'

After an hour the Mannings' corpses were cut down and buried, ironically enough, beneath the same type of paving stones within the prison as those under which they had buried Patrick O'Connor.

The Press in general and the satirical magazine *Punch* in particular made much of Maria Manning's choice of gallows garments, one edition even including an acerbic item entitled *'Fashions for Old Bailey Ladies'* reporting, tongue-in-cheek, how;

'At the elegant reunion on the occasion of the late *Matinée Criminelle* at the Old Bailey, the lovely and accomplished Lady X......... carried off *les honneurs* with her lovely *Manteau a la* MANNINGS, trimmed with *ruche en gibbets* and *têtes de port bouffonées*. The neck is surmounted with a running cord ... la CALCRAFT, which finishes in a *noeud couland* in satin, under the left ear. With the *chapeau* is worn a *bonnet de pendue*; this sweet cap can be arranged to cover the whole face and is likely to be thus worn during the approaching season.'

Her funereal appearance is believed to have given rise to the bestowal of the name 'Black Maria' on the type of police vehicles used to convey prisoners to gaol, although this term was already in use in the USA in the 1840s, being derived from that of Maria Lee, a large coloured lady, owner of a lodging house in Boston, who frequently assisted the police to subdue struggling miscreants.

Over the months and indeed years following the Mannings' executions, crowds flocked to Mme Tussaud's to gaze, not only at the effigy of Frederick in his black suit, his wife in the now legendary costume, and that of their victim, positioned near a scale model of their kitchen showing where the body had been buried, but also the actual crowbar with which Patrick O'Connor had been so brutally slain.

Charles Dickens was later to refer to the executioner, this time in another letter to the newspaper, saying 'Mr. Calcraft, the hangman, of whom I have some information in reference to this last occasion, should be restrained in his unseemly briskness, in his jokes, his oaths, and his brandy.' Briskness, perhaps, in order to despatch the victims without delay; jokes and oaths, hardly, for he was known for his reticence on the scaffold, and the only brandy available was that given occasionally to victims to calm their nerves. By 1868 however, the famous author would seem to have changed his opinion of the hangman, for in an August edition of *All the Year Round*, a weekly journal published by him, Dickens included an article by an unidentified clergyman who had given spiritual solace to a murderer on the scaffold. Far from denigrating Calcraft, the cleric wrote 'I can see him as I write, a mild, gentle-faced man, his eyes full and grey, though small and sweet in their expression.' The padre then went on to describe the execution; 'the hangman then went on to fix the rope, with long pains to arrange the knot in the most merciful place; and there was a fall and something was swaying to and fro, till at last it became steady. Then there was the noise of the crowd, and it woke up into life, to go about its business.'

CHAPTER FIVE

CALCRAFT IS CHARGED WITH NEGLECT

As the years went by, the general public became accustomed to seeing comprehensive reports of executions in the newspapers of the day, and were only too aware of the authority with which William Calcraft controlled everything taking place on the scaffold, down to the minutest detail. Judge their surprise, therefore, and no doubt their malicious delight when, on reading the *Times* of 7th and 14th March 1850, they saw an account of the feared executioner appearing in court, not for the purpose of surveying his next victim, but as a defendant!

Those crowding the public gallery in the Worship Street Police Court, Shoreditch, would have noticed that Calcraft was showing his age. With the passage of time – he was now forty-nine years old – he had become thickset, and his full straggly beard and unkempt hair, previously grey, was now white, and they listened intently as the charge was read out; that he had refused to support his seventy-four-year-old mother Sarah, at that time living in a workhouse (a parish hostel for the homeless, such refuges not noted for their luxurious lifestyle) in Hatfield Peveril near Chelmsford, Essex. In evidence Mr Shee, one of the officers of the parish, stated that he had visited the defendant at his home in Hoxton and found him pursuing his occupation as a shoemaker. Upon being reminded of his family commitments and responsibilities, Calcraft refused to contribute towards his mother's upkeep, leaving him, Mr Shee, no alternative but to take out a legal summons against him.

Calcraft is Charged with Neglect 53

As evidence regarding Calcraft's income was essential to the court before reaching a decision as to his culpability, the case was adjourned for seven days. When the hearing was resumed, Calcraft was absent from the Court; the Governor of Newgate Prison however, was present, and as the defendant's immediate employer he stated that Calcraft was paid one guinea a week by him for his services. The defendant not having appeared, the magistrate ordered that an arrest warrant be issued, but before this could become effective, Calcraft arrived. Once there, he had the embarrassment of having to face his destitute mother across a packed courtroom, and having to listen while she explained that she had been staying with her married daughter for two years but eventually had no alternative but to seek the charity of the parish. Heaping further shame on her son's head, she went on to complain that she had not seen him for three years, and although she had written to him on three occasions asking for his help, she had not even had one reply.

William Calcraft was then ordered to stand and face the Bench, and give his reasons for being unable to support his mother. As quoted by the *Times*' reporter, he said "Well, I should be very happy to support her if it was in my power, but it is not; and as to what she says about the profits I derive from my shoe-making business, I can assure you that I have not earned a penny at that for a great number of weeks. I have sustained a very severe personal injury, in fact you never saw such an arm as I have got. I can neither get my coat on nor off without assistance, and after being confined to bed with it for more than two months, I had a doctor's bill sent to me for £10.3s.6d., which I am totally incapable of paying at present, and he must wait for it. I admit that I receive a guinea a week from the city, but that is all we have to live on, and when you deduct 4s.6d. out of that for rent, and the cost of a Sunday's dinner, you will find there is not much left."

Then, evidently in the hope of eliciting some sympathy from the Bench, he continued "It is not for want of feeling, that I don't support my mother; she was in much better circumstances than I am, she had a large quantity of good furniture and a number of silver spoons, and I can't see why she applied to the workhouse people at all." He was then asked whether he had any children, to which he answered that he had three, adding that although they were now grown-up, they were still an expense to him. The magistrate, evidently sceptical, exclaimed sternly "Well, in accordance with an act as old as the reign of Queen Elizabeth, you are clearly liable for the support of your mother, and so I feel it my duty to make an order on you for the sum of three shillings per week for your mother's support as long as she remains chargeable to the workhouse, together with the costs attendant upon the present proceedings against you." The costs, as declared by Mr Shee, amounted to £1.9s.6d., the magistrate then stating that this sum would be included in the order.

Calcraft, obviously taken aback, replied defiantly that the Bench may make the order if they liked, but that it was wholly beyond his power to pay up. He went on to ask the parish officer, perhaps with a hint of sarcasm, what he, the defendant, would be paid if he took his mother home and looked after her; this offer was rejected by Mr Shee, who then retorted that perhaps Mrs Calcraft might prefer to remain in the workhouse! To this Mrs Calcraft agreed, saying she would not be safe in London for as long as a week, and that she would much rather stay in the workhouse.

At that, William Calcraft seemingly capitulated for, as the *Times* reported 'The defendant thereupon leant over his mother, expressing his willingness to take care of her, and with much apparent feeling, told her that he was very sorry she should have had to come there at all. And upon the order being made, and one of the officers coming forward to help her out of her chair, the defendant pushed him aside and, gently raising her, with his arm round her waist, he carefully supported her out of the Court.' Perhaps he had assumed that she did have enough with which to support herself – but at least he might have behaved like a dutiful son and replied to her letters!

One of William's two sons, Thomas, who died on 7 October 1925, coincidentally the very day on which his own granddaughter Muriel was born, *was* doubtless dutiful to his father William – and also to his Sovereign, for when old enough he joined the Household Cavalry; obviously his father's profession did not prohibit him from being selected for one of the distinguished regiments which carried out guard duties for Queen Victoria. One would like to think that his proud parents William and Louisa joined the large crowds that attended the parades and reviews frequently taking place in the City, there to watch their son as, with his colleagues, he escorted the royal coach.

Of course the newspapers of the day did not devote all their column space to Calcraft's misdemeanours; just as contemporary readers are regaled by 'zany' news items, so were their Victorian counterparts. In that year, 1850, it was reported that at a London circus, the 'Lion Queen' had been attacked and mauled to death by a tiger she had recently introduced into her act. The animal had obviously decided to prove that her title did not apply to one of his breed. Another animal story concerned a balloonist, a Mr Green who, despite vigorous protests by the SPCA, got airborne sitting astride a horse. A Mr Peters also received some attention from the press; charged with stealing a duck from Kensington Gardens, he received a three months gaol sentence, while in Warwickshire Richard Manks surely qualified for an unusual record, that of walking a thousand miles in a thousand hours, one mile every hour on the hour. Doubtless he rested for the balance of each sixty minutes, but the report does not specify whether he headed in one direction during the four days and sixteen hours of his perambulation, turned back when the half way stage of five hundred miles had been reached, or indeed returned to base at the end of each hour. And today's readers, appalled by the intensity and noise of London's traffic and yearning for the reputed 'good old days', should think again; Victorians were overwhelmed by the sheer multitude and cacophony of the thousands of vehicles crowding the City's streets; lumbering omnibuses, two-seater cabs, hackney coaches, gigs, vans, large and small wagons bringing provisions to the markets, manure carts, butchers' trucks, all drawn by horses. Nearly 15,000 vehicles traversed London Bridge every twelve hours and the annual number of horses crossing Westminster Bridge was no fewer than eight million! Apart from the tons of manure deposited by them, should one animal slip on the greasy surface and fall, a back-up of miles could ensue with the inevitable consequences; road-rage is not a modern phenomenon, and in those days all drivers had whips!

April 1850 found Calcraft in Cambridge, where one Elias Lucas was appearing in court charged with murdering his wife. Obviously she was not present; at least not all of her, for a gruesome exhibit was produced in evidence, namely a tin box containing part of her stomach and intestines!

Lucas was a well-built man in his mid-thirties who worked on a farm owned by a Mr. Cross at Castle Camps, a small village some eighteen miles from Cambridge. He had married his wife Susan in 1846 when she was aged sixteen, their marriage reportedly a happy and contented one. She had a sister, Mary Reader who, having left her employer, a carpenter in nearby Castle End, on grounds of ill-health, moved in with Susan and her husband, and found work as a servant in Mr Cross' house. It was then that an illicit affair began between Elias and Mary, one that would result in the deaths of all three.

Arsenic being available on the farm for the purpose of exterminating rats, Lucas acquired some of it, determined to rid himself of his wife so that he and Mary could marry. On 21 February 1850 he persuaded his lover to mix some of the deadly poison in food she had prepared for the evening meal. Susan duly ate the food and soon after complaining about the nauseating taste, collapsed. Doctor Cramer was sent for and on arrival he found Mrs Lucas dead. On examining her he saw that her fingers were 'clenched as a bird's claw and the body was supernaturally blue, the symptoms making me believe that she had died from poison. Under such suspicious circumstances I refused to sign a death certificate.'

Mary Reader, affecting innocence of the cause of the tragedy, stated that there was no poison in the house, further saying that her sister had had a disease of the chest and that after the meal, had vomited in the garden and had exclaimed: "I am a dead woman."

In court Doctor Cramer stated that he performed the post mortem and found two grains of metallic arsenic in the stomach, after which he had placed that organ and the intestines in a bladder and taken them away. Further witnesses testified that Lucas had frequently said he wished he was a single man again and that, together with the testimony of the police that they had discovered fifteen ounces of the poison in the kitchen, sealed the fate of the two murderous conspirators.

The members of the jury were out for but a short period before returning with a guilty verdict, upon which Mr Justice Wightman donned the black cap and condemned both Elias and Mary to death.

As reported in the local newspaper 'On hearing the verdict pronounced, Lucas, who had conducted himself throughout the trial with the greatest levity, even laughing at the sight of the tin box containing his late wife's viscera, waved his hands, vociferating: "I am not guilty, goodbye, ladies and gentlemen, I am innocent." But later, while in the condemned cells, the awful realisation of their fate caused them both to confess, Lucas saying:

"I deserve to be hanged! I brought it on myself!" and expressing his sanguine hope and confidence that the Almighty would forgive him. Mary Reader too, confessed that because of the infamous passion she had for Elias, she had allowed herself to be persuaded by him to mix nearly a tablespoon of arsenic into her sister's food, and she stated her bitter regret at ever having done so.'

In the edition of 13 April 1850 a graphic account of the executions was published, describing how 'shortly before twelve o'clock the culprits were removed from their cells, when the Executioner commenced the ceremony of pinioning their arms and preparing them for the awful trial they were about to undergo. The mournful cavalcade then slowly proceeded, the chapel bell tolling a solemn sound, towards the platform erected in front of the principal entrance to the gaol, and which, by means of a ladder, the culprits ascended, accompanied by the Reverend Mr. Roberts, the Governor of the Gaol, Mr Orridge, and Calcraft, the well-known 'finisher of the law'.

'Shortly after, the wretched beings were placed under the fatal beam' continued the report 'and after a few moments spent in prayer, the ropes being adjusted, on a signal then being given, the fatal plank fell, and the wretched beings were launched into eternity, in sight of the countless multitude of spectators who, filling the avenues and surrounding the Castle Hill, had assembled to witness the melancholy exit of two youthful criminals who had alike outraged the ties of nature and the sacred ordinances of God. The bodies, after hanging the usual time, on being cut down, will be buried within the precincts of the prison.'

After the executions copies of an expiatory poem, allegedly composed by the doomed couple (although more likely by an enterprising pamphleteer!) were sold as a dreadful warning to others who might be similarly tempted; these are included in Appendix 3.

Such was the revulsion felt by the public towards the couple who had committed such a ruthless crime, that little criticism was directed by the newspaper – or even from those around the scaffold – at Calcraft; no doubt he appreciated the welcome change!

Headgear rather than neckwear caught the attention of the media in 1849 when T & W Bowler of Southwark invented the bowler hat, apparel which, although first worn by Norfolk gamekeepers, soon showed every sign of becoming popular throughout the country. Traditionally-minded readers will no doubt be relieved to know that William Calcraft refused to submit to fashion's demands, and continued to appear on the scaffold wearing his tall odd-shaped hat. But quite likely he and Louisa had an edifying day out at the Great Exhibition in the Crystal Palace, Hyde Park, which was ceremonially opened by Queen Victoria on 1 May 1851.

Also in that year there was an apparent reduction in the taxes people had to pay. Since 1784 an annual tax had been levied on the number of windows in peoples' houses, ranging from 2s.3d. (about 11p.) per window up to eight windows, to 7s.6d. (37p.) each for up to 39 windows. This imposition, at a time when farm labourers, for instance, existed on wages of 8s. (40p.) a week, resulted in bricked up windows and darkened rooms. The tax was finally abolished on 24 July, and while no doubt window cleaners reaped the benefit, the general public soon realised that other taxes were inevitably increased!

In March 1852, Calcraft had to travel north to Derbyshire, to despatch a man who had committed a truly horrendous murder. Anthony Turner, a tailor who lived with his wife and child in Lane End, a village near Belper, about eight miles from the county town, had a part-time job collecting rents for a Mrs Phoebe Barnes, the owner of property in the locality. However he had defaulted on money he owed her, and finally losing patience with him, she sent him a note informing him that she no longer intended to employ him.

Determined to get his revenge, Turner borrowed a large bacon-slicing knife from Mr Husland, the owner of the local grocer's shop, exclaiming that he was going to kill Mrs Barnes with it. Any intention the grocer may have had of informing the police was thwarted by Turner, who forthwith went directly to his victim's house. The door was opened by the maid who, on being told that he wished to see her mistress, went upstairs, returning to say that Mrs Barnes had nothing whatsoever to say to him. At that, insensate with rage, Turner pushed the girl to one side and mounted the stairs.

Thoroughly alarmed by the man's aggressive attitude, the maid ran next door to the residence of the Reverend Bannister, that cleric immediately responding by going to Mrs Barnes' rescue; but alas, too late. Even as he entered the house, Turner, the bloodstained knife grasped in his hand, was descending the stairs, and in the struggle that followed, the reverend gentleman managed to wrestle the attacker to the floor and then go to the bedroom – where a ghastly sight met his eyes! As described in one of the melodramatic broadsheets of the day 'Mrs Barnes lay on the ground, her head literally severed from her body, one of her thumbs also cut off, as if in struggling to prevent the murderous knife from lacerating her throat. Medical aid was immediately in attendance, but life was extinct.' A severed head usually is fatal.

Turner had escaped into the night, and the police lost no time in issuing a description of the wanted man: "aged about 45 years, height approximately 5 feet 8 inches, he has very small black eyes and is believed to be wearing a pair of drab trousers and a black coat".

It was not until Monday night, two days later, that Superintendent Wragg and a fellow officer named Taylor received information that Turner had been seen near his home in Lane End, to where they immediately proceeded. Locating their quarry, who had taken refuge in an upper room of a nearby house, the senior officer, pausing only to light a candle and draw his night-stick, entered the bedroom, in time to see Turner raise the knife to his own throat, meanwhile exclaiming frantically "It's all over!"

Wragg closed with the man, striking him several times with his stick, and despite the candle having been extinguished in the mêlée, thereby plunging the room into Stygian darkness, both officers managed to overpower Turner and deprive him of the weapon. He was then arrested and conveyed in a cart through the large crowd of people attracted by the commotion, to the lockup.

At his trial he was charged with wilful murder, and such was the overwhelming evidence against him that the jury were out only three hours before bringing in a verdict of Guilty. The atmosphere in court was admirably described by a reporter the next day; 'His Lordship put on the black cap and in tones which thrilled every heart in court, he said "Anthony Turner, after a long and painful investigation, to which all parties have devoted themselves with exemplary attention, a jury of your country has been compelled to perform the painful duty of pronouncing you guilty of murder – of murder which, at all times black and dreadful – becomes in your case doubly black and dreadful!" His Lordship then sentenced the prisoner in the usual terms; he was then removed from the Bar of the court in a state of stupor.'

Early on the morning of 26 March 1852 a few spectators had already started to gather; to quote a local newspaper 'a concourse of people there certainly was, and so there would have been at a foot race or a balloon ascent; but until previous to noon, a person could walk conveniently over the open space in front of the scaffold, and as twelve o'clock approached, numbers of mechanics and labourers arrived from all directions, with the apparent intention of passing away their dinner hour.' The crowd then rapidly increased in size, another paper regretting the fact 'that a large proportion of the multitude consisted of women and children, the women especially being very numerous. We also noticed' the editorial continued 'a great number of females with babes at the breast. One woman in Vernon Street had no less than eight small children with her. They were all dressed up for the occasion, and no doubt she thought she was giving them an intellectual treat. Indeed the scene resembled a pleasure fair than anything else.'

Just before midday the prisoner was taken from the condemned cell and led across the yard to the gatehouse. Entering that building, he was escorted up a spiral stairway to an upper room, where Calcraft proceeded to pinioned his arms. The two men then stepped out through a doorway on to the scaffold that had been erected on the left-hand side of the principal entrance to the gaol.

Seemingly resigned to his fate, Turner – who had earlier confessed his guilt and admitted throwing the knife he had used, on to a neighbour's fire – offered no resistance as the hangman capped and noosed him; wasting no time, Calcraft operated the drop, his victim's struggles lasting only a matter of minutes. There was little commotion among the crowd; indeed one journalist reported that 'there was no manifestation of feeling on the part of those gathered round the scaffold, and after looking at the lifeless body for some time, they quietly dispersed. The public houses were soon filled after the execution, in consequence of the great numbers from the country requiring refreshments.'

An hour later, the body was cut down, and William Barton, a local sculptor who lived in North Street, Duffield Road, took a cast of the head before the corpse of murderer Anthony Turner was finally buried in the prison cemetery.

Calcraft is Charged with Neglect

Over the next few years Calcraft had to travel across the Border several times, when ordered to execute Scottish criminals, one particular journey being to despatch two murderous brothers, Michael and Peter Scanlan. They had been employed at a lime works in Fife, and occupied rooms in a lodging house next to a shop owned by Margaret Maxwell, a friendly woman who, having initially allowed them a certain amount of credit on their purchases, finally ran out of patience and refused to extend that facility. Their reactions were violent and merciless; on the night of 16 February 1852 they broke into the house and savagely beat the woman to death.

A resultant search of the house by the police found that a silver watch was missing, as was a sum of money; bizarrely, a copy of the New Testament had also been stolen. The two brothers immediately came under suspicion and after further investigations, were brought to trial at Edinburgh on 14 June. In court they had little to say in their defence and, being found guilty, were sentenced to be hanged at Cupar, south of Dundee, on 5 July. On hearing their fate, the Scanlons protested their innocence, calling the judge and members of the jury 'damned asses!'

Cupar not having its own scaffold, one was borrowed from Edinburgh, its component parts being loaded on to wagons and re-assembled some little distance from the town's prison. Being similarly bereft of a hangman, the London executioner was sent for, and so Calcraft started out on his thousand mile round trip. Arriving at the gaol the hangman inspected the scaffold and gallows, finding them to his satisfaction, and on the fateful day travelled in the bus chartered to convey the cortège to the site, accompanied by the priest, and seated next to one of his victims, a macabre sight to those lining the bus route! Nor were avid spectators the only ones there. As a precaution against any escape bid being attempted by the Scanlans' workmates, not only were four hundred citizens sworn in as special constables to reinforce the local police force, but the vehicle was escorted by regular soldiers of the 42nd. Regiment and the 7th. Hussars.

The two men, dressed in white moleskin suits, mounted the scaffold, there to embrace each other in a final farewell. Even as Calcraft pinioned them, they continued to swear that they were not guilty of the murder, but forgave all those who had condemned them to death. Suddenly, on seeing Peter's sweetheart in the crowd, waving frantically and weeping, Michael exclaimed "Look, Peter, there's Marget!"

A dramatic moment then occurred, for just as the hangman released the drop, a fierce thunderstorm broke over the town, causing the thousands packed around the green to scatter and seek cover, thereby averting any of the mob scenes which usually occurred after a hanging.

And as it was a double execution, Calcraft received £30, some of which was to reimburse him for his travel expenses.

Some months later the hangman had an even greater distance to travel, it being nearly six hundred miles to Aberdeen, where George Christie was to be executed on 13 January 1853. Greed was the motive, drink the impetus, when Christie, aware of the fact that Barbara Ross, owner of a local farm, had sold two pigs, returned drunk after a convivial session in the city's taverns and decided to deprive her of the proceeds of the sale. At her first signs of resistance he seized an axe and with it killed, not only her, but also her five-year-old grandchild.

Arrested later, suspicion became a certainty when the police discovered several of the woman's valuables in his house. Denial was useless, hanging inevitable, and when Calcraft pinioned him on the scaffold, the priest asked him if he had anything to say. Showing no emotion, he replied "No". And the eight thousand or so spectators watched as Calcraft released the trap and the unrepentant murderer went to meet his Maker.

Hardly had Calcraft had time to get home and make a shoe or two when, in March of that year, he had to travel north again, this time to the Scottish Borders, and once more climb the steps of the Edinburgh-owned scaffold, to meet, for the first and last time, one John Williams.

In order to traverse many roads in this country in those days, tolls had to be paid for their upkeep (a 19th century Road Tax), the money being exacted by toll-keepers who lived in cottages along the routes. Whatever dispute arose between Williams and Andrew Mill, toll-keeper at the Cleek-him-in-Toll, near Lauder, situated betwixt Jedburgh and Edinburgh, is not known, but the outcome was horrifyingly obvious, for Andrew Mill was later found dead.

Shortly after 11.30 on the cold wet morning of 12 March 1853 Williams was brought out of Greenlaw's County Hall; clad in prison garb of flannel trousers and jacket, his chains were struck from his ankles by the local blacksmith and he was led to the scaffold. There, although capped and pinioned, he was allowed to hold a handkerchief, the dropping of which would signify the completion of his prayers and his readiness for death. Calcraft waited, his hand on the lever; the handkerchief dropped – the trapdoor almost simultaneously following suit.

Solo hangings were always well-attended but when more than one victim was to be despatched, the dedicated patrons of the scaffold turned out en masse. And so it was when Hans Smith M'Farlane and Helen Blackwood were sentenced to death for the callous murder of a ship's carpenter, Alexander Boyd. They had been out drinking with him and others, and on their return to their house in the New Vennel, Glasgow, they drugged him with whisky and snuff. They then proceeded to rob him of his clothes and money and finally pushed him through the lofty window, either the lethal cocktail or the fall resulting in his death. The robbery and murder were seen by two small boys who were being looked after by Helen Blackwood and had earlier been tucked up for the night under the bed.

At their trial in Edinburgh, at which they were both sentenced to death, the woman declared "We have not got justice – there is a higher Judge for us. We are innocent!" They were escorted back to Glasgow's North Prison and there M'Farlane requested the Governor's permission to marry Helen Blackwood, but the application was refused and arrangements were made forthwith for their execution.

Little did the crowd of forty thousand who crowded round the scaffold on that day, the 11 August 1853, expect to see anything more than what they had anticipated – an execution, yet in fact it was to be nothing less than two funerals and a 'wedding'! For as Hans and Helen stood side by side on the drop, the clergyman standing nearby and the hangman poised to operate the bolt, the expectant silence of the crowd was broken by M'Farlane as, in a determined voice, he said: "Helen Blackwood, before God and in the presence of these witnesses, I take you to be my wife; do you consent?" Without hesitation Helen replied, "I do!" "Then" Hans replied, "before these witnesses I declare you to be what you have always been to me, a true and faithful wife, and you die an honest woman."

The clergyman, not unsurprisingly caught unawares, quickly gathered his wits and in a loud voice exclaimed "Amen!" But Calcraft, although doubtless realising that he was inadvertently playing the dual roles of both best man and the bride's father, also realised that, as the Finisher of the Law, he dared not allow sentiment to interfere with his duty; drawing the bolt, he sent the couple on their way – together.

The hangman must have been relieved when, about a fortnight later, he was ordered to carry out another execution, not, this time, in the far north of the country, but at Lancaster Castle, a notable landmark in the city of Lancaster. His victim was Richard Pedder, a boatman who lived in the little village of Hambleton, not far from Fleetwood, and who plied his trade in the nearby Wyre estuary.

On 18 April 1853 local police were called to his house, where they found Mrs Pedder lying dead in the garden, she having been killed by a shotgun fired through the open kitchen window. Her husband was in a distraught condition and attempted to commit suicide by shooting himself; disarmed, he was arrested and taken along Carr Lane, now the A588, to Stalmine, where he was confined in the police station there.

Despite initially confessing to the murder of his wife Betty, at his trial early in August at the Castle Assizes, his lawyer sought to claim that it was accidental. The jury, although wasting little time in finding Pedder guilty of murder, nevertheless recommended mercy, but the plea was rejected by the judge, as was a later petition submitted by the townsfolk, and the prisoner was sentenced to death by hanging, the execution to take place on 27 August of that year.

The *modus operandi* in respect of those being executed at Lancaster Castle involved the victims being brought from the prison's chapel, situated within the building, into the 'Drop Room', where they were pinioned in readiness. In the outer wall of the room were, and still are, large double doors, their upper halves being glazed; these doors opened inwards, revealing a sheer drop of six feet to the ground outside, and this area, at the rear of the Castle and facing the nearby church of St Mary, was in a recess of the castle's walls, and so became known as 'Hanging Corner'.

The original arrangement was for the victim to be noosed by a rope attached to a beam that extended outwards above the doors; when dead, the body was not cut down but was swung back into the cellar immediately beneath the Drop Room through an opening below the double doors. The cellar was also accessible via a trapdoor in the floor of the Drop Room, which allowed the hangman go down, cut the body free and deposit it in the coffin waiting there.

In later years major structural alterations took place. When an execution was due to take place, gallows were erected outside in Hanging Corner, two strong posts being fitted into square holes chiselled in large circular stones set in the ground, and then joined by a crossbeam. Beneath the beam the six-foot high scaffold was positioned, butting against the wall, the cortège thereby leaving the Drop Room via the doors and stepping straight on to the boards.

After the execution, the body was again swung from where it hung suspended beneath the level of the trap, back into the cellar as before, the opening being screened from morbid spectators by black curtains. A method of mass production – or rather, extinction – was made possible by the considerable distance between the posts, the crossbeam being capable of accommodating several felons at the same time, the greatest number being eleven, hanged in March 1801.

This then was the arrangement in place when Pedder was due to meet his Maker. On the evening prior to the fateful day the gallows were erected in Hanging Corner, and by early morning thousands of spectators had flocked in on foot and horseback, by cart and by coach, by road and by rail, from the surrounding towns and countryside. To control them, nearly fifty police officers were on duty, and shortly before midday Pedder was brought to the Drop Room, where he was given the last sacrament, after which Calcraft entered, carrying his 'tackle', the hangman then proceeding to pinion the condemned man's arms.

The *Lancaster Gazette*, in its next issue, reported how the Chaplain led the grim procession out on to the scaffold, where Pedder, contrite and resigned to his fate, thanked the prison governor and warders for the considerate way in which he had been treated. Mounting the steps, the tragically short rope attached to the beam immediately above his head, he faced the vast multitude packed into the restricted area around the scaffold, many sitting on the church wall opposite, and bowed respectfully, then said "May the Lord Jesus receive my soul."

Calcraft stepped forward, first pulling the white cap down over Pedder's head before positioning the noose about the man's neck. Allowing a few moments for all formalities to be completed, he then withdrew the bolt. Pedder's body dropped a mere two feet or so, to writhe momentarily before hanging motionless. Slowly the crowd dispersed, Calcraft completing his task an hour later by descending into the cellar, bringing the body in and cutting the rope, after which it was interred in the prison grounds.

Obviously no-one can possibly know what it must feel like to be hanged, but a credible description of the effects was postulated by Calcraft after officiating at an execution at Lancaster Castle – and it may well have been following that described above. As quoted in a guidebook by Thomas Johnson, published in 1893, the hangman said 'Well, I have heard that when you are tied up and your face turned to the Castle wall and the trap falls, you see its stones expanding and contracting violently, and a similar expansion and contraction seems to take place in your own head and breast. Then there is a rush of fire and an earthquake; your eyeballs spring out of their sockets; the Castle shoots up into the air, and you tumble down a precipice.' Doubtless an assessment as realistic as anyone can get, from one who should know.

> In London in 1854 the dreaded cholera disease struck again, and although the epidemic was for the first time identified as being water-borne, 10,000 people died. Also water-borne were fish in Regent's Park, where the first ever public aquarium in this country was opened. Knowing Calcraft's love of fishing, he could well have been among the early visitors. On the wider scene, Britain declared war on Russia, the Charge of the Light Brigade monopolised the headlines and the bravery of the cavalry earned the plaudits of the general public.

Calcraft started the year 1854 in Scotland again, this time to despatch William Cumming, who lived in Leith on the Firth of Forth. Despite claiming that his wife had got drunk and then fallen down stairs, thereby sustaining fatal injuries, the Edinburgh jury did not believe him and found him guilty, a verdict contrary to the opinions of the thousands attending his execution on 25 January, the cheers and shouts of encouragement to the condemned man causing Calcraft to waste little time in pinioning and noosing his victim. Whether the hangman in his haste had failed to secure Cumming's arms securely enough, or the condemned man had somehow succeeded in loosening his bonds, is not known, but as the hangman released the drop, Cumming managed to push the white cap up, revealing his face – and the horrified crowd watched his contorted features as his body gyrated slowly and helplessly, suspended from the gallows' crossbeam.

Girvan is a small town on the west coast of Ayrshire and it was there on the night of 22 December 1853 that Alexander Cunningham carried out his cruel and calculated plan to murder his wife Janet. They had been separated for some time, for reasons not known; perhaps his simmering hatred reached its zenith, or perchance he had met another woman. Whatever it was, it resulted in him taking his gun and going to the weaver's shop where he knew his wife would be working at that hour.

Reaching the building he looked through the window into the brightly lit room, and saw his wife operating her loom. Whether he was unable to get a clear shot at her, or whether, sadistically, he wanted her to look down the muzzle of the weapon, was not recorded; the fact remained that he attracted her attention by tossing gravel at the window; as she did so, he pulled the trigger, killing her outright. The evidence was overwhelming; the trial, on 19 April, short and conclusive – as was Calcraft's rope on 11 May 1854.

A gun also featured in an horrific murder committed by Joseph Meadows in the following year, his victim similarly seeing the death-dealing weapon pointing at her. And in like fashion the murderer faced the equally death-dealing William Calcraft on 28 July 1855.

Meadows, a young man of 23 years of age living in Dudley, Staffordshire, was in the habit of frequenting a public house, the Sailor's Return, where he met Mary Ann Mason, a seventeen year old who worked in that hostelry. They fell passionately in love with each other but, whether in order to conceal their relationship from her parents who might otherwise find out about their relationship from the other habitués of the pub, or for some undisclosed reason, they pretended to be brother and sister.

Their romance blossomed, the couple meeting as often as they could, but the fact that Mary Ann, determined to succeed at her first job, served the customers in a friendly manner, aroused in Joseph an all-consuming jealousy, unwarranted feelings which were to lead to the ultimate death of both young lovers.

The climax came on 12 May. Meadows, after a heavy drinking session the previous evening and having had little sleep brooding over the imagined infidelity of his girl friend, could stand his vengeful thoughts no longer. Early that morning he took a carbine (a short-barrelled lightweight rifle used by cavalry) belonging to his employer, a member of the local regiment, and entered the tavern.

In those days drinking took place at all hours, and at his trial evidence was given that Meadows joined Mary Ann in the kitchen and sat drinking there until mid-morning. Then without any apparent reason, and oblivious to the presence of two other customers, he suddenly produced the gun from beneath his coat and shot the young woman, killing her outright.

He made no attempt to escape, and on the arrival of the police, admitted that he had killed her because he had been jealous, adding that "I was determined that if I could not have her, no-one else would."

At his subsequent trial at Worcester on 17 July 1855 little defence could be raised in the face of such testimony as that given by one of the witnesses, William Ingram, who described the scene that day in the Sailor's Return, saying "I wondered what had happened; the report knocked my cap off. I went over to the prisoner and said to him 'You've murdered her – what did you do that for?'"

Such overwhelming evidence had but one result, the jury unhesitatingly bringing in a verdict of Guilty. Nor did the judge, Chief Baron Pollock prevaricate in sentencing the prisoner to be hanged for the awful crime.

From the condemned cell Meadows wrote a long and rambling letter to Mary Ann's parents, expressing his contrition, and blaming it on his excessive drinking. On meeting Calcraft on the Worcester scaffold at eight o'clock on the morning of 28 July 1855, he had but three words to say; "Do it quickly." The hangman nodded and complied – well, at least as quickly as his three foot long rope would allow.

In that year the executioner and his family moved from Islington to Poole Street, off the New North Road, Hoxton, one not without piscatorial advantages, the house being only a matter of yards from the Regent's Canal – more fishing for William! And no doubt they sent off their change of address letters to friends by using the six experimental post boxes set up by the Post Office in London in April of that year.

CHAPTER SIX

PANIC ON THE SCAFFOLD

William had often said that he rarely remembered much about his victims, or even who they were, but he could hardly have forgotten the appalling struggle he had while hanging Esther Hibner, who had to be restrained in a straitjacket, or the young, hysterical Sarah Thomas, carried screaming up the scaffold steps. And little did he anticipate that when executing William Bousfield on 31 March 1856, a man condemned to death for murdering his wife and three children, he was destined to have to cope with an ordeal as traumatic as any of those he had previously experienced.

He should really have suspected that all was not going to be straightforward when, on entering the cell, he found his victim sitting on the bed, his head bowed, seemingly oblivious to everything that was taking place around him. Encountering no resistance, Calcraft briskly pinioned the man, noticing as he did so that Bousfield had somehow injured himself, his face being badly burned.

That this could have happened at all was explained in the *Times* of 1 April, the newspaper including in its report of the execution 'The public is aware that the condemned cell which was formerly the receptacle for prisoners condemned to death during the short period allowed them by law after sentence, is no longer made use of; but the prisoner is placed in a sufficiently comfortable room, with a good fire, and watched day and night by one of the officers of the gaol.' The fire might well have been good, but the officer not as watchful as he should have been, for Bousfield had attempted suicide by throwing himself on the fire, not being rescued until he had suffered severe facial burning.

Apparently totally incapacitated, Bousfield could only stand upright by being supported by a warder and it was obvious that he was unable to walk; accordingly four prison officers carried him to where the gallows awaited. The crowd watched with horrified fascination as, the victim being too limp to stand unaided, a chair was brought out and placed on the trapdoor, the warders then seating Bousfield in it.

Calcraft, his task ostensibly simplified by this arrangement, pulled the hood down over the man's head, positioned the noose and then released the drop. The trapdoor opened, the chair descended into the pit, and Bousfield fell the length of the rope. Satisfied that, apart from a minor hiccup or two, everything had gone according to plan, Calcraft left the scaffold – and it was then that the unimaginable happened.

As mentioned earlier, the *Times* covered the execution extensively, and its reporter's description left his readers in no doubt as to the dreadful scene that ensued. 'The sound of the falling drop' he wrote 'had hardly passed away, when there was a shriek from the crowd "He's up again!" and, to the horror of everyone it was found that the prisoner, by a powerful muscular effort, had drawn himself up completely to the level of the drop, that both feet were resting on the edge of it, and that he was vainly endeavouring to raise his bound hands to the rope.

One of the officers immediately rushed up on to the scaffold and pushed the man's feet from their hold, but in an instant, by a violent effort, he threw himself across to the other side and again succeeded in getting both his feet on that edge of the drop. Calcraft, who had earlier received a letter threatening to shoot him if he hanged Bousfield, had wasted little time in vacating the scaffold, but was then urgently recalled; he seized Bousfield, but it was with considerable difficulty that he forced him off the scaffold boards, and he was again suspended. The short relief the wretched man had obtained from the constriction of the rope by these desperate efforts had probably enabled him to respire and, to the astonishment and horror of all the spectators, he for a third time succeeded in placing his feet upon the platform, and again his hands vainly attempted to reach the fatal cord. Calcraft and two or three other men then forced the wretched man's feet from their hold, and his legs were held down until the final struggle was over.'

The crowd's vocal reactions to these ghastly proceedings can well be imagined, a further touch of the utterly macabre being added to the scene as, the victorious end of the Crimean War having just been announced, all the bells of the churches in the vicinity of Newgate were pealing merrily in celebration!

In many of the executions about this time Calcraft had back-up assistance when necessary. This was provided by other hangmen, one being Evan Evans of Carmarthen, the affluent son of a Welsh lawyer, who enjoyed being known as 'Evans the Hangman' while in Wales, although later changed his name to Robert Anderson, that being the name of his grandfather. Able to afford many hobbies, he became friendly with Calcraft over the years, despite maintaining that executions should be performed by professionals such as prison warders, rather than brutes who only did it for fame and money!

Another assistant on some occasions was the Stafford executioner, George Smith of Dudley, but not on 14 June 1856, when the multiple poisoner Dr William Palmer was due to mount the scaffold steps, for Smith was the No.1 and Calcraft not even invited, the authorities no doubt economising by using their local man rather than pay William's travel expenses. Not that Calcraft was not interested in the case, far from it, for the *Daily Telegraph* reported that during the Old Bailey trial he was seen among the crowds congregating outside the court agog to hear the verdict.

The newspaper went on to deplore his presence there 'exhibiting himself to the gaze of hundreds of respectable people, his every movement indicating an ardent aspiration that he would be called upon to make an official operation on the jugular vein of the unfortunate Palmer.' The editor classed his presence as 'an outrage upon decency' and 'questioned the propriety and good taste of those who allowed the common hangman to tread the precincts of a public building where are congregated none but persons of respectability, for none could look upon that man who, for the sake of filthy lucre, traffics in human blood, without feeling that they came in close proximity to a public character that society detests.' They neglected, however, to condemn the government of the day, elected by the 'respectable' people, for making hanging the penalty for murder, and the learned judge who condemned Palmer to death; hardly logical.

In August of that year Calcraft travelled southwest to Dorchester, there to carry out another execution, one that was to be in complete contrast to that of Bousfield. His victim was Elizabeth Martha Brown who, having discovered that her husband, a man twenty years younger than herself, was having a torrid affair with another woman, seized her opportunity on finding him in a drunken stupor and promptly slew him with an axe. Any defence she may have had was brushed aside, not only by the jury, who found her guilty of murder, but also by the judge, who sentenced her to death.

In her final moments, Elizabeth showed not the slightest sign of fear; on the contrary, for although the scaffold was some distance away and the prison van was ready to convey her, she expressed a wish to walk there and proceeded to do so, escorted by the usual retinue of officials. The scaffold was high, having been erected on top of the gaol's imposing gateway; there being eleven steps to the first level, Elizabeth calmly mounted them, then stood patiently while Calcraft pinioned her. A further nineteen steps led up to the gallows and, despite the fate awaiting her and the inherent difficulty in maintaining her balance, her wrists being secured to the leather belt around her waist, with unbelievable composure she followed Calcraft.

The hangman had never concealed the fact that he disliked having to execute women, and perhaps this accounted for his lapse of memory, for he completely forgot to bind the woman's ankles together, a precaution which would not only prevent her from lodging her feet on the edge of the drop, but the strap itself, by securing her long dress tight around her ankles, would also maintain some decency in the proceedings by stopping the garment rising as she descended.

This oversight was not lost on the *Times* reporter present, whose subsequent report emphasised the fact that Calcraft, having left the scaffold to operate the drop, remembered just in time and returned to rectify his error before finally carrying out the execution. And just as today, when many youngsters manage to obtain access to cinemas showing 'adult only' films, so in those days teenagers seized the opportunity to watch a real live hanging. One of those was a Dorchester schoolboy, sixteen-year-old Thomas Hardy, the young genius who would grow up to be a renowned novelist and poet, but was now just a lad who, in order to get a good view, had scaled a nearby tree, hanging on to its branches as the unforgettable scene unfolded before him. That it was unforgettable is evidenced by his recounting, many years later, 'how he marvelled at the marble-like covered face of the hanging woman in the misty rain, the tight black gown setting off her shape as she swung back and forth on the rope.' Oblivious to any poetic overtones, Calcraft stolidly cut her down an hour later and then went home.

A sectarian argument – a drunken fight between two miners, Peter M'Lean and Thomas Maxwell, and the latter fell dead – having being struck with a heavy stone, then stabbed with a clasp knife. It happened on 15 November 1856 near the Scottish town of Bathgate on Saturday, the traditional drinking night, and M'Lean was soon arrested and charged with murder.

He appeared before three judges of the Edinburgh's High Court, and the presence of one, Lord Deas, boded ill for him. The honourable gentleman was not noted for the lenient verdicts he handed down; on the contrary he had earned the nickname of 'Lord Death' and the 'Hanging Judge' by the criminal classes, and had once been heard to declare 'that he would clear the city of thieves by his exemplary sentences of fifteen or twenty years penal servitude, so that he could hang up his watch and chain to a lamp post, go for a walk – and on returning, find them both intact'!

M'Lean was found guilty by a majority vote and despite a recommendation for mercy by the jury, he was sentenced to be executed at Linlithgow, West Lothian, on Monday, 2 February 1857. Calcraft arrived a few days earlier, even though the scaffold, borrowed from Edinburgh again (!) had not yet arrived. And because the Court had issued a dire warning that if anything went awry in the proceedings, 'those responsible would answer at their higher peril', the magistrates arranged for an assistant hangman named Peddie, from Dundee, to be present as a stand-in, should Calcraft fall ill or meet with any misfortune at the hands of M'Lean's fellow-miners. Further precautions were taken; to guard against any attempt to rescue the condemned man, who was being held in a cell in the old prison in the town square, police officers were brought from Edinburgh and two hundred and fifty special constables also sworn in, this force being reinforced by soldiers of the 5th Dragoons to control the large crowds expected to attend the execution.

The scaffold was not delivered until early on the Monday morning, when carpenters hastily assembled it in front of the County Hall. Calcraft subsequently inspected the structure and attached the halter to its beam, while police and troops lined the barriers, behind which a multitude of spectators were already gathering. The hangman then went to the gaol and, after pinioning his victim, he, together with the warders and other officials, accompanied the condemned man to the scaffold. M'Lean mounted the steps and, facing the sea of upturned faces, exclaimed in tremulous tones "Good people, take warning by me; avoid evil company and drink, and keep the Sabbath." Calcraft, as professional as ever, then drew the bolt – and justice had been done.

In June Queen Victoria distributed sixty-two Victoria Cross medals for outstanding bravery in the Crimea to soldiers on parade in Hyde Park. One wonders whether Calcraft and his wife joined those watching – and whether Louisa had been tempted to wear any of the latest fashions created in Paris, 'Cage-crinolines', wide, bell-shaped frameworks suspended from female hips, beneath voluminous dresses, being much in vogue across the Channel. These were totally impractical, especially in busy streets, and in March 1863, according to the *Penny Illustrated Paper*, so large were the crowds gathered to watch the Prince of Wales' wedding to Princess Alexandra of Denmark that many women daringly unhooked and stepped out of their crinolines, discarding them where they lay! Men's fashions however changed but little at that time; William would have had no need to update his appearance, his hirsute facial appendages already conforming with masculine requirements of moustache and side whiskers; though judging by his portrait it is doubtful whether he was ever tempted to use the newly-introduced hair 'cream', macassar oil!

Every edition of the *Lancaster Gazette* printed on Monday, 31 August 1857 must have sold out in record time, for it described in extensive and graphic detail the execution of murderer Edward Hardman, which had taken place in that city on the previous Saturday. Textiles being one of the major industries of the area, and Hardman's profession being that of a shoemaker, he had doubtless been able to procure a quantity of antimony potassium tartrate (tartar emetic), a highly poisonous salt used in the treatment of leather and fabrics; together with other poisons, he administered this colourless and odourless chemical to his wife Ellen, her death being a particularly agonising one.

Their marriage had not apparently been a particularly harmonious one, and by February 1857 it would seem that the husband was already administering some kind of noxious substance to Ellen, for he wrote to her father, William Holden, informing him that she had been suddenly taken ill. Mr Holden visited the house and after comforting her, returned home, only to receive another letter a few days later, reporting a worsening of her condition.

Shortly afterwards Hardman, together with a friend, John Ashburner, went to the nearby town of Preston, where Hardman bought half-a-pound of arsenic 'to exterminate bugs', he explained, but those troublesome pests were not his target, for during the following week Ellen's health rapidly deteriorated, her skin growing cold and clammy, her joints aching. The local doctor was sent for, but by then she was beyond medical help, and her death was attributed to gastroenteritis with complications.

Following her funeral, rumours detrimental to Edward's character reached the ears of the authorities, gossip hinting that he had a strong motive for causing his wife's death because of his involvement with another woman. To clear his name it was decided to disinter the corpse and perform an autopsy – but far from establishing his innocence, a warrant for his arrest was issued, for traces of both tartar emetic and arsenic were discovered in her body.

His trial, which took place in Lancaster's Crown Court in August 1867, was almost a formality, the evidence forthcoming from John Ashburner and the chemist, together with the results of the post-mortem, proving conclusive. After a mere twenty minutes consideration the jury returned to deliver a verdict of Guilty; the learned judge concurred and immediately passed sentence – death by hanging.

As word spread, people from all over the county of Lancashire made their way to the city by train, in carts and on foot. Calcraft arrived on the Friday and after reporting to the Governor of the Castle and inspecting his quarters therein, went for a stroll. His previous appearances on the Lancaster scaffold had made him easily identifiable to the local residents and he soon found he was being followed by a large and excited crowd; to shake off pursuit he made his way back to the Castle via the front door of a nearby inn, departing through the back door without even pausing for a tankard of ale!

Meanwhile Hardman, incarcerated in his cell, while refusing to admit guilt, nevertheless stated that the tartar emetic he had given to his wife – whom he loved dearly, he said – was for medicinal purposes. Obviously resigned to his fate, he expressed his appreciation for the compassionate treatment he had received from the Governor and his staff.

At about ten o'clock on his last evening he had a large supper, then went to bed, getting up some seven hours later to kneel and receive the last sacrament before eating a surprisingly substantial breakfast. The morning was spent closeted with his priest in the prison chaplain's office until, at about twelve o'clock, he was conducted to the chapel where Calcraft and other officers of the law were waiting. The moment had arrived.

In accordance with legal requirements he was asked whether he saw any reason whereby the law should not take its course, a question to which he gave a negative response. The hangman then strapped the waist belt around his prisoner and, securing the man's arms, proceeded to lead him out to the scaffold and the eagerly waiting crowd.

As reported later in the *Lancaster Gazette*, the gathered assembly, a captive audience for those of religious persuasion, had for some hours been listening to lectures on the perils of imbibing hard liquor and the need to lead a pure, Christian life, the accompanying fervent singing of hymns successfully averting any of the unruly behaviour which usually took place at such events.

The sonorous tolling of the Castle bell heralded the imminent appearance of the cortege, a silence descending on the spectators as Calcraft positioned the condemned man immediately under the gallows-beam, the silence being broken only by the prayers spoken by the priest. Edward Hardman was evidently at breaking point, his features drawn, his face as white as a sheet, although he managed to remain motionless as the world he had known vanished from his view for ever, the white cap being drawn down over his face, and through the thin material he felt the rough caress of the hempen noose as Calcraft positioned it around his neck. For a long moment time seemed to stand still; the boards beneath his feet trembled as the supporting bolt was withdrawn; he felt the trapdoors fall away, the halter tightening remorselessly around his neck, then – eventually – oblivion.

The body remained suspended for an hour, Calcraft reappearing to cut the corpse down and supervise its conveyance within the Castle limits. The crowd, seemingly shocked by the spectacle they had just witnessed, dispersed slowly and sombrely, the almost inevitable riotous unruliness being noticeable by its absence.

Such however was not the case later when, at nearing midnight, workmen arrived and commenced to dig a grave by the church wall immediately opposite to the scaffold site, for they were greeted by a drunken mob of two hundred or more. Most of the police having been withdrawn after the hanging had taken place, little could be done to restrain the troublemakers from pelting the black coffin with stones as it was carried out and slowly lowered into the grave. Reinforcements were summoned and it was with some difficulty that the fractious elements were routed, the deplorable occurrence reflecting badly on the city's otherwise proud reputation.

On a summer's day in June 1857 the good ship *Martha Jane* moored in Liverpool Docks, one of its crew-members, Able Seaman Groves, wasting little time in reporting to the authorities the appalling events which had taken place at sea en route from the West Indies – nothing less than the sadistic torture inflicted on one of his fellow sailors, Andrew Rose, savage beatings and merciless punishments which had resulted in the man's eventual death.

Following an investigation three men were arrested and charged with the crime, Captain Henry Rogers, First Mate Miles and Second Mate Seymour. Testimony was given by the ship's crew that, following the brutal treatment to which Rose had been subjected, his lacerated and mutilated body had been thrown into the sea on the orders of the captain.

At their trial at Liverpool Assizes two months later, on 19 August, it was disclosed that the deceased had attempted to jump ship in Barbados and had been forcibly returned to the ship by port officials, the ship's officers taking reprisal by repeatedly scourging him without respite during the subsequent voyage. All three were found guilty and sentenced to death, but following the intervention of the Home Secretary, the sentence passed on the two subordinate officers was reduced to that of life imprisonment. This mitigation was probably due to the fact that ships' captains bore the ultimate responsibility for everything taking place on board, and the master of the *Martha Jane* had obviously made no attempt whatsoever to restrain his officers.

Captain Rogers awaited his fate imprisoned in the condemned cell in Kirkdale Gaol situated near the Liverpool docks where his ship still rode at anchor, and in the last few days left to him, was frequently visited by his grieving wife and two of his five children. But on the morning of 12 September a more unwelcome visitor entered his cell: William Calcraft. He had, as was his wont, spent the night in the prison, and wasted little time in preparing his victim for execution, pinioning him securely.

Outside, the crowd of fifty thousand or more were growing impatient, a thunderous roar from them sending the seagulls flocking skyward in alarm as, at midday, the grim procession appeared and mounted the scaffold steps. Escorted by the hangman and, in accordance with the law, accompanied by the prison governor, the sheriff and the chaplain, Captain Rogers allowed himself to be positioned on the drop. Despite his bound wrists he managed to shake hands with Calcraft, though failed to admit his guilt, simply averring that he had taken no active part in the maltreatment of the murdered sailor. He did not, and could not, however, deny his personal responsibility.

One of the punishments inflicted on the suffering Andrew Rose was that of being suspended from the ship's yard-arm, a rope about his neck, there to swing, half-strangled. Appropriately enough then, similar retribution was meted out to the condemned man, the deck being the scaffold, the 'yard-arm' Calcraft's gallows, and the strangulation was allowed to take its full course until all movement ceased.

The Liverpool lyricists had as usual been busy thumbing through their rhyming dictionaries, the product of their endeavours hawked around the town that day being quoted in Appendix 3. And a later edition of the local newspaper carried an advertisement announcing that a wax effigy of the murderer had been placed on display in the city's Chamber of Horrors, the figure clad in the clothes actually worn by the murderer on the scaffold; the hangman had as usual exercised his right to claim the garments, and then passed them on to the museum – at a price. Selling verses was all right for some people; Calcraft also was never averse to adding a little something to supplement his standard fee of £10 per execution!

Some weeks later, the hangman was back in Scotland again, the far north-east this time, in Aberdeen, tasked with despatching itinerant hawker John Booth. Returning from one of his sales trips, Booth visited a local tavern and, hearing gossip circulating about the morals of his wife during his absence went home and accused her of being unfaithful to him. In the violent row that followed he attacked her with a knife; she fled, taking refuge in her mother's home nearby, hotly pursued by her husband. On attempting to enter the house, Booth found himself face-to-face with her mother, who tried to eject him; maddened by her interference, he drew his knife and stabbed her to death.

At Aberdeen Circuit Court on 24 September 1857, presided over by Lord Hope and Lord 'Death' Deas, Booth stood trial. Under the circumstances there was little testimony brought in his defence and he was sentenced to be hanged. And on 21 October, standing on the scaffold, his arms pinioned, he confessed his guilt. Calcraft waited patiently until his victim had finished his long speech before deftly hooding and haltering him; seconds later the trapdoors fell, the sound of the impact reverberating along the street. Similar echoes were never to be repeated, for Booth's execution was the last to be carried out in that city.

There can be few deaths more agonising than those brought about by drinking prussic acid, yet that was the appalling way in which John Thompson gained his revenge on Agnes Montgomery for spurning his advances.

Thompson, also known as Peter Walker, thereby arousing suspicions that he already had a criminal record, was determined that Agnes would pay for thus ignoring him and so sent an errand boy to Glasgow charged with buying sixpenny-worth of prussic acid. If challenged, the boy was to claim that it was for use by a portrait painter. Thompson then poured some of it into a bottle of beer and on 13 September 1857 he went to visit Agnes, who lived alone in Eaglesham, a small village situated some eight miles south of Glasgow.

At his subsequent trial at Glasgow Circuit Court, a three day hearing lasting from 22 to 24 December 1857, Agnes' next door neighbour testified that on hearing a loud noise she looked out of the window and saw the accused leave the deceased's house; becoming concerned, she investigated, to find her neighbour writhing in excruciating pain. Further evidence was forthcoming, a small girl playing nearby telling her mother that she had seen the accused actually entering Miss Montgomery's house.

Thompson had fled the scene and set out on foot for Glasgow. En route he decided to pay a call on a Mr and Mrs Mason, at whose house he had once lodged. It would seem from what subsequently transpired that for reasons unknown, he bore a grudge against the couple, for he bought a bottle of whisky and augmented the contents with the remainder of the prussic acid. Invited in by the Masons, he offered them a drink, the taste of which, Mr Mason later stated, was awful, and his wife declared made her feel dizzy and blurred her vision. The police were summoned, Thompson later being apprehended and taken into custody.

The Mason's testimony, linked to the suspicious death of Agnes Montgomery, resulted in the exhumation of the young woman's body, a post mortem revealing the existence of poison. In the face of such overwhelming evidence, suicide by such means being ruled out, Thompson was found guilty, and on the cold winter's day of 14 January 1858, those waiting expectantly around Paisley's scaffold watched as the London hangman led the condemned man up the steps to the gallows. Thompson, accompanied by clergymen – to whom he had earlier confessed that at the age of nine, he had pushed a playmate into a quarry, thereby drowning him – seemed stunned, and Calcraft quickly prepared the murderer for his well-deserved fate. Unusually, it was reported that when the hangman operated the drop, several spectators were seen to faint 'and the groaning and yelling of the crowd could be heard a mile away'.

> London residents endured a sweltering heat wave that summer, even Members of Parliament deploring the 'Great Stink', referring to the pungent odours of rotting garbage in the City and especially along the banks of the Thames. In the following year, 1859, the National Portrait Gallery opened, and while William Calcraft may not have been interested in that particular event, it is likely that Louisa experimented with some of the recipes contained in *A Book of Household Management*, better known as Mrs Beeton's Cookery Book, which was first published in serial form that year. It is not known whether William was a cricket fan; if he was, no doubt he anxiously followed the performance of 'twelve Cricketers of England', the first overseas tour, which sailed to Canada and the USA in September 1859.

Horsemonger Lane Gaol, south of the river, on the flat roof of which, in 1849, the Mannings had been executed, provided the venue for the hanging of William Godfrey Youngman, a man whose crimes were truly horrific; no less than the murders of his sweetheart Mary Streeter, his mother and two brothers on 16 August 1860. This virtual massacre took place in a house on the Walworth Road, not far from the Elephant and Castle, although details of the actual circumstances are scarce. Whether he had a violent row with his sweetheart and his mother and brothers intervened, or whether the altercation took place between him and his relatives, in which his sweetheart became involved, is unclear, although some sources aver that his motive was to claim insurance on their deaths. Whatever his reasons, the fracas resulted in the deaths of all four, the victims being first stabbed, then their throats cut.

On 4 September nearly thirty thousand people crowded the area in front of the gaol, jeers and abuse greeting the murderer as, escorted by Calcraft and other officials, he appeared on the scaffold. The hangman must have been impressed and doubtless pleased by the composure shown by his victim as he secured the man's arms; displaying no sign of nerves, Youngman said calmly "Strap my legs tight and be sure to shake hands with me before I go."

This latter request was frequently made to Calcraft in the course of his work, one which he rarely refused, no matter how heinous the crimes committed by his victim, it signifying that the hangman was acting purely impersonally, in his role as an instrument of the Law rather than as an individual.

For a long minute Youngman stood motionless; then, as the hangman withdrew the bolt, the crowd applauded with tumultuous cheers; and Mme. Tussaud's sculptors prepared to get busy again.

> There was plenty to fill the newspapers in 1860; the rebuilding of Parliament was finally accomplished; the first 'Open' golf championship was held, at Prestwich; and from then on, if pugilists wished to fight, they would henceforth have to wear boxing gloves, the last major bare-knuckle fight having taken place. It was between Tom Sayers and the American John Heenan, over 42 rounds, for a prize of £200 each, the venue being Farnborough, Hants; the result was a draw.

Calcraft had by now been hangman for over thirty years, his appearance before the general public being as familiar as are today's television news presenters, albeit his news being bad for at least one member of his audience. His 'uniform' occasionally drew adverse criticism from the Press, to which his terse comment was "There didn't ought to be no newspapers!". His relations with the gentlemen of Fleet Street were always fraught. One journalist reported that, on attending an execution with a colleague, they made their way to where the scaffold stood. There being no sign of the executioner, his companion said "I wonder whether that bloodthirsty scoundrel, Calcraft, has arrived!" Next moment an awesome figure emerged from the dark cavity beneath the scaffold, where he had been checking the drop bolt; looking at the newspaper man, he growled "The bloodthirsty scoundrel is here!"

Admittedly he seemed rarely, if ever, to have his hair and beard combed or cut, and that, together with his pockmarked features, must have appeared fearsome to those he was about to hang. When the occasion demanded, of course, he could make the necessary effort; once invited to the sheriffs' dinner to celebrate the last day of the court sessions, he raised his glass of wine to the gathered assembly. Serjeant-at-Law Ballantyne was present, and afterwards described the hangman as a decently dressed, quiet-looking man. Referring to Calcraft's salutation, he declared "This he drank to the health of his patrons, and expressed with becoming modesty his gratitude for past favours and his hopes for favours to come."

Calcraft's favourite fishing grounds, the nearby Regent's Canal, flows south and east, joining others to become the Grand Union Canal. And it was only a matter of yards from that waterway, as it flowed through Stepney, that a rent-collector named Walter Thomas Emms, despite repeated calls at the house of his employer, received no reply, and finally, on 17 August 1860, the police broke in, to find the body of a woman who had sustained serious head wounds.

The dead woman was Mrs. Mary Emsley who lived at No. 9 Grove Road, just off the Mile End Road in Stepney. A wealthy woman, she owned a number of properties, the rents of which were collected by Emms. She had no enemies, as far as was known, and the police quickly concluded that as there were no signs of a disturbance in the house, she must have been acquainted with her brutal assailant, who had attacked her without warning.

Another employee of hers was James Mullins, and when it was discovered that although he was an ex-police sergeant, nevertheless he had a criminal record, he became the prime suspect. Despite all their efforts, the police failed to find any evidence directly linking Mullins with the crime and so took the somewhat unusual step of offering a reward for information that might lead them to the murderer. And who should come forward to claim the reward but Mullins, who declared that he had actually seen Walter Emms hiding packages in a shed next to his house. When confronted with this, Emms vehemently denied involvement; moreover he produced a watertight alibi. Mullins' evidence was then investigated more thoroughly, the police taking him to where he said he had seen Emms conceal the packages – and it then became immediately obvious that from that viewpoint, he would not have been able to see inside the shed! Further evidence incriminating Mullins was forthcoming when police searched his house, property identified as belonging to Mrs Elmsley being found; the case against Mullins was incontrovertible, the outcome of his trial inevitable.

In the condemned cell, no doubt he kicked himself for claiming the £300 reward; had he not done so only suspicion rather than the charge of murder would have been levelled against him. As it was, the only kicking he did occurred on 19 November 1860, on the end of Calcraft's rope. And shortly afterwards, ghoulish-minded visitors mounting the Grand Staircase in Mme. Tussaud's would, on turning right into the Main Vestibule, find the entrance to the Chamber of Horrors, its number of exhibits now increased by one. And within the foreseeable future, they would be able to study the contorted features of the murderous models in much more detail, Joseph Swan having invented the electric lamp in June of that year.

New Year 1861 saw Calcraft travelling north again, this time to Dumbarton where, after being tried at Glasgow, Patrick Lunnay was sentenced to be hanged for stabbing to death a fellow lodger, James Cassidy, in a drunken brawl on 11 November of the previous year. Insisting he was not guilty, nevertheless he showed 'callous indifference' as Calcraft positioned the noose, the crowd of 2,500 waiting with their usual macabre expectancy as the hangman went below and drew the bolt.

Most of Calcraft's victims were guilty of killing relatives, friends or ordinary strangers; rare it was that men committed parricide (slew their 'pa', their fathers); so rare, in fact, that twenty-year-old George Smith, guilty of murdering his father Joseph, was dubbed by the local press as 'The Ilkeston Parricide' after the Derbyshire town in which he lived.

The tragic saga started in April 1861 when a young woman named Emma Eyre accused Smith of being the father of her newborn child. Smith, who regularly divided his time between drinking and womanising, hotly disputed her claim, although there was little doubt as to his involvement. Over a few beers he decided to sidestep his responsibilities by fleeing to France, but had not gone many miles before realising that he had insufficient funds for the journey anyway, so he returned home and stole his father's bank book.

He then went to Nottingham, where he attempted to draw £14 from a bank, but this proved unsuccessful, authorisation by his father being required. Thwarted, he returned to Ilkeston and took to the bottle again, during which he was heard to say that if his father caused any trouble over the bank book, he would shoot him. With what money he had left, he bought a pistol and ammunition, and went home, but his father had gone out; later, however, after having had more to drink, he returned, to find his father sitting in a chair, with his head resting on his hand. When his son entered, he said "George, you must not go on so; you come in at all hours of the night, and I don't think you get any better – but worse." At that Smith drew the pistol out and fired, killing his father instantly.

On 29 July he appeared before Mr Justice Willes and after a trial that attracted much attention from the local press, he was found guilty and sentenced to death. In the dock he defiantly proclaimed his innocence and vowed to repeat it on the scaffold, yet two days later he must have repented, for he admitted his crime to Mr Sim, the Prison Governor of the Vernon Street Gaol, Derby. Yet despite his confession, he still believed that his sentence would be commuted and, as reported in the *Derbyshire Advertiser* 'the condemned man enjoyed his meals, slept soundly, and has gained in weight.' He was guarded by four warders, turnkeys, namely Messrs. Hind, Mountenay, Benson and Holmes, and on realising that there would be no reprieve he asked one of them to obtain copies of suitable hymns for him to sing on the scaffold, though he admitted that he doubted whether he could face the crowds who would attend his execution.

Early in the morning of Friday 16 August 1861 Smith rose and ate a hearty breakfast, tea and beef being the main constituents, and was joined at eleven o'clock by the Rev. Mr Heron for Holy Communion and prayers. Those moments of spiritual support were soon followed by the arrival of the Sheriff who, in accordance with legal procedure 'demanded the body of Smith.' The official procession then formed up, consisting of the condemned man escorted by warders, the Sheriff, Mr

1a.
William Calcraft:
the "classic"
picture

1b. William Calcraft:
A rare mid-19th
century photo

2a. Calcraft
wielding the whip

2b. Calcraft's short-
drop noose

3a. A typical deathmask

3b. Dissection in Surgeons' Hall

4a. Newgate Prison

Newgate Prison – much associated with William Calcraft

4b. Old Newgate Gateway, c.1750

The windmill was for ventilation

4c. Multiple hangings at Newgate Gallows, c.1783

5a. Newgate Prison: the scaffold inside the prison

5b. Newgate Prison: Outside this door, public executions were held

6a. Derby: Vernon Street Gaol

Other prisons associated with William Calcraft

6b. Wandsworth: whipping post

6c. Horsemonger Lane gaol

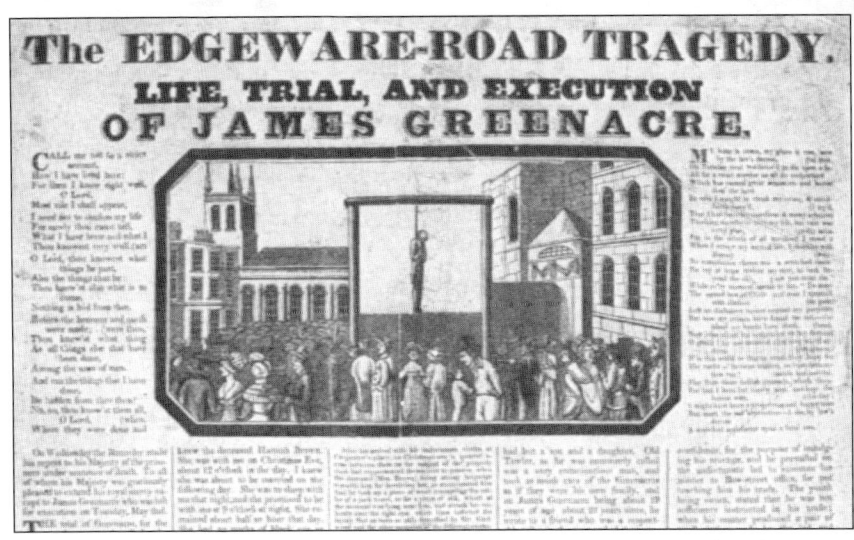

7a. A broadsheet from the Greenacre trial

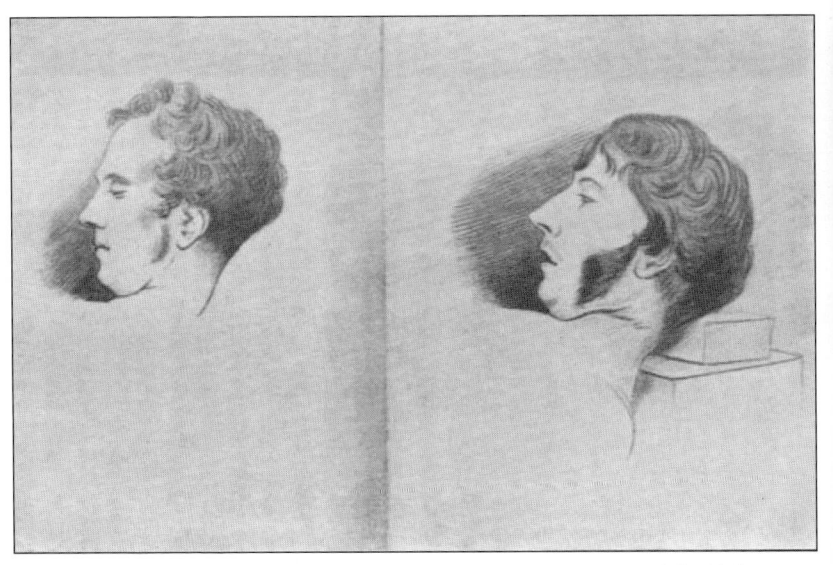

7b. John Head, *alias* Thomas Williams   John Bishop

8a. Convict imprisoned in the Black Hole

Those who were spared Calcraft's rope were transported to the penal colonies of Australia in convict ships similar to the sailing ship *Success*. Until the exile of prisoners ceased in 1867, this vessel was one of many which conveyed human cargoes in such harsh and brutal conditions that many convicts died en route

8b. Punishment by the cat-o'-nine-tails

8c. The compulsory salt bath, the victims scrubbed with salt water

Gisborne the surgeon, the chaplain, the Prison Governor and, of course, William Calcraft. En route the party passed through the prison yard, Smith taking the opportunity to bid farewell to several of his fellow prisoners, warning them to abstain from strong drink, the cause of his downfall, and to express a wish that he might meet them in Heaven. Solemnly they continued their way through the gatehouse and out via the spiral stairway to where the scaffold stood.

It was claimed, perhaps somewhat inaccurately, that about sixty thousand spectators, townsfolk, workmen, tradesmen and colliers had assembled to watch the murderer pay the penalty, the large attendance of young females among them being particularly remarked on; many of the women present carried baskets, and had evidently come prepared with their dinners. Itinerant news-vendors plied their wares, down-at-heel artists sold penny portraits of the condemned man, and over the hubbub of obscene singsongs and earnest Scripture readers could be heard the cry "Pork pies all hot – hot, oh!"

When led on to the drop, Smith fell on his knees and after praying loudly, faced the dense crowd and said "Goodbye, my friends, goodbye", a farewell which, according to the *Derbyshire Advertiser* 'evinced great emotion, women shrieking and beseeching God to have mercy on his soul, and sturdy men were completely overcome by the touching scene, and gave evidence of a feeling that could not be resisted.'

Then a hypnotic silence fell on the spectators as Calcraft dropped the hood over the condemned man's head and followed by positioning the noose around his neck. Then, at seven minutes past twelve precisely – and accompanied by a blood-curdling scream from someone in the crowd – the hangman drew the bolt, those watching later asserting that although death seemed to be instantaneous, Smith's pendant body was later seen to shudder, and ten minutes elapsed before his corpse hung motionless.

An hour later the body was cut down and taken back into the gaol. There, Mr Barton, the sculptor, got busy with his clay and took a cast of the head and face to be put on show in Mr. Sims' museum in the town, following which, the body was examined by Mr Gisborne, the surgeon who, by some esoteric analytical process not recognised by medical textbooks, was then able to diagnose the murderer 'as having five parts animal, and the nerve to kill ten men.' The body, fully-clothed, was then buried within the grounds of the gaol and covered with quick lime.

The immense crowd, under the watchful eyes of the Sheriff's traditional escort, the javelin-men, sitting astride their horses, and officers of the Derby police force, dispersed in a quiet and orderly manner. As, no doubt, after collecting his fee, did the hangman.

It was not the practice of the Victorians to allow such an event to pass without utilising it for the benefit of the younger generation who were so prone to temptation. Accordingly on the following Sunday evening, the address given by the Rev Erskine Clark at St Michael's Church was 'The Lessons to be Learned by the Ilkeston Murderer's Confession', the *Derbyshire Advertiser* and doubtless the subsequent issue of the parish magazine reporting that 'the attendance of young men had been invited by the circulation of small handbills, and not withstanding that these had been very sparingly distributed, by half-past eight o'clock, the church was completely filled. The congregation was chiefly composed of the working classes and exclusively of the male sex, of whom there could not have been fewer than five hundred present – a sight most unusual and impressive. As Mr Clarke, in plain but earnest language, pointed out the moral of the late tragic occurrence, the attention of every member of that large congregation was arrested; and it was manifest that the words which fell from the preacher's lips operated powerfully upon the minds and consciences of many present, the effect of which may, by God's grace, be seen after many days.'

Some months later, in April 1862 to be exact, Calcraft had to go once again to Derby, there to hang Richard Thorley. That young man – he was only twenty six years of age – was born in Leather Bottle Yard in that town and being strong and well-built, obtained a job in a local foundry, though later became a boxer of some renown in the area. His future seemed promising, but all that was to end when his young wife suddenly died; overwhelmed by his loss he took to drink, despite all the efforts of a family friend, Eliza Morrow, to help him get over the tragedy. In his more sober moments he turned to Eliza for female company and could perhaps have been restored to his former carefree and ambitious self had he not become so attached to her; indeed so attracted that he became jealous about her casual friendships with other men. And when one night he saw her in the company of a soldier, his reactions were inevitable, the outcome fatally inexorable – getting hopelessly drunk, he took his razor and, going to Eliza's home in Court No. 4, Agard Street, he slit her throat.

His arrest by Detective Sergeant Thomas Vessey took place later that night and he was subsequently jailed in Vernon Street Prison. At his trial, witnesses described seeing the actual attack, and the surgeon, Mr. Joseph German gave evidence of the wounds inflicted, those near the right ear, the mouth, the cheek and the neck being so severe as to cause death within a minute. Little could be said in Thorley's defence and, as reported in the *Derby Gazette* 'during the learned judge's summing up, the prisoner leaned his head on his hand, and it was said that brandy was administered to him.' He was found guilty and sentenced to die on 11 April 1862.

His execution drew the usual large crowds, it being estimated that while waiting for the appearance of William Calcraft and his victim, most of the twenty thousand or so spectators joined in raucous choruses, many listened to the religious speeches exhorting all and sundry to shun strong drink, and some, at the back of the crowd, even hired the telescopes and opera-glasses at exorbitant rates from those of Derby's enterprising opticians who had been professionally farsighted enough to seize the opportunity thus offered.

Except in a multiple execution or where a victim put up a violent struggle, spectators spent more time in waiting for something to happen than when it actually took place, and so it was that day outside Vernon Street Gaol. The singing and shouting stopped abruptly as Thorley, Calcraft, and other officials suddenly appeared; the condemned man's voice rose in prayer as the hangman proceeded to position him beneath the fatal beam, bind his ankles together and draw the cap down over his head; then the drop fell, 'sobs being heard in every direction'.

Mr Barton, the sculptor, might well have been there later, to take a cast of the head but Mr. Bally, the phrenologist, certainly was, and did. After studying the contours (the 'bumps') of the victim's skull, he solemnly pronounced that Thorley's prominent features were indicative of firmness and hope, though somewhat lacking in self-approbation and self-esteem; had the felon been given a good education, Mr. Bally concluded, he would have made an excellent mechanic. Alas, William Calcraft had thwarted any such ambitions that Thorley may have had in that direction.

In contrast to the so-called 'last words' of condemned men usually sold around the scaffold, Richard Thorley expressed his feelings in a letter dictated by him at 11.20 am on the morning of his execution, minutes before being led out to the gallows. Addressed to his 'Dear Friends and Companions' it continued 'Before bidding adieu to this world, I wish to give you a few words of advice which I hope you will profit by. You all know my downward career, from my first neglecting my Sunday school, till the day I committed the dreadful deed for which my life is justly forfeited. You will know that I was too fond of gambling and the alehouse, and although now I am almost ashamed to confess it, that I was one of the 'Fraternity' styling themselves the 'Derby Fancy'. But you see in my fate the result of such a wicked course of life, and I beg of you as a last dying favour, not to follow in my footsteps. Avoid the alehouse, which is the school of crime. Avoid gambling in every shape, and instead of spending the Sabbath day in such degrading, sinful pastimes, attend some place of worship where you will hear what brings true pleasure to the mind.' Continuing in the same vein, the letter concluded 'I have addressed these few words of advice while I am waiting in the room on my way to the scaffold and I sincerely hope for the good of your own souls, you will learn a lesson by my sad experience. I now take my dying farewell of you all, and I trust we shall one day meet in Heaven.'

Whether any of the onlookers did in fact take the awful lesson to heart is not known, but Victorian society in general sincerely hoped so, and the broadsheet sold in large numbers that day, allegedly 'written by a Lady'; it so encapsulates the moralising and almost mitigating sentiments of the times, that it is considered worthy of including it in its entirety – in Appendix 3.

> Calcraft may have had to travel to Scotland frequently, but the stone needed to clad the six thousand tons of iron which formed Southwark Bridge, opened some years earlier, had been laboriously transported from Scotland. And it was across that bridge and the neighbouring London Bridge that thousands of terrified Londoners fled in 1861 to escape the flames which devastated much of Southwark's houses and the warehouses lining the river's edge.
> On a lighter note, prospects of a new type of holiday for the gentry were introduced by one Thomas Cook, his firm of travel agents offering for the first time, a continental tour, which

included six days in Paris. It is doubtful that Calcraft and family took advantage of the opportunity, London working classes of those days finding Margate or Brighton much more affordable.

CHAPTER SEVEN

POISONERS AND PIRATES GET SHORT SHRIFT

Surely there can be nothing more disconcerting for a hangman who, having hooded and noosed his victim, reaches for the bolt, only to have the procedure suddenly brought to a grinding halt by someone running up the scaffold steps waving a piece of paper – especially when he had had enough problems already in subduing the person he was about to hang. Yet this is precisely what happened to Calcraft on 29 April 1862 at Dumfries, just across the Scottish Border, when Mary Reid had been sentenced to death.

Mary Reid, otherwise known as Mary Timney, had for a long time not seen eye to eye on matters with a neighbour, Ann Hannah, to put it mildly, and the issue came to a head on 13 January 1862. During a violent argument she struck her adversary with a cloth beetle, a heavy hand tool used in pounding cloth, and clubbed her to death, although at her trial on 8 April before the notorious Judge Deas at Dumfries Court, she claimed that it had been in self defence, Ann Hannah having attacked her first. She was found guilty and sentenced to be hanged in the town on 8 April, petitions subsequently raised on her behalf being rejected.

Her execution was a particularly lamentable occasion. By now in a state of nervous collapse she had to be half-carried up the scaffold steps by two warders, the large crowd watching William Calcraft intently to see how he would cope with the situation. Thus supported, she was positioned on the trapdoors, Calcraft somehow managing to slide the hood over her head.

Poisoners and Pirates Get Short Shrift   91

The thin material hardly stifled her desperate pleas as she begged for mercy on account of her four offspring, her pitiful cries only spurring Calcraft on to bring the execution to a speedy conclusion. Wasting no time he quickly dropped the noose over her head and made to release the bolt – stopping in his tracks as a roar from the crowd heralded the arrival of a messenger!

Hurrying up the steps, the messenger handed a letter to the Prison Governor who, together with the sheriff, chaplain and warders, was present on the scaffold. For a long moment an eerie hush hung over the proceedings while the Governor scanned the contents, everyone present assuming that a last-minute reprieve had been granted. And then the Governor announced that the letter was from the editor of a London newspaper requesting him to despatch an account of the hanging as soon as possible – and so the execution should therefore continue! Even as the shocked crowd listened almost unbelievingly to the statement, Calcraft acted; the trapdoors parted – and Mary's pathetic voice ceased abruptly as the rope tightened about her neck.

In the financial accounts subsequently compiled by the Town Council, the cost of transporting the scaffold from Edinburgh, together with the associated expenditure, amounted to £100; Calcraft, doubtless relieved by the successful end to a particularly distasteful episode, received his fee of £20 plus his expenses, and wasted little time in returning home. But if he thought he had rid the world of one female murderer, he little realised the depth of iniquity to which the woman he was due to hang six months later had sunk; not content with one victim, this woman was a multiple killer. Before that, however, there were other scaffold candidates requiring his attention.

Between May and September 1862, in two towns only six miles apart, no fewer than three children, one police officer and three men, two of them brutal murderers, met their deaths.

The first crime took place in the heart of Manchester on 16 May when Evan Mellor, an agent acting on behalf of property owners, was stabbed to death by William Robert Taylor, a tenant of one of the buildings owned by Mellor's employers. According to reports in the local papers at the time, a boiler had exploded with the building, killing one of Taylor's children, and a prolonged dispute had followed over possible compensation and rental agreements. Matters came to a head when Taylor and his wife

Martha visited Mellor's office. A fracas ensued in which Mrs Taylor reportedly pointed a gun at the agent; her husband then attacked him with a knife and in the violent struggle that followed Mellor was repeatedly and fatally stabbed.

The couple were promptly arrested, and shortly afterwards a further tragic discovery was made when the dead bodies of their three children were found at their home. Subsequent post-mortems failed to reveal the cause of the deaths; no traces of identifiable poison were found, no arrests made. Instead both parents were sent for trial at Liverpool Assizes, charged with the murder of Evan Mellor.

The facts of the case spoke for themselves, and as far as the husband was concerned, little defence other than insanity could be raised. This plea was not upheld, and while Martha Taylor was found innocent of the charge, not having taken active part in the crime, William Taylor was found guilty and sentenced to death.

The vicious murder, together with the mysterious death of the three otherwise healthy children, sent waves of shock and horror through the city's residents, gory details filling page after page of the local and national newspapers. But scarcely had the furore died down than another murder in the district sent reporters rushing to the scene at Smallshaw near Ashton-under-Lyne, a town but a few miles away, where a police officer had been shot whilst in the performance of his duty.

It would seem that a serious controversy about pay and conditions had arisen between the owners of local brickworks and their employees, to the extent that attacks had been carried out on the works' premises, thousands of bricks being wilfully destroyed. And on the 28 June 1862 two police officers on patrol in the Smallshaw area encountered a gang of seven or eight men armed with clubs and guns. Upon being challenged the men retaliated; shots were fired, one hitting and wounding Sergeant Harrop, a further fusillade of shots mortally wounding his fellow officer, Police Constable William Jump, a married man and father of five young children. The gang escaped in the darkness but the authorities not only offered a reward of £200 but also brought in reinforcements to search the surrounding district. However it was not until September that their efforts resulted in the capture and arrest of five men, one of whom, George Ward, was put on trial and found guilty of murdering the constable.

Poisoners and Pirates Get Short Shrift 93

Meanwhile William Taylor had been languishing in durance vile, confined in the condemned cell in Kirkdale Gaol, since May. Such a long delay between sentencing and execution was most unusual; perhaps the authorities hoped that, given time to reflect, he might become conscience-stricken and confess to the murder of his three children, the cause of their deaths still not having been established. But there seemed little prospect of that, one newspaper quoting his boastful assertion implying that he had indeed killed them but that the surgeons would never discover by what means. Now, however, with another murderer being due to be executed at Kirkdale Gaol, there was no point in waiting any longer, and so orders were given for Calcraft to attend on 13 September 1862 and carry out a double execution.

On arrival in Liverpool the hangman, aware of the details of the two cases from newspaper reports, must have realised that although he would have the crowd's full support when despatching the suspected multiple child-murderer Taylor, he could be in real danger when Ward appeared on the scaffold, ugly rumours having circulated that large numbers of the murderer's fellow strikers might demonstrate their sympathy with their 'hero' in more violent ways than simply booing and hissing. The police too were taking no chances; at the prospect of the scaffold being rushed by a mob of burly workmen hurling half-bricks, two hundred officers were brought in to control the vast crowd. But the executions turned out to be almost an anticlimax, the spectators doing little more than watch intently as Calcraft positioned the two men next to each other on the drop, pinioned and hooded them, then shook their hands before departing to release the trapdoors. Accompanied by the usual audible gasp from the crowd, the drop fell, neither victim struggling for longer than a few seconds before swaying slowly in deathly unison.

At the customary press interviews given afterwards, Captain Gibbs, the prison governor who, together with the chaplain, had of course been present on the scaffold, informed the journalists about the surprising admission made by Taylor before the noose tightened, that the three children had died as long as eight days before he had murdered Mellor – but his reasons for killing them, and the method he had used, died with him. And Calcraft packed his tackle into his canvas bag, collected his double fee of 2 guineas, and went home.

Catherine Wilson, although attractive, nevertheless possessed a diabolically fiendish nature. In 1853 she obtained employment as housekeeper to a Mr Peter Mawer, an elderly gentleman who lived in Boston, Lincolnshire, gaining his trust by nursing him when the gout from which he suffered became unbearable. She gave him his medicine, a remedy named colchicum derived from the dried seeds or corms of the autumn crocus which, when taken in small doses, brought relief, although was lethal if taken in large quantities. So devoted was she in her ministrations that Mr Mawer made the grave error of promising that he would leave everything to her in his will – and thereby sentenced himself to death!

In the October of the following year, poor Mr Mawer died. His doctor, having prescribed the colchicum, decided that his patient, desperate to relieve his pain, must have taken an accidental overdose. Catherine, her crocodile tears very much in evidence, collected her legacy from the solicitors, her belongings from the house, and departed for the bright lights of London.

While enjoying herself in the capital on the proceeds of her new-found wealth she became enamoured of a man named Dixon and together they moved into an apartment at 27 Alfred Place, Bedford Square, just off Tottenham Court Road. They introduced themselves to Mrs Soames, the landlady, as Mr and Mrs Wilson, and proceeded to revel in the high life; but her partner was an alcoholic and when drunk, he brutally beat her, unaware of the fact that together with her belongings and the money from the will, she had also brought the remaining quantity of colchicum!

Towards the end of 1855, for – to him – some unknown reason, he suddenly started to feel ill, and his condition rapidly deteriorated. Mrs Soames commiserated with Catherine, especially when her tenant explained that her husband had been consumptive for years and could not be expected to survive this latest attack. Nor did he. The local physician, Dr. Whidburn, was summoned to sign the death certificate and, not being their regular medical man, insisted on a post mortem, despite the widow's grief and her plea not to cut her dear husband up 'because he had always been horrified at the thought of his body being mutilated'. No trace of tuberculosis was found, but as the doctor had no reason to suspect anything untoward, further analysis was considered unnecessary, and the death certificate was accordingly signed.

This tragedy under her roof brought Mrs Soames and the grieving Catherine closer together and they became great friends, to the extent that Mrs Soames did not hesitate to lend the 'widow' sums of money whenever she asked for it. From Catherine's point of view there was only one way to repay such generosity – with colchicum!

Scarcely twelve months had passed before ill-health unaccountably overtook Mrs. Soames. She was of course assiduously nursed by her friend, who never failed to administer her medicine; five days afterwards, the landlady died in agony. Dr Whidburn attended again and another post mortem took place. Death by natural causes being assumed, another death certificate was issued. Catherine was flushed with success, having literally got away with murder – again. There was obviously nothing to prevent her from doing it again – and again.

She had another friend, a Mrs Atkinson who, together with her husband, kept a millinery shop in Kirkby Lonsdale, Cumberland (now Cumbria). They had met in 1860 when Mrs Atkinson was visiting London, and while shopping, the lady had somehow mislaid her purse, a loss that conveniently allowed Catherine to go on another spending spree. Some weeks later Mrs Atkinson wrote to say that she was coming to London again to purchase some stock for the shop. Seizing the opportunity, Catherine promptly suggested that her friend should stay with her in her new home in Loughborough Road, Brixton, south-west London. Mrs Atkinson gratefully accepted, with the inevitable result that a few days later Mr Atkinson received a telegram informing him that his wife was seriously ill and that he should come at once. And within hours of his arrival, his wife was dead.

The doctor attending was completely mystified as to the cause, but Mr Atkinson refused to agree to a post mortem, Catherine having used the same strategy in telling him that on her death bed his wife had implored her not to let anyone cut her body up. And as for the large sum of money with which Mrs Atkinson had intended to buy new stock, Catherine expressed her surprise that his wife had not written and informed her husband that en route to London by rail, she had felt unwell, got out at Rugby and, while resting on a seat on the platform, her money had been stolen. And Catherine also explained that the diamond ring she was wearing had of course been given to her by her late-lamented friend for looking after her.

Catherine Wilson's murderous career continued undetected, other victims being innocently duped to swallow the toxic colchicum until in February 1862, nine years after her first murder, she employed the same well-proven method as before, by becoming nurse to an elderly and frail lady, Mrs Sarah Carnell who lived in Marylebone. Once again she tended her charge; again was promised a large legacy, and again the perfect opportunity presented itself. Unfortunately however Catherine had used up all the colchicum, so had to resort to other means. On being asked by her employer to collect some of her usual medicine from the chemist, Catherine did so. On her return she said she had also brought a 'soothing draught', which would make her patient feel better. Pouring some into a tumbler she offered it to Mrs Carnell, who hesitated, exclaiming that the glass felt hot. Urged to drink it, that it would warm her up, the woman did so, only to spit it out again – to stare horrified as the mouthful of liquid she had rejected, burned holes in the sheets! The game was up; Catherine Wilson made a speedy exit from the house. It was not until six weeks later, in April 1862, that she was arrested, charged at Marylebone Police Court with attempted murder, and put on trial.

In court she was accused of switching Mrs Carnell's usual medicine for oil of vitriol (sulphuric acid). Her lawyer suggested that it was accidental and no fault of his client's; the chemist's assistant, a youth of fifteen, must have given her that by mistake, but the judge scornfully rejected that theory, pointing out that had the lad given a bottle of sulphuric acid to the prisoner in the dock, it would have become red-hot and burst while she was carrying it back to the house!

The jury was sent out to consider their verdict, and while they were doing so, the defence lawyer was approached by a man who identified himself as a detective of the Lincoln police force. After complimenting the lawyer on his efforts to get his client exonerated, he added that if her counsel won the case and she were found not guilty, she would then be in more trouble than she could ever imagine – for he had warrants for her arrest on no fewer than seven murder charges.

Meanwhile, to Catherine, waiting fraught with anxiety in the dock for the jury's verdict, all seemed lost. Eventually the jurors filed back into the courtroom and for some reason known only to themselves, the foreman delivered the result of their deliberations – not guilty! Catherine Wilson, surprised and delighted at having been given the benefit of the doubt, stepped from the dock – and was immediately arrested by the Lincoln police officer.

She was held in prison while further extensive enquiries were made. Investigations into the deaths of Messrs Mawer and Dixon, Mrs Atkinson and Mrs Soames, together with the attempted murder of Mrs Carnell, were instituted, corpses were exhumed, post mortems carried out. The results were beyond doubt, the doctors conducting the autopsies agreeing that the colchicum seeds had been infused and probably administered to her patients and partners in such 'health-restoring' drinks as brandy, wine, or tea. At her subsequent trial at the Old Bailey, Catherine Wilson listened apparently unconcerned as the damning evidence mounted against her, betraying not a flicker of emotion even when the judge donned the black cap and sentenced her to death.

On execution day, 20 October 1862, twenty thousand spectators crowded the area around Newgate to watch retribution overtake a woman who had committed so many horrific crimes, but she ignored the jeers and catcalls as the hangman placed the noose around her slim neck. Catherine Wilson had needed several drops of colchicum to despatch her victims – William Calcraft required only one drop to despatch his.

> London's thoroughfares were changing considerably in that and the following year. The construction of the Thames Embankment had begun, and one wonders whether Calcraft, en route from his house in Shoreditch, went out of his way to have a look, or even travel on the newly opened Tube which ran from Paddington to Farringdon Street – the first Underground railway system in the world. And if his wife Louisa ever wanted to experience a 'first', she could have gone shopping in William Whiteley's Universal Provider shop in Bayswater- the first departmental store in the country, which opened for business in May 1863. On the other hand she could have become a customer at the CWS, the Co-operative Wholesale Society, which was established in that year.

And still on the subject of drops – if George Woods and Duncan McPhail had been content merely to have a drop to drink with Ann Walne that day in November 1862, instead of robbing and murdering her, they would not have had the one that William Calcraft subsequently arranged for them to take. But when

'Chorley Tom', Thomas Bowling, a poacher and ex-convict, told them that following the sale of a cow, the old lady would have money in the house, the two men, together with Daniel Carr and Benjamin Hartley, found the prospect irresistible and proceeded to make plans to visit Ribchester, where Mrs Walne lived.

Ann's badly injured body had been found by neighbours on 11 November and the police, in the shape of Sergeant Whiteside and other officers from nearby Preston and Blackburn, were soon on the scene, the officer later describing to the inquest jury what he saw on entering the room. "She lay sprawled on the bed, naked from the waist down, her head and face covered in blood which still oozed and dripped. Her hands had been roughly fastened by the wrists to the bedposts, while a piece of ragged shawl was tied tightly round her throat." Their further search revealed that the little cottage and the adjoining room in which she sold ale, known as the 'Joiners Arms', had been thoroughly ransacked and any money that might have been there was missing.

A reward of £100 was offered for information leading to the arrest of those responsible, Thomas Bowling wasting no time in coming forward to inform on his friends and claim the cash, following which the four men were arrested. One of them, Benjamin Hartley, a weaver, sought to save his skin by turning Queen's Evidence, and gave the police a detailed description of exactly what had happened at the lonely cottage that night. Armed with crowbars, sticks and a pistol, the men had broken in and, because the old woman had, not unnaturally, screamed in terror while they were searching for the money, Daniel Carr went up to the bedroom and struck her several heavy blows with a loaded stick he carried, after which Woods tied her wrists to the bed-head. Having found the money, the gang then fled, dividing the spoil among them and disposing of their weapons. The latter were discovered later, with the assistance of Hartley, and proved conclusive evidence at their trial on 30 March 1863 at Liverpool Assize Court.

However, only two men appeared in the dock. Because of his cooperation, no evidence was offered against Hartley, and when the Kirkdale prison warders entered Carr's cell they found him having breathing difficulties so severe that he was in a state of collapse. Medical aid was immediately summoned, but too late, for the accused man died without regaining consciousness.

In court the evidence of witnesses proved overwhelming, local men coming forward to state that on passing the scene of the crime that day, they had noticed four sets of footsteps in the snow; moreover other statements were produced by railway staff describing the men who had purchased tickets at the nearby railway station early on the morning in question.

Desperate efforts were made by the defence to cast doubt on their veracity; Bowling's evidence was also challenged on the grounds of self-interest as he was claiming the reward, and on Hartley for similar reasons. Although the trial dragged on for weeks, the outcome was never in doubt, but because the murder was not considered to have been premeditated, the jury added a rider recommending mercy to their verdict of guilty. The judge might have agreed with the verdict but he certainly didn't agree with the recommendation, for he then proceeded to don the black cap.

On the fatal day, Saturday 25 April 1863, the condemned duo also wore caps, albeit of a contrasting colour, placed over their heads by Calcraft and held in place by his nooses. The local newspaper later remarked on the resigned composure of Woods and commented that his companion showed every sign of extreme apprehension. The Rev. Appleton read the appropriate Biblical verses, but for Woods and McPhail the Altar of Justice was the scaffold, and the Service itself, conducted by the hangman, was brief and conclusive, for after shaking hands with the two members of his flock, he stepped back and drew the bolt. The opening of the trap and the tightening of the ropes were accompanied by the exultant roar from the rest of the 'congregation', a journalist among them reporting how 'Woods dropped heavily and remained motionless, but McPhail struggled frantically for nearly a minute before he too paid the price'; Ann Walne had been avenged.

A robbery which ended in murder meant that Calcraft had to visit Scotland again, his victim this time being John 'Sodger' Reilly, his nickname earned by being an ex-soldier of the 60th Rifles, although by the time of his crime he was a labourer. He had attacked a woman walking along the road that led from Holytown to Newhouse, near Motherwell in Lanarkshire, and in the struggle, inflicted fatal injuries on her. When her body was found, a hue and cry was raised, but Reilly had already fled south, first to Biggar, then across country to Hawick, crossing the Border into Northumberland.

When eventually arrested, it was alleged that he confessed to the murder, but later, in court, he withdrew it, claiming he was innocent. No credence was given to his plea, and on 16 May 1863 he felt Calcraft tighten the pinioning belt about his waist, saw the throng of onlookers gathered round the scaffold outside Glasgow's South Prison and, for but a fleeting second, was aware of the boards beneath his feet falling away.

In January 1864 the hangman travelled to Liverpool again, there to accept once more the hospitality of Kirkdale Gaol's Governor, Captain Gibbs, preparatory to despatching an ex-policeman named Luke Charles. The condemned man had been found guilty of murdering his wife Mary, the victim of what the Victorians called the 'eternal triangle', the other member of that particular geometric configuration being Luke's intended fiancée Ellen Ford.

Charles had been a police constable in Bury, Manchester, following service with the Irish constabulary, and it was while living over there that he had met Ellen, a young woman who was so enamoured of him that, unaware he was already married, moved into lodgings in Bury in order to plan their wedding. She subsequently returned to her home in Ireland, satisfied to await the moment when Luke would join her there. From his point of view however, there was one major obstacle; prior to a marriage the traditional banns called for the knowledge of any impediment why the ceremony should not take place. In this instance the impediment was poor Mary Charles; so she would first have to be removed.

In February 1863 Luke and his wife left their dwelling, telling friends they were going to visit Mary's sister, Julia Dunn, who lived in Pendleton, about six miles away, near Salford. Luke returned alone, and a month or so later Julia, not having heard from her sister, contacted Luke, only to be told that she had gone to Ireland to visit her mother. Her further enquiries only elicited the same negative response, even after Luke had returned from yet another visit to Ireland, for the purpose, of course, of visiting Ellen Ford. Now seriously concerned about her sister's whereabouts, Julia went to the police and voiced her worries. Those worthies promptly checked their files and among the records of unidentified bodies was one of a woman found floating, ironically enough on St Valentine's Day, 14 February, in the Manchester, Bolton and Bury Canal, a Lancashire waterway which meandered, as it still does, through Prestolee,

Ringley, Pendlebury, Brindle Heath – and Pendleton! Following a verdict of 'Found Drowned' the corpse was interred in Salford Cemetery at the council's expense.

On the canal path had also been found a nightdress, a cloak and a nightcap; on the third finger of the dead woman's left hand was a wedding ring. All these items were taken for safe custody to Salford Workhouse, and it was there that they were recognised by Julia as belonging to her sister Mary. No injuries were apparent, but this did not necessarily discount the possibility of foul play; a sudden push leaves few bruises.

Despite adhering to his original story that his wife had gone away, Luke Charles was the chief suspect, his evasive manner, his unsatisfactory replies over the past few months and the evidence of his duplicity given by Ellen Ford, leaving the police – and the judge and jury – in no doubt as to his guilt.

So convinced were the police that they had the right man that, according to local newspapers, several mysteries remained unsolved, all involving that nightdress. If, as stated by Charles, he and his wife had indeed gone to her sister's home, how could Mary have left the house without her sister seeing that she wore her nightdress, covered only by a cloak, always assuming that there would have been some compelling reason why Mary would have wanted to go out anyway, in that particular state of *dishabillé*? If, on the other hand, the couple had gone to Pendleton – as they must have had, the body being found in the nearby canal – but had stayed elsewhere in the town, surely Mary would have insisted on visiting her sister and mentioned the proposed visit to their mother.

Did he murder her first, then push or throw her in, or did she die by drowning? If murder, where did it take place? If in her sister's house or elsewhere in the town, surely someone would have heard a struggle or must have noticed her subsequent absence. And how did Charles get Mary, if alive, to the canal? It seems out of the question that she actually walked there so minimally clad; yet if already unconscious or dead, the possibility that he carried her limp form in his arms seems equally untenable. It was an industrial area, mills lining the banks of the canal, workmen and women going to work even before dawn; the spectacle of a scantily dressed woman, or a man carrying one such in his arms, would have attracted rather more than casual comment. And the theory that Mary went to the towpath fully dressed and in daytime, there to be murdered and stripped, her nightdress then being put on her by her husband in order to deceive the police that it happened at night and that Mary was in the habit of sleepwalking, was unlikely, albeit conceivably feasible, but Charles never claimed such an alibi.

However there was no mystery at all about the circumstances surrounding Luke Charles' death, which took place on Saturday 9 January 1864, nor was there any need to question any of the five thousand or so witnesses regarding the identity of the man who caused it; William Calcraft never pulled any strings to avoid his responsibility – just the rope from his pocket and the trapdoor bolt from its socket.

Until the late 1700s the remains of executed criminals were displayed to the public as deterrents. To warn travellers coming to the City from the south to behave themselves, heads were exhibited on London Bridge, the only bridge crossing the river into London for hundreds of years. Those entering from the north saw the gallows at Tyburn and were similarly apprised. But what of those coming via the river Thames itself, seafarers bent on committing maritime mischief? The solution was obvious; to display the corpses of such offenders by hanging them in chains along the river banks on the approaches to the City, at Wapping and Bugsby's Hole near Blackwall, among other places.

The authority set up to legislate on all maritime matters was the Court of Admiralty, which was responsible for trying and sentencing everyone committing ship-borne crimes, even minor offences such as stealing ropes, anchors and suchlike items of chandlery from dockyards and wharves. Death sentences were, appropriately enough, carried out near the water's edge, at Execution Dock, the method being, as the historian Holinshed pointed out 'that pirates and robbers by sea are condemned in the Court of Admeraltie and hanged on the shore at lowe water mark, where they are left till three tides have overwashed them.' There, swaying with the tides, the bloated and waterlogged bodies provided dire warning to the crews of the scores of ships entering the Pool of London, medieval records showing that over three hundred pirates were executed along the Thames each year.

Five of Calcraft's victims could well have suffered a similar ghastly fate had it not been for legislation passed during the reign of William IV (1830-1837) which stipulated that 'crimes committed on the high seas are henceforth to be tried at the Central Criminal Court' in other words, the Old Bailey. The five

Poisoners and Pirates Get Short Shrift 103

men in question were Blanco, Lopez, Leone, Duranno and Watts, four being natives of Manila, the chief port of the Philippines, the fifth a Levantine. They were all crew members of the good ship *Flowery Land*, bound for Singapore when, on 10 September 1863, they mutinied and murdered not only the captain, but also his brother, the first mate, the steward and the cook. Only one man escaped, the second mate, who then alerted the authorities and so brought about the capture of the pirates.

Their executions at Newgate provided Calcraft with yet another record, that of being the last hangman to perform a multiple execution in public, all five being hanged at the same time. And the opportunity to watch as many on the drop as that, instead of the more usual one or two, provided the general public with an occasion that was not to be missed. Nor did they.

On Sunday the 21 February 1864 at least five thousand people started to gather for the next day's big event. Three of the newspapers of the day, the *Times*, *Morning Herald* and *Morning Star* gave wide coverage, between them describing how 'the throngs had poured in from the dens of St Giles, the sinks of Somerstown and the purlieus of Whitechapel. Costermongers rubbed shoulders with dapper clerks and shopboys, hot-potato-men cried aloud, and persons with greasy trays invited the public to buy still more greasy pastry. Roughs reviled each other at safe distance and bedraggled women in gaudy rags pushed about with more than masculine effrontery.' One Newgate shop 'was doing a roaring trade selling muddy coffee and sticky cakes'; Calcraft, observing the latter, no doubt looked back with some nostalgia to the days when he sold pies around the scaffold! Pickpockets had a field day, despite the legislation passed in earlier days that 'Whereas persons in contempt of God's commands, and in defiance of the law, are found to cut pockets and pick purses, even at places of public execution, while executions are being done on criminals; be it therefore enacted that all such persons shall suffer death without benefit of clergy.' Thieves too made hay while the sun shone – or rather when it didn't. At the sight of a respectable onlooker they would move in menacingly 'and in an instant the victim would be surrounded, hustled, divested of all his valuables, and sent hatless and coatless away. If he resisted, he was beaten; if he cried out, he was garrotted.'

Not everyone present was of the lower classes, of course. All the rooms of the surrounding houses had been hired, at an exorbitant price, well in advance, in much the same way as corporate suites are booked at today's sporting stadiums, their wealthy occupants passing the time by drinking and playing cards, their culinary repasts varying from chicken and tongue, ham and cakes, washed down with sherry or champagne.

At about three o'clock on the Monday morning, the shouting and general hubbub rose to a crescendo 'as the base of the scaffold was dragged out of the gaol by a team of horses. Hooting, catcalls and other oaths greeted the men employed to erect the gallows.' More jeers and abuse heralded the arrival of the police. More than eleven hundred constables of the combined City of London and Metropolitan forces, some of them mounted, together with their superior officers, arrived, taking up their positions around the scaffold and the surrounding area, their presence becoming even more necessary by dawn when the Underground railway disgorged further hordes of spectators.

And at seven a.m. the star of the show arrived – William Calcraft himself! As later reported in the *Morning Herald* 'His entrée was hailed with a kind of familiar but suppressed hum of recognition from those in front of the gallows, which was acknowledged by a slight bow and a smile of strange and sinister character. After a close scrutiny of the flooring of the scaffold and the mechanism of the drop, he quickly retired.'

An hour later he made his way to the condemned cells and pinioned each man in turn, tightening the black leather belts he had brought, securely around their waists and arms. They then took their places in the procession which consisted of the prison governor, sheriffs and under-sheriffs, the chaplains, prison warders and other officials, and proceeded two-by-two along the narrow corridors and through the prison cemetery, a stone passageway about eight feet wide, open to the skies but covered by a grating, hence its name the 'Birdcage Walk'. Beneath the paving stones over which they walked lay the corpses of previously executed prisoners and where their bodies, covered with quicklime, would also be buried.

On reaching the press yard within the prison the cortège was a little early, so the prisoners were allowed to sit on a bench for a few minutes. One of the officials, noticing that they were obviously overwhelmed at the prospect of their impending execution, instructed that each be given the usual drink of brandy, but hardly had they had time to drink it than the clock of St Sepulchre's Church opposite the prison started to strike eight o'clock and the Newgate bell began to toll. First to be led through the black draped doorway and out on to the scaffold was Blanco, escorted by two warders; to the deafening roar and cries of "Hats off! Hats off!" from the crowd, he was followed by Leone, Durrano and Watts, Lopez being last. Calcraft, keeping a close eye on his charges, suddenly noticed that Blanco was on the point of collapse. Stepping forward he and the assistants with whom he had been provided for the occasion, caught the man just in time and with difficulty placed him in a chair, which was then dragged into position on the drop. The others were led forward to their designated places, apparently resigned to their fate, but Lopez nodded and smiled at the crowd.

Newgate scaffold had been designed to accommodate up to twenty-two victims at the same time, and old prints show all five of the *Flowery Land* quintet standing in line, identically white-hooded and noosed. Calcraft, having completed his preparations, went below and for a moment a deathly hush fell on the throng – to be followed by a resounding cheer as the bodies of the Five Pirates dropped seemingly only a distance of inches, first to jerk and twist, then slowly rotate with the momentum of their fall. And the prison bell fell silent.

As mentioned earlier, the sheriffs, chaplains and other officials then adjourned to the prison, there to partake of the traditional hearty breakfast before returning at nine o'clock to witness Calcraft cut down the bodies. The crowds had long since dispersed and the hangman and his assistants had no difficulty in transporting the limp corpses back into the prison, where they were examined by the staff-surgeon. After he had made the necessary entries in the prison records certifying 'that they could never slay or sin again', the bodies were taken to the Birdcage Walk, there to join the many others interred beneath the paving stones. And on the wall above their graves were carved their initials 'B L D L W', these letters accompanied, unusually, by further identification of their crime, 'Ship Flowery Land Feb. 22 1864' being added. Thirty-eight years later, in 1902, Newgate Prison was demolished to make room for the present Old Bailey Central Criminal Court of Justice. The remains of those buried beneath the paving stones of Birdcage Walk were exhumed without ceremony and conveyed to Ilford, there to be re-interred in the City of London Cemetery.

CHAPTER EIGHT

A 'FIRST CLASS' MURDERER – AND OTHERS

P irates killing their captain on a ship in foreign waters was not an entirely unknown occurrence during the reign of Queen Victoria, but the murder of a passenger on a London railway train filled the public with shock and disbelief, more so because the attack occurred in a *first* class compartment, of all places! Yet that is precisely what happened to Thomas Briggs, a senior bank clerk travelling from Fenchurch Street station to Hackney Central, north-east of the City, on the evening of 9 July 1864, his badly injured body being seen lying by the railway line by the driver of a train heading in the opposite direction. Medical examination revealed that his death had been caused by several severe blows to the head, delivered, it was later ascertained, by his own walking stick, after which he had been thrown from the train. Moreover his personal possessions, including his gold watch and chain, were missing and, oddly enough, the silk top hat he always wore.

On locating and searching the train involved, the police had no difficulty in identifying the compartment in which the assault had taken place, two passengers boarding it having already reported finding copious bloodstains soaking into the seats. Also in the compartment was Mr Briggs' silver-topped walking stick, heavily bloodstained, and a black beaver hat, the discovery of the latter leaving the police in no doubt that the murderer, in his haste, had fled, wearing Mr Briggs' elegant headgear.

Descriptions of the missing valuables and the hat were circulated throughout the City, a response being forthcoming two days later from a London jeweller named, appropriately enough, Mr Robert Death. He reported that he had in his possession a gold chain matching the description, which had been brought in by a man with a foreign accent, who exchanged the chain for a similar though less expensive item.

That early success presaged an imminent arrest, but then the trail went cold. However, an alert cab driver named Matthews read one of the notices offering a reward of £300 for information on the case, and the jeweller's macabre name attracted his attention, it being the same as that printed on the inside of a jewellery box which had been given to his daughter by a German friend, Franz Muller. Moreover he, Matthews, had also recently bought a couple of black beaver hats, one for himself, the other for the German. Ironically, if Muller had gone to a jeweller having the name of Smith or Jones, the killer might never have been caught. On such incidental facts..............! As it was, the cabman furnished the police with the vital information, adding that Muller had left for the United States on the *SS Victoria* four days previously.

Determined not to be thwarted, the police ascertained the date on which that ship was due to arrive in New York and also the fact that another, much faster ship, the *SS City of Manchester*, was due to depart and would reach New York three weeks before the *Victoria* docked. Accordingly two police officers and Messrs Death and Matthews, the latter two gentlemen accompanying them in order to identify their quarry, embarked on the ship and, together with officers of the New York police force, were present on the quay as Muller came down the gangplank. Despite denying all knowledge of the murder, he was identified by the witnesses, and when Mr Briggs' gold watch was found in his luggage he was arrested and taken into custody.

His extradition was applied for and granted; on 16 September he arrived under escort at Liverpool and travelled by rail to London. While in prison petitions on his behalf were raised by the German Legal Protection Society, German nationals and sympathisers in this country; from the Continent the King of Prussia even sent telegrams to Queen Victoria requesting clemency be shown. All to no avail however, for on 27 October 1864 Muller appeared in the dock at the Central Criminal Court. Despite his defence council claiming that he had an alibi and also attempting to accuse Matthews of the crime, the jury were out for a mere fifteen minutes, returning to deliver a verdict of guilty.

Monday 14 November saw the customary crowds gathering at Newgate, the scenes being just as lawless and chaotic as those at other executions, other perhaps than the vocal renditions of popular music hall songs, and a sinister couplet – in which all those participating swayed rhythmically from side to side as they chanted in macabre unison "Oh My! Think I've got to die!"

In the condemned cell Muller rose at six o'clock, dressed, and was then joined by the prison chaplain, the Rev. Davis, and Dr Louis Cappel, pastor of the local German Lutheran Church, for prayers. Later the usual officials arrived and the German was escorted to the press room where Calcraft waited. The hangman had arrived earlier and despite the multitude thronging the surrounding streets, had managed to reach the gates of the gaol without being recognised, thereby avoiding the usual harassment. Muller, pale but obviously holding himself in check, stood motionless while the hangman pinioned his arms and removed his neckerchief and shirt collar in readiness for the noose. Then it was time for him to face the crowd, the gallows, and his Maker.

In its report the *Times* described how the murderer 'took with a steady step his place beneath the beam, then, looking up and seeing that he was not exactly beneath the proper spot whence the short black link of chain depended, he shifted a few inches and then stood quite still. Following close came the hangman, who at once pulled a white cap over the condemned man's face, fastened his feet with a strap, and shambled off the scaffold amid low hisses.'

Dr Cappel, holding the condemned man's hand, prayed with him and asked whether he was guilty or innocent of the dreadful crime, to which Muller replied that he was innocent. Again the pastor questioned him, saying "I ask you now, solemnly and for the last time, have you committed this crime?" There was a brief pause, then Muller murmured "Ja. Ich habe es gethan." ("Yes, I did it"). And before the sound of the words had died away, Calcraft operated the drop.

The hangman had done his job more efficiently than usual, for the newspaper described the final moments. 'Those who stood close to the apparatus could just detect a movement twice, an almost imperceptible muscular flicker that passed through the frame. This was all, and before the peculiar humming noise of the crowd was over, Muller had ceased to live, though as he hung, his features seemed to swell and sharpen under the white cap so that the dead man's face at last stood out like a cast in plaster.'

That description was more appropriate than the reporter could have imagined, for a plaster cast of the head was in fact taken before the corpse was buried within the prison precincts. Prior to that, however, the inevitable melee broke out, the journalist describing how 'even before the slight slow vibrations of the body had ended, robbery and violence, loud laughing, oaths, fighting, obscene conduct and still more filthy language reigned round the gallows far and near. Such too the scene remained with little change or respite, till the old hangman, Calcraft, slunk again along the drop amid hisses and sneering enquiries of what he had had to drink that morning. After failing once to cut the rope, he made a second attempt more successfully, and the body of Muller disappeared from view.'

Inevitably the pamphlet purveyors were doing a roaring trade among the spectators, selling copies of the victim's 'Last Words'. English not being Muller's mother-tongue, it is hardly likely that he would have composed such verses during his final hours in the condemned cell, but the fruit of the pamphleteers' literary endeavours may be seen in Appendix 3.

Immediately following the execution a message was despatched by the undersheriff to the Home Secretary stating that 'By direction of the sheriffs I have the honour to acquaint you that the prisoner Muller has at the last moment, just before the drop fell, confessed to the German minister of religion attending him, that he was guilty of the deed for which he suffered.' This notification was no doubt welcomed by the authorities, confirming as it did the judgment of the court.

Needless to add, Madame Tussaud's inventory of wax figures was later increased by one, and Calcraft's professional record also increased by the same number, that of hanging the first man to commit a murder on a train in this country!

In March 1865 William Calcraft made his farewell appearance before the good folk of Lancaster when he executed Stephen Burke, a forty-year-old tailor, for murder, it being the last public execution to take place in that city. The scenario was almost pure Dickensian in its drama; it had been snowing heavily, and it also involved six young children who, by five minutes past midday, would be orphans, for the condemned man was their father; his crime, the murder of their mother.

The ghastly offence took place at their home in Preston, Lancashire, at the end of January that year, when neighbours summoned the police to investigate a disturbance. On forcing an entrance the officers discovered that Mrs. Mary Ann Burke had been brutally beaten to death by her habitually drunken husband, their young daughter giving evidence to that effect at the subsequent trial. On hearing her account of the frequent quarrels and violent attacks which had taken place in the house, the court had no hesitation in finding him guilty and accordingly sentenced him to death, the execution to take place at noon on Saturday, 25 March that year.

Contrary to normal practice, work on assembling the gallows at Lancaster Castle's Hanging Corner, opposite the Church, started earlier than usual, the grim edifice being completed before dusk on the Friday. This was not done out of consideration for the prisoners asleep within the Castle – the usual practice was to erect it during the night – but to avoid the difficulties in transporting the heavy beams and component parts through the large numbers of spectators expected to arrive early in order to ensure a good view of the grim proceedings. And arrive they did, being reinforced the next morning from all over the county, reaching the city on foot and by horse-drawn vehicles, special excursions also having been laid on by the railway companies.

The *Lancaster Gazette* reported that some of Burke's closest relatives had been allowed to visit him on the Friday, speaking to him through the large aperture in the cell door through which, when necessary, food could be passed; his youngest child, a baby of four months old, was also handed to him in that manner. Rocking it in his arms, he paced the floor in an obviously disturbed state of mind, so distraught that a special watch had been kept on him in case he attempted to commit suicide.

Calcraft had been warned of this and so ensured that, as twelve o'clock approached, his victim was closely escorted as the procession left the Drop Room and assembled on the scaffold. Burke, now the cynosure of hundreds of pairs of eyes, became visibly agitated, Calcraft wasting little time in drawing the cap over the man's head and positioning the noose around his neck. In the moment of intense silence that followed, the hangman operated the lever; the drop fell, Burke apparently dying almost immediately. Being clad in a white shirt and trousers, the white cap covering his head, his now slowly swaying body made an eerie sight silhouetted against the black walls of the ancient Castle.

One wonders whether, once William arrived back home in London, he or Louisa read 'Alice in Wonderland' to their children or grandchildren as a bedtime story, the book having just been published. They definitely had no worries about the safety of the youngsters while crossing the road; that year the *Road Locomotion Act* came into force, compelling all drivers of road 'locomotives' not to exceed 4 mph and to be escorted by three attendants, one of whom had to walk in front carrying a red flag! If the vehicles of the newly formed Metropolitan Fire Service had also to conform with that ruling, many a fire must have burned itself out before the crews arrived!

Of all the murder cases with which Calcraft had been associated, surely the one which proved to be his *magnum opus* was that of Dr. Edward William Pritchard in July 1865, a case which not only attracted wide public attention and condemnation but also involved the hideous murder of two women, an anonymous letter, the later discovery of the charred remains of a servant girl, and such incongruous items as a skull, some teeth, and a pair of elastic-sided boots! It was also an execution that could well have ended disastrously because of Calcraft's clumsiness.

Dr Pritchard was a vain and egotistical Walter Mitty type, an erstwhile naval assistant surgeon and the son of a Royal Navy captain, he professed to be a close friend of Garibaldi, the Italian patriot and revolutionary, whom he had never even met, and gave talks about countries he had never visited. That would have been accepted and tolerated as merely eccentricity, had he not also had been a charlatan, a womaniser – and a poisoner.

He and his wife Mary Jane ('Minnie') had been married for fifteen years and had five children when, in 1860, they moved to Berkley Terrace, Glasgow, where Pritchard established his surgery. However, four years later a fire destroyed their residence, a maid dying in the flames; local gossips, aware of the good doctor's philandering ways with women, hinted at his close involvement in the conflagration.

The family subsequently went to live in Clarence Place, Sauchiehall Street, Glasgow, where Pritchard proceeded to have an affair with a teenaged servant, Mary M'Cloud, promising to marry her in the event of his wife's death. And when the young girl became pregnant, the doctor employed his medical skills in carrying out an abortion.

Early in 1865 Minnie fell ill, her husband diagnosing a

stomach upset. Her mother, Mrs Jane Taylor, came and nursed her but on 25 February, after eating some tapioca pudding, inexplicably fell ill herself and within weeks had died. Despite Dr Patterson, a local practitioner, suspecting narcotic poisoning, Pritchard overrode his opinion and signed the death certificate, stating that the cause of death was due to apoplexy.

Three weeks later, on 18 March, Minnie also passed away, her grieving husband diagnosing the cause of her death as gastric fever, and proceeded to sign her death certificate also. Then, doubtless planning how he would spend the proceeds from the insurance policy he had taken out on Minnie's life, he went to her funeral – only to be arrested on his return home, an anonymous letter having been sent to the authorities casting doubt on the cause of her death. Both corpses were subsequently exhumed, autopsies revealing the presence of aconite and tartar emetic (antimony potassium tartrate, a colourless, odourless poison) in both of the bodies.

At his trial at the High Court of Justiciary in Edinburgh on 3 July 1865, the Right Honourable John Inglis presiding, damning evidence was given by a local chemist who testified that the prisoner had frequently purchased antimony from his pharmacy. Despite his defence counsel claiming that both murders had been committed by the young maid, Mary M'Cloud, the jury was out for less than an hour, and returned a verdict of guilty. Dr Pritchard was then sentenced to be hanged at Glasgow on 28 July.

The date of the execution happened to coincide with the annual Glasgow Fair, the council having to order the removal of some of the shooting galleries, roundabouts, sideshows and similar attractions, in order to make room for what was definitely not a side-show, the scaffold itself, around which, as the time drew near, approximately 100,000 spectators thronged, order being maintained by the presence of 750 policemen.

The *Edinburgh Scotsman* of 28 July gave a definitive account of the proceedings, the following excerpts describing how: 'the prisoner retired to bed a little before midnight on his last night and although he was somewhat restless at first, he soon fell into a deep sleep and slept soundly until five o'clock in the morning. Later he partook of some coffee and bread, and appeared quite prepared for the dreadful ordeal which he was to go through.

'A number of people whose duties led them to take part in the dismal proceedings were admitted early to the Old Court, among them being a number of modellers from Edinburgh who had received the sanction of the authorities to take a cast of the culprit's head after execution, to enrich the collection of similar curiosities in the museum of the Phrenological Society.

'Eventually the clergyman and officials came to the cell to administer to the man during his few remaining moments. When the clock struck eight the magistrates entered the courthouse and took their seats on the bench, and a few minutes later the solemn voice of the officiating clergyman was heard from the cell below, reading a portion of the 90th psalm. Then the small party ascended the steps from the condemned cell and everyone in the courtroom rose to his feet and stretched eagerly to catch a glimpse of the prisoner as he stepped firmly through the dock (in the floor of the dock was an aperture through which stairs led to the cells, hence the final words of judges at the end of a trial "Take him down", thereby avoiding the necessity to lead the prisoner out through the body of the court). The prisoner then advanced to the front of the table above which sat the magistrates on the bench.

'The wretched man' continued the newspaper report 'had his arms pinioned, the hangman having performed this painful part of the ceremony in the cell. Dr Pritchard was clad in deep mourning and on his left hand he wore a black kid glove. He seemed to have bestowed some care on his toilet; his clothes were neatly arranged and his thin flowing hair and long beard were carefully trimmed.

'The certificate for the custody of the prisoner having been handed over, the grim procession was formed again and moved off through the passage leading towards the scaffold, led by two officers in scarlet livery. The prisoner bore up with wonderful composure and the only sign of fear he betrayed was a slight trembling in the limbs. As he ascended the steps of the scaffold he stumbled slightly on the top step but regained his balance and on reaching the drop he stood firm and erect.

'His appearance on the elevated platform was the signal for a deep howl of execration from the immense crowd. Calcraft stepped on to the scaffold with the doomed man and was received with a few groans and hisses. Quietly, and with an expertness that showed him to be well accustomed to his awful work, the executioner stationed his victim above the drop and busied himself in the grim work of his office. The white cap was expeditiously drawn over the head of the culprit and the fatal noose adjusted about his neck.

'The prominent figure of the executioner, his head covered with a black skull cap and his long white beard lending to his aspect a sort of venerable air, strongly attracted the attention of the crowd and drew forth repeated sounds of recognition. The dread preparations completed, Calcraft stepped back a pace or two on the scaffold and anxiously surveyed the rope that was to suspend his victim. He seemed satisfied with the result of his scrutiny, for he again immediately advanced, examined the noose about the prisoner's neck, taking particular care to see that the man's beard was free from its influence, and then grasped the unhappy man by his ungloved hand and shook it kindly and almost affectionately in token of farewell.

'This token of feeling on the part of the aged executioner seemed to meet with the approval of the crowd, and once more the hoarse murmur spread throughout their ranks. Firmly the prisoner stood above the drop, showing little if any trace of agitation except for an occasional quiver of the legs, and several times Calcraft, as if morbidly anxious that no mistake should occur, examined the rope and drop to see that all was clear. After finally completing his scrutiny he pulled the bolt and the body of the prisoner swung with a sudden jerk into space.

'The unhappy man did not die without a struggle. For an instant after the drawing of the bolt no motion was perceptible in the body, but it soon swung quickly around, the whole form quivering and the hands working with a muscular action. But this soon ceased and ere ten minutes had lapsed his body hung perfectly motionless upon the rope in the dull air of the morning.'

Another reporter described Pritchard's final contortions as 'after the bolt was drawn he shrugged his shoulders more than half-a-dozen times, his head shook and his whole body trembled violently.'

The body remained hanging until fourteen minutes to nine, when Calcraft proceeded to lower it. In doing so he momentarily lost his grip of the rope and the body fell suddenly and violently on to the coffin which was resting on two trestles below. Part of the bottom of the coffin was knocked out by the fall but fortunately it was repaired by a number of workmen who were present, and the body, having been stripped, was conveyed into the courthouse where, after the Edinburgh modellers had taken a cast of the corpse's head in order to satisfy the needs of the Phrenological Society, the body was buried in the gaol courtyard at ten o'clock.

Forty-five years later, the buildings were demolished and the site excavated. The remains of those who had been buried there were exhumed and among them were found the skeleton and skull of William Pritchard, together with his elastic sided boots; so well preserved were the latter, that a souvenir hunter promptly stole them!

If season tickets had been introduced by 1866, no doubt William Calcraft would have availed himself of one, for in January of that year he had to pack his little black bag and again catch a train to Scotland, this time travelling nearly four hundred and fifty miles north to Montrose. The murderer this time was Andrew Brown, an axe-wielding seaman who, on 6 September 1865, while aboard the schooner *Nymph* some miles off the coast of Forfarshire, without warning slew the skipper, John Greig, while that unfortunate gentleman lay asleep in his bunk. Another member of the crew, Pert by name, managed to wrest the weapon from Brown and throw it over the side, although even without the axe, the murderer must have somehow subjugated his fellow crew members, for he then took command of the vessel and took it into harbour at Stonehaven.

Once ashore, he went to his mother's house, and whilst there he was arrested by the local police. At his trial in Edinburgh on 8 January 1866, despite having previously claimed to have borne the skipper a grudge, he pleaded insanity, but the jury refused to accept this and brought in a verdict of guilty, although a few members also recommended that a merciful sentence be handed down. However no such leniency was shown. Brown was sentenced to death, and on the 10 January 1866 he was taken under strong escort on the long road journey round the Firth of Forth to Forfar and its prison.

On the 31st of that month he was given the privilege of having a special train in which to travel from Forfar to Montrose, a coastal town some miles away. The scaffold, loaned by the Aberdeen authorities, had been erected in the main street and, anticipating the need for crowd control, one hundred and fifty special constables had been sworn in. However that measure was not necessary, no more than three and a half thousand spectators gathering around the gallows, waiting patiently for the gruesome entertainment to begin.

Andrew Brown, having been earlier pinioned by Calcraft, was led out and assisted up the scaffold steps. There, apparently resigned to his fate, he was positioned on the drop, standing motionless as the hangman hooded and noosed him. The crowd watched with awed fascination as Calcraft operated the drop and the body at first twitched, then hung limp.

After the corpse had been removed for burial in Forfar Prison, Calcraft left for home. As well-behaved as the crowd had been, nevertheless they vented their contempt on the hangman, hissing him as, escorted by forty policemen, he made his way to the railway station; it was obvious that unless his victim had actually murdered and dismembered helpless women and children, Calcraft would continue to be abused and vilified every time he appeared in public!

One dark evening in December 1865 Alexander McEwan, a baker's vanman, was travelling alone along a road near Vicar's Bridge, Blairingone, near the town of Dollar in Perthshire, when a man suddenly sprang from behind the hedge and opened fire with a gun, fatally wounding McEwan before robbing him. Police enquiries led to the arrest of Joseph Bell, a local poacher who had recently borrowed a gun because, as he admitted, he was penniless. Yet when searched, he was found to be in possession of goods and a sum of money, the total of which added up to that originally carried by the vanman. Further evidence was forthcoming, the footprints left by Bell's boots exactly matching those at the scene of the crime, and a gun found under Vicars Bridge was identified by the man who had previously lent it to the poacher.

Although absolute proof was not forthcoming there was so little doubt of Bell's involvement that the jury at his trial in Perth on 24 April 1866 took less than thirty minutes to bring in a verdict of guilty, the judge, Lord Ardmillan concurring wholeheartedly and sentencing Bell to be hanged in the town on 22 May.

The usual preparations were set in motion; sheriffs, under-sheriffs and the chaplain were informed; the use of the Aberdeen scaffold was requested and subsequently hauled across country on carts, on arrival being erected against the prison wall; workmen told to erect crowd control barriers at strategic places; police officers detailed to report to specific locations at specific times, and of course William Calcraft received a letter from the prison governor giving him the details and requesting that he head north once more.

Arriving at Perth on the day before the execution, the following morning he went to the condemned cell, there to pinion a prisoner who was still stubbornly resisting the chaplain's plea that he should confess and so clear his conscience. Two thousand or so citizens of the town and from local villages crowded the street outside the gaol; Calcraft went through his grim routine of hooding and noosing; and as the drop fell the muffled voice of the condemned man could still be heard proclaiming his innocence.

The Victorians, convinced that sinners would be consigned to the infernal regions, there to be consumed by fire and brimstone, no doubt noted with satisfaction the appropriate fate suffered by Thomas Grime for the murder of James Barton, whose body was then thrown into a furnace, for after a short but conclusive meeting with the hangman, the killer's evil soul would of a certainty be dispatched to Hades for all eternity.

On 2nd January 1863, Barton, a fifty-five year old man, was at work on the night-shift maintaining the boilers in Bawk House Pit, at Haigh, a village situated near Wigan, Lancashire. Workmen coming on duty later found him absent and the boiler fires out. Two of the men were Barton's sons who, in order to raise steam in the boilers, relit the furnaces, little realised that by doing that, they were burning what was left of their father, for during later examination of the ashes, fragments of charred bones were discovered. What was not found, however, was any trace of the large and valuable silver watch James Barton always carried.

In the weeks, months and indeed years following, extensive investigations were carried out, but the trail had gone cold. However in 1865 a number of arrests took place and so-called confessions made, some alleging that the evidence had been disposed of, the much-sought-after watch being thrown in the nearby Leeds and Liverpool canal; accordingly that particular stretch of the waterway was subsequently drained and searched, with negative results, but the wide report of that event was instrumental in finally solving the murder mystery.

The newspaper account of the canal dredging was read by a young man named James Grime who, on reading about the distinguishing features of the watch in question, must have felt his blood run cold as he realised that that very timepiece was the one which his brother Thomas once had in his possession and was now owned by James himself! The police were informed and proceeded to interview Thomas, at that time serving a prison sentence in Dartmoor for theft. The suspect admitted being at the scene of the murder but implicated a confederate named William Thompson and accused him of committing the murder and then pushing the body into the furnace, Barton having threatened to report him for poaching on the Haigh Hall estate.

At the trial on 13 August 1866 before the Liverpool Assize judge, the prosecution found no corroborative evidence to incriminate Thompson; Grime had admitted his involvement in the murder and moreover had been in possession of the victim's watch; therefore whether or not another man had struck the actual death-dealing blows, Grime was equally responsible.

The jury agreed, taking only a matter of minutes to deliver a verdict of guilty. Pale but imperturbable, Grime stood motionless in the dock as the judge pronounced the death sentence, the execution to take place at a time to be appointed, at Kirkdale Gaol in that city.

In the condemned cell Grime, a devout Roman Catholic, made peace in accordance with his religious beliefs by informing the Prison Governor Captain Gibbs that he exonerated Thompson and others he had implicated. And on 1 September 1866, after eating a good breakfast and then praying with his priest, he was conducted to where William Calcraft waited. With arms pinioned, he was escorted by the officials and chaplain to where the black-draped scaffold had been erected.

The rain had stopped, the sun had come out – and so had the crowds in their thousands, watching with ghoulish fascination as the hangman briskly capped and noosed his man. From beneath the white hood came words audible only to those nearest to the scaffold, the last, pitiful words Calcraft had so often heard spoken by his doomed victims; "Lord Jesus, receive my soul." And the trap doors fell.

Grime's corpse was buried in the grounds of Kirkdale Gaol, but not before the usual practice was carried out, a death mask being taken of the face for scientific study.

CHAPTER NINE

THE STRAIN STARTS TO TELL

In April 1867 the pamphlet printers were in profit again when James Longhurst paid the penalty, a booklet entitled *Gallows Verse and Worse*, privately printed in 1903, reporting how, having been found guilty of murdering seven-year-old Jane Sax on 28 June 1866 'he was executed this morning on top of Horsemonger-Lane Gaol. Since his condemnation he has expressed contrition for his crime and hoped that God will forgive him. Notwithstanding the prisoner appearing to be in a state of mind becoming his awful position, when he was taken down from the condemned cell to the yard to be pinioned, a frightful scene ensued; the moment the culprit saw Calcraft, the executioner, approach him with the straps to pinion his arms, he started back with an aspect of terror depicted on his countenance, and began to struggle violently with the turnkeys. The chaplain spoke to him and endeavoured to calm him, and this for a moment appeared to have the effect, but upon the executioner requesting that the culprit might be taken outside, as he could not see to fasten the straps properly, another fearful struggle ensued, and it required five warders to hold him, and it was necessary to throw him to the ground while he was being pinioned, and one or two of the turnkeys were very much hurt by the kicks they received.

The prisoner's conduct seemed to be actuated by an uncontrollable horror of the executioner and the apparatus of death. After he had been secured he walked quietly by the side of the chaplain until he arrived at the steps leading to the scaffold, and immediately he caught sight of the gibbet his horror appeared to return. He again struggled violently as well as he was able, and was forcibly dragged up the steps and held under the beam by several turnkeys while the rope was adjusted round his neck, and as speedily as possible the bolt was drawn, and after a few struggles the wretched youth ceased to exist.' The verses accompanying this account are included with others in Appendix 3.

Calcraft's personal roll-call of violent victims, which already included such struggling protesters as Longhurst, Bousfield and Hibner, was due to be increased by one, namely John Wiggins. As reported in the *Illustrated Police News*, that gentleman was arrested and sent for trial, the charge being 'that on or about a certain date in July 1866 he did, with malice aforethought, kill and murder his concubine, Agnes Oates, by cutting her throat at their home in Limehouse.' At his trial in the Old Bailey, his plea of innocence and his claims that Agnes had attacked him and then committed suicide with the knife, were rejected out of hand by the court and he was found guilty, the judge decreeing that the execution should take place outside Newgate Prison at 8am on 15 October 1867.

Although news of the verdict and sentence were widely circulated throughout the City, surprisingly few turned up to gather around the scaffold at the appointed time, the streets in the vicinity of Newgate being no more crowded than on an ordinary, non-execution day. This was because of a badly planned fixture-list of hangings, another execution having been scheduled to take place at 10 am that same morning at Horsemonger Lane Gaol when a man named Louis Bodier was due to meet his Maker; coincidentally for the identical crime to that committed by Wiggins, of murdering his partner. Another hangman had therefore been detailed to perform that particular execution, there not being sufficient time for Calcraft to despatch Wiggins, wait the stipulated hour, cut his man down, then travel across the river and make his way through Southwark to the other gaol. Not that Calcraft was disappointed at the small attendance at Newgate; on the contrary, he was probably only too grateful, for the smaller the crowd, the less abuse he would be subjected to, though subsequent events would prove to him that he had been sadly mistaken. And whether the crowd was small or large certainly made no difference to Wiggins.

Just prior to 8 am the condemned man was escorted to the press yard, there to be joined by the inevitable party consisting of the Prison Governor and the Ordinary, the sheriffs, under sheriffs, newspaper representatives, and of course Calcraft, the latter then proceeding to secure the man's arms in the usual manner. As he did so, Wiggins protested at the tightness of his bonds. Whether the hangman obligingly loosened them slightly is not known; if he did, he certainly had good reason to regret his humane action later.

On reaching the scaffold the condemned man ignored the shouts and whistles of the onlookers and ascended the steps without hesitation, but on being led towards the trapdoors, he held back, despite all Calcraft's efforts to urge him forward. The hangman beckoned for assistance and was joined by first one, then two burly warders. Wiggins, a well-built and muscular young man, fought violently to free himself from their grasp, and it was not until no fewer than four warders had seized his arms and legs that they managed to propel him into position beneath the beam. Further force was then necessary to make him stand still while Calcraft, now desperate to despatch his victim before even more trouble erupted, pulled the white cap over his head, but his efforts were partly thwarted as Wiggins somehow managed to dislodge the cap sufficiently with his mouth and shouted to the horrified spectators "I am innocent! Cut my head off but don't hang me! I am innocent!" His plea to be decapitated rather than hanged was probably engendered by the fear, common among criminals, of being subsequently dissected while not quite dead, due to the short drop.

Whether Calcraft had in fact slackened his bonds earlier, or whether they had become loosened during his superhuman struggles, the result was that Wiggins suddenly found himself able to reach up with his hands and grasp the rope suspended above him. Frantically he swayed from side to side in his attempts to put his feet anywhere other than on the trapdoors, but the combined efforts of the warders proved too much for him; the epic conflict came to an abrupt end as, for a brief moment, they held him just long enough for Calcraft to drop the noose over his head. Hardly pausing to position it around his victim's neck, the hangman swiftly operated the drop, and the spectators' cries of consternation and disgust were stilled as the victim's body twitched in its death throes. And William Calcraft left the scaffold as quickly as possible, no doubt wondering how he was to explain the cause of the débâcle to the officials conducting the enquiry that would inevitably follow.

By now it was evident that the strain was starting to take its toll on the hangman. For decades, he had been the target of abuse and derision without allowing it to affect him to any great extent; he accepted it as an occupational hazard, par for the course, and once he had hanged his victim and left the scaffold site, he could mentally shrug his shoulders and forget about it. But when, in 1867, he had to execute three Irish Fenians, William O'Meara Allen, Philip Larkin and Michael O'Brien (aka Gould), all that changed; routine insults were replaced by intimidatory and sinister threats, and he received letters warning him of dire retribution should he proceed with the hangings, one printed in the Manchester newspapers threatening 'Sir – if you hang any of the gentlemen condemned to death at the New Bailey prison, it will be the worst for you. You will not survive afterwards.'

His three victims were members of the Irish Republican Brotherhood, an association that did not hesitate to use violence in pursuance of their political aims. Two of their leading members were Colonel Kelly and Captain Deasy, both of whom were arrested in Manchester in September 1867. While being taken into custody, the horse-drawn prison van in which they were travelling was ambushed by some of their supporters, the vehicle being forced to stop when the horses were shot and injured by a man firing a revolver. Another man, Peter Rice, scrambling on top of the vehicle, forced open the ventilator on its roof and fired his pistol into the inside of the van, killing the prisoners' unarmed escort, Sergeant Brett. Rice then ordered a woman prisoner to get the keys from the dead officer's pocket and unlock the van doors. In the mêlée which followed, during which more shots were fired and bricks and other missiles thrown by the mob, the two Irish prisoners escaped and were never recaptured.

In the roundup of suspects which followed, William O'Meara Allen, Philip Larkin and Michael O'Brien were arrested and, although not having fired the shot which killed Sergeant Brett, they were, in the eyes of the law, adjudged guilty of taking part in an illegal act which resulted in murder and so were sentenced to death, execution to take place on 23 November 1867 at the New Bailey Prison, Salford.

Soon after 7 am on that fateful morning the condemned men were roused and given breakfast consisting of coffee and toast; this was followed by prayers with their padres. Calcraft and his deputy, Armstrong, a Welshman from Newport, Monmouthshire, then entered the condemned cells, there to pinion their victims and escort them up the long flight of steps leading to the scaffold erected immediately outside the prison walls. Armed soldiers and police manned the barricades lest any attempt at rescue be mounted by members of the IRB, but the crowd was unusually small in number, perhaps out of sympathy for the doomed trio, perhaps due to the weather, which was bitterly cold and foggy.

On the scaffold Calcraft and Armstrong wasted no time in lining the men on the drop and covering their faces with the customary white caps, then dropping the nooses around their necks. The men's ankles were then strapped together, and at that moment Larkin was seen to sway as if about to collapse, and only regained his balance after assistance was given by the two hangmen.

It was only then, with almost indecent haste that Calcraft, his nerves now near breaking point, rapidly departed below the scaffold – and the trapdoors parted, the three victims falling to their deaths. But the cruelly short length of Calcraft's ropes dictated that only one, Allen, would die mercifully quickly, for as vividly described in John O'Dea's definitive book *Story of the Old Faith* published in 1910:

'The other two ropes, stretched taut and tense by their breathing, twitching burdens, were in ominous and distracting movement. The hangman had bungled! For Larkin and O'Brien the drop was too short. Canon Cantwell and Father Quick (their spiritual councillors) had retired as soon as the bodies fell. So had the Governor and the other prison officials. None remained but Father Gadd, old warder Kirtland and the hangman. Calcraft then descended into the pit and there finished what he could not accomplish from above. *He killed Larkin.* (Father Gadd was later to relate how the executioner adopted his usual method of speeding a victim's demise – or shortening his suffering – this time, not by pulling the man's legs, but 'by climbing on to Larkin's back'.)

Then, continued O'Dea's account 'he turned his attention towards O'Brien, but O'Brien was in the Monsignor's charge and he forbade the hangman to touch him (by pulling *his* legs in like manner). Poor O'Brien's hands were clasped within the Monsignor's own. His fingers touched the crucifix the chaplain held. For three-quarters of an hour he breathed and for three-quarters of an hour the good priest knelt, holding the dying man's hands within his own, reciting the prayers for the dying. Then the long drawn out agony ended. O'Brien, the last of the three was dead. After a while the bodies were cut down and Father Gadd saw them buried in quicklime within the unhallowed precincts of the city.' The bodies were actually interred in the grounds of the New Bailey prison but years later, when that gaol was demolished, the remains were removed and re-buried in the surrounds of Strangeways Prison, Manchester.

Final statements written by the three men were subsequently printed in the Irish press and are included in Appendix Two. And shortly after the executions black-edged Mass cards were distributed in commemoration of their deaths; beneath symbolic images of sorrowing women and the Holy Ghost, appeared the inscription;

'Of your charity pray for the souls of WILLIAM PHILIP ALLEN, aged 19 years. MICHAEL O'BRIEN, aged 30 years. MICHAEL LARKIN aged 30 years. The three unfortunate men who were executed at the New Bailey, Salford, on Saturday Nov. 23rd. 1867. Their profound love of 'Poor Old Ireland' and the Fenian cause induced them to attack the Police van in Hyde Road, Manchester, on the 18th of September and release COL. KELLY and CAPTAIN DEASEY (sic) from custody. They were tried by Special Commission and sentenced to death on Friday Nov. 1st. MAY THEY REST IN PEACE.'

As for Calcraft; having carried out the sentences imposed by the court in accordance with his duties, and still fearing an attack by those who had threatened reprisals should he do so, he hastily left Manchester as quickly as he could, not daring to relax until the lights of London welcomed him home.

In April of the following year he added yet another record to his achievements, that of being the last executioner to hang a woman in public. His victim was Frances Kidden, an attractive young woman whose happily married existence was marred only by the fact that she and her husband had not been able to have a baby. Her outraged reactions upon discovering that her husband had had a child by another woman can therefore be well imagined, reactions which drove her to kill the man she loved, the man who had so cruelly deceived her. And so, on 2 April 1868, she stood silently on the drop in the market place in Maidstone, Kent, resigned to her fate as Calcraft, much as he hated having to execute a woman, hooded and noosed her; then, having deprived her unfaithful husband of his life, she forfeited her own.

The Strain Starts to Tell   125

After hanging Frances Kidden, Calcraft had barely time to go home and get a night's sleep before catching an early train next day and travelling to Salford, there to stay overnight in the New Bailey prison before carrying out a double hanging on 4 April.

One of condemned men awaiting the hangman's attention was Miles Weatherill, and there had been little doubt that the good folk of Todmorden, a village perched high on the bleak windswept Yorkshire moors, had been shocked and appalled, not only at the two brutal murders he had committed, but that one of his victims should have the local clergyman, the Reverend Mr. Plow. In the opinion of many of the residents Weatherill was the last person to have done such a thing; he had been well brought up, and attended the village Sunday School regularly – yet had he been less religiously disposed, an elderly man and a young woman would not have met such savage deaths, for it was there that he met and fell in love with another worshipper, Sarah Bell.

Sarah was a member of the parsonage's domestic staff and the liaison that blossomed between the two was frowned upon by the clergyman and his wife in view of Sarah's youth, to the extent that they forbade her to associate with him further. Despite that, however, love triumphed, the two lovers continuing to meet secretly, until a rift appeared in their relationship, a rift apparently caused by Jane Smith, another maid at the parsonage who, Miles believed, for reasons of jealousy or personal rivalry, had not only informed her employers of Sarah's disobedience, but had also vilified him to his girlfriend. This suspicion was borne out when, the clergyman having dismissed Sarah for ignoring his ruling, she moved to York and declared she wanted nothing further to do with him.

Inflamed by this rejection, he was determined to get even with the two people responsible, the Rev. Plow and Jane Smith. Accordingly, late at night on 2 January 1866, he went to the Parsonage and on meeting the clergyman, savagely attacked him with an axe. Alerted by the commotion, members of the staff came to the rescue, but Weatherill then entered the building and, encountering Jane Smith, shot her dead before finally being overpowered.

The Reverend Mr Plow succumbed to his injuries shortly afterwards, and so Weatherill was charged with causing his death in addition to that of the maid. In view of the overwhelming evidence from the numerous witnesses, little defence was possible, and at his trial he stood in the dock, head bowed, as the spine-chilling words of the judge echoed round the courtroom:

"The sentence of the law is that, for the crimes of wilful murder, you will be taken from hence to the prison from whence you came, and taken from thence to a place of execution, and be there hanged by the neck until you are dead, and that your body then be taken down and buried within the precincts of the gaol from whence you were taken. May the Lord have mercy on your soul."

And so the condemned cell in the New Bailey received Miles Weatherill, there to await his fate.

His companion on the scaffold was to be twenty-seven-year old Timothy Faherty, an ex-soldier who, after discharge from the Army, had obtained employment in one of the many weaving mills situated near the Manchester and Ashton-under-Lyne Canal in Droylsden, Lancashire. Among his fellow loom operators was Mary Hanmer, an attractive brunette with whom he became deeply enamoured, but alas, she gave no indication that she felt the same about him, on the contrary, for she had already expressed her intentions to commit herself only to a man who was a Roman Catholic and moreover one who abstained from intoxicating liquor. Faherty met the first qualification but definitely not the latter, occasionally drinking heavily with his mill-mates.

Matters came to a head on Christmas Day 1867 when, after having had a few festive beers, he visited Mary in the hopes that she would respond to his affectionate feelings for her, only to find her attitude towards him cold and contemptuous; insensate with fury, he picked up a poker and dealt her several violent blows, so violent that she died shortly afterwards. His trial in court, presided over by Mr Justice Lush, was as short as was that of Weatherill, culminating in the same sentence – death by hanging.

By dawn on Saturday 4 April 1868 the first few score of spectators had started to gather around the scaffold outside the gaol, their numbers having grown to several thousand by execution time, eight o'clock. Faherty, his face drawn and pale, was the first to be brought out by Calcraft, who then proceeded to hood and noose him. There followed for Faherty a nightmare scenario which was totally undeserved no matter how appalling his crime, for due to some inexplicable delay, several minutes elapsed before Weatherill was escorted on to the scaffold, and

The Strain Starts to Tell 127

Faherty was left standing on the drop, unable to see anything, petrified by the thought of his rapidly approaching demise; not knowing whether he was to die by himself or wait until he had been joined by the other man; any second expecting the trapdoors to suddenly fall away beneath him, without further prayer or warning.

It must have seemed an interminable length of time to the doomed man before the creaking of the boards heralded the arrival on the scaffold of Weatherill, the chaplain Father Gadd, the prison officers and of course mine host, William Calcraft. The hangman slipped the white hood over Miles Weatherill's head, keeping it in place with the noose around his neck, and then, as a token of grim farewell, he shook the bound hands of his two victims. To Faherty at least it must have been almost with relief that he heard the bolt being drawn from its socket – the last sound that either of them heard before they plunged downwards, their bodies writhing as if in impotent protest against the mercilessly short rope, until eventually all life slowly ebbed away. The spectators slowly dispersed, the members of the unofficial scaffold fan club among them being filled with disappointment at the prospect of having to travel elsewhere, perhaps even as far as London, should they wish to witness any further hangings, for these were the last to be held in public in Lancashire.

Calcraft however was only too pleased to head towards the capital; wasting little time in cutting down the corpses, he collecting his double fee and caught the next train home to his family. Doubtless he was relieved that the current spate of executions were those of 'ordinary' criminals and not the recent Fenian-type political hangings, with their overtones of lurid threats to his life and limb. But how wrong he was.

On the afternoon of 13 December 1867 a violent explosion occurred at the Clerkenwell House of Detention in London, a barrel of gunpowder having been detonated immediately outside that prison. The bomb was so destructive that sixty yards of the prison wall were demolished, houses opposite collapsed, windows over a wide area were shattered and no fewer than six people were killed outright, six more dying of their wounds shortly afterwards. A later report stated that 'a further five subsequently died from causes attributable to the explosion; one young woman is in a mad house; forty mothers were prematurely confined and twenty of their babies died from the effects of the explosion on their mothers; others of the children are dwarfed and unhealthy, and one mother is now a raving lunatic. One hundred and twenty persons were wounded, fifty going into St Bartholomew's, Gray's Inn Lane and King's College Hospitals; fifteen are permanently injured, with loss of eyes, legs, arms, etc., besides twenty thousand pounds worth of damage to person and property'. In an abortive attempt to release one of their leaders, Richard O'Sullivan Burke, imprisoned therein, the Fenians had struck again.

Over the next few days suspects were rounded up and one of them, Michael Barrett, was identified by witnesses as the one who had lighted the fuse on the barrel. At his trial in the Old Bailey, despite his defence that he had been in Glasgow at the time of the explosion, an informer, Patrick Mullany and others testified to the contrary, and Barrett was found guilty and sentenced to death. Which meant that Calcraft would have to hang him.

If the executioner had been apprehensive when faced with the task of despatching the three Fenians, one can only imagine his state of mind at the prospect of hanging another, this time one who had caused the violent death, not just of one police sergeant, but those of at least twelve innocent people, and of injuring many others. He was fully aware that the public's outraged reaction to the casualties, the sympathy of many towards the cause of the Irish Republican Brotherhood, and the fact that this execution was to be the last held in public. It would attract a larger and more volatile crowd than ever before, and despite having some of them on his side, he would also be the target of abuse and even, perhaps, of more sinister retaliation by active supporters of the condemned man. Indeed prior to carrying out recent executions the threats had continued, one letter putting it into so many words, saying; 'I am writing to tell you to take care, for as sure as I have a pen in my hand you will be shot tomorrow morning about eight o'clock. I suppose you think you got home very well when you hung the Fenians last November but you won't get home alive again. This is plain English. There will be about 200 Fenians in the morning with loaded revolvers ready to fire off at you, so give this up as a bad job this time. So look out, nothing can save you this time. My parting shot to you is to pray to God before you go on the scaffold. Goodbye, from A FENIAN'

Although nothing untoward had happened on the earlier occasion, ominous warnings such as this were enough to unnerve even the youngest and self-confident of men, and Calcraft, now sixty-eight years of age, was no hero dedicated to accepting all risks in order to avenge outrages against society in the name of the law. His state of mind can well be imagined; he would be standing as if on a stage set high above the crowd, the cynosure of all eyes, a virtually unmissable target for anyone seeking to kill the very symbol of 'foreign' domination – the English hangman himself.

The execution did in fact attract more avid spectators than usual, a reporter of the *Times* painting a dramatic word-picture of the scene in the edition published the next day, 27 May 1868, an account repeated in *Reynold's News* three days later:

'Yesterday morning, in the presence of a vast concourse of spectators, Michael Barratt, the author of the Clerkenwell Explosion, was hanged in front of Newgate. In its circumstances there was very little to distinguish this from ordinary executions. The crowd was greater, perhaps, and better behaved; still, from the peculiar atrocity of the crime for which Barratt suffered, and from the fact of its being probably the last public execution in England, it deserves more than usual notice.

'On Monday the barriers were put up, and on Monday night a fringe of eager sightseers assembled, mostly sitting beneath the beams (of the barricades) but ready at a moment's notice to rise and cling to the front places they had so long waited for. There were the usual catcalls, comic choruses, dances, and even mock hymns, till towards two o'clock, when the gaiety inspired by alcohol faded away as the public houses closed, and popular excitement was not revived until the blackened deal frame which forms the base of the scaffold was drawn out in the dawn, and placed in front of the door from which Barrett was to issue.

'Its arrival was greeted with a great cheer, which at once woke up those who had been huddled on doorsteps and under barricades, and who joined in the general acclamation. The arrival of the scaffold did much to increase the interest, and through the dawn people began to flock in, the greater portion being young women and little children. Never were these more numerous than on this occasion, and blue velvet hats and huge white feathers lined the great beams which kept the mass from crushing each other in their eagerness to see a man put to death.

The crowd was most unusually orderly, but it was not a crowd that one would like to trust.

'It is said that one sees on the road to the Derby such animals as are never seen elsewhere (pickpockets, thieves, swindlers – author); so on an execution morning one sees faces that are never seen save round the gallows or near a great house-fire. Some laughed, some fought, some preached, some gave tracts, and some sang hymns; but what may be called the general good-humoured disorder of the crowd remained the same, and there was laughter at the preacher or silence when an open robbery was going on. None could look on the scene, with all its exceptional quietness, without a thankful feeling that this was to be the last public execution in England.

'Towards seven o'clock the mass of people was intense. A very wide open space was kept round the gallows by the police, but beyond this the concourse was dense, stretching up beyond St Sepulchre's Church (opposite the prison) and far back, almost into Smithfield – a great surging mass of people which, in spite of the barriers, kept swaying to and fro like waving corn. Now and then there was great laughter as a girl fainted, and was passed out hand over hand above the heads of the mob, and there was a scuffle and a fight, and then a hymn, and then a sermon, and then a comic song, and so on from hour to hour, the crowd thickening as the day brightened, and the sun shone out with such a glare as to extinguish the very feeble light which showed faintly through the glass roof above where the culprit lay.

'It was a wild rough crowd, not so numerous nor nearly so violent which thronged to see Muller (who murdered Thomas Briggs on a train some four years earlier – author) or the pirates die (the *Flowery Land* murders). In one way they showed their feeling by loudly hooting a magnificently attired woman who, accompanied by two gentlemen, swept down the avenue kept open by the police, and occupied a window afterwards, right in front of the gallows. This temporary exhibition of feeling was, however, soon allayed by coppers (coins, not police officers! – author) being thrown from the window for the roughs to scramble for.

'The convict Barrett had retired to rest about ten o'clock on the previous evening, and having spent a somewhat restless night, rose at six yesterday morning, dressed himself, and engaged in prayer. Shortly afterwards he was joined in his cell by the Rev.

James Hussey, attached to the Roman Catholic chapel in Moorfields, who had attended him regularly since his conviction, and who remained with him until the last.

'By a predetermined arrangement, and contrary to the usual practice, the convict was not pinioned in the Press room, as it is called, but in his own cell and, this process over, he was conducted to the drop by a private way, accompanied by his priest and attended by the executioner and three or four warders, the prison bell and that of St Sepulchre's Church, hard by, tolling the while. The Sheriffs and Under-Sheriffs who, with others, stood in a group in a gloomy corridor behind the scaffold, just caught a glimpse of the doomed man as he emerged with his attendants from a dark and narrow passage, and turned a corner leading to the gallows. He was dressed in the short claret-coloured coat and the gray striped trousers, both well worn, by which he had become familiar to all who were present during his protracted trial. His face had lost the florid hue it then wore, and in other respects he was a changed man.

'With the first sounds of the bells came a great hungry roar from the crowd outside, and a loud, continued shout of "Hats off!" till the whole dense, bareheaded mass stood white and ghastly looking in the morning sun, and the pressure on the barriers increased so that the girls and women in the front rank began to scream and struggle to get free. Amid such scenes as this, and before such a dense crowd of white faces, Barrett was executed. His clergyman came first. Barrett mounted the steps with the most perfect firmness. This may seem a stereotyped phrase but it really means more that is generally imagined. To ascend a ladder with one's arms and hands closely pinioned would be at all times difficult, but to climb a ladder to go to certain death might try the nerves of the boldest.

'Barrett walked up coolly and boldly. His face was as white as marble, but he still bore himself with firmness, and his demeanour was as far removed from bravado as from fear. We would not dwell on these details, but from the singular reception he met as he came out upon the scaffold. There was a partial burst of cheering, which was instantly accompanied by loud hisses, and so it remained for some seconds till, as the last moment approached, the roars dwindled down to a dead silence. To neither cheers nor hisses did the culprit make the slightest recognition. He seemed only attentive to what the priest was saying to him, and to be engaged in fervent prayer.'

Because of his vulnerability Calcraft probably kept as close as possible to his victim; wasting no time, he strapped Barrett's ankles together, slipped the cap over the man's head, then dropped the noose round his neck. As he did so, Barrett turned his head and, in a muffled voice, asked the hangman to adjust the rope. The reason why he did so was not reported; perhaps in his haste Calcraft had positioned it wrongly, perhaps so that it was pressing on Barrett's chin. The hangman could even have thought that the condemned man was delaying the proceedings so as to allow a fellow republican in the crowd to get a shot at him; whatever the possible reason, Calcraft quickly readjusted it, then swiftly moved away – and drew the bolt.

As usual, discrepancies occurred between the various reporters present. The *Daily Telegraph* man described how 'there was a convulsive heaving of the chest and shoulders, and a quick movement of the legs' but conceded that 'death was speedy, the pallor of the neck showing infallibly when it had taken place.' Whereas the *Times* journalist said 'Barrett never moved. He died without a struggle'. But the latter spoke for both papers in reporting that 'It is worthy of remark that a great cry rose from the crowd as the culprit fell, a cry which was neither an exclamation nor a scream, but it partook of the sound of both. With the fall of the drop the crowd began to disperse, but an immense mass waited till the time for cutting down came, and when nine o'clock struck there were loud cries of "Come on, body snatcher!", "Take away the man you've killed!" etc. The hangman appeared and cut down the body amid a storm of yells and execrations as has seldom been heard even from such a crowd. There was nothing more to be seen, so the concourse broke up with its usual concomitants of assault and robbery. The body, on being taken down, was placed in a shell (a temporary coffin) and removed to an adjoining building in the presence of the Sheriffs and Under-Sheriffs, the Prison Governor and surgeon, and the Ordinary. There, the rope having been removed from the neck and the leathern straps by which the legs and arms had been pinioned, the surgeon certified that life was extinct. The expression on the face was marvellously serene and placid, and the features composed to a degree irreconcilable at first sight with the notion of a violent death, though the lips and parts of the forehead were unusually livid. Towards the evening the body was buried in the accustomed place within

9a. Daniel Good and Jane in the stable

9b. Daniel Good in the Condemned Cell

10. China statues of the Mannings. The case of Maria and Frederick Manning attracted considerable attention. Almost 2,500,000 broadsheets of the execution were sold.

Frederick George Manning. Manning's Solicitor. Mrs. Manning's Solicitor Maria Manning.

11a. The Mannings, drawn in court by Robert Cruikshank

11b. The execution of the Mannings

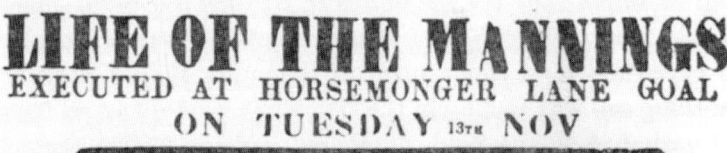

LIFE OF THE MANNINGS
EXECUTED AT HORSEMONGER LANE GOAL
ON TUESDAY 13th NOV

SEE the scaffold it is mounted,
  And the doomed ones do appear,
Seemingly borne wan with sorrow,
Grief and anguish, care and pain.
They cried the moments is approaching,
  When we together must leave this life,
And no one but the least compassion,
On Frederick Manning and his wife.

Though married yet she was espoused
  With O'Conner all was right,
And oft he went to see Maria
Frederick Manning's lawful wife.
At length they plann'd their friend to murder
  And for his company did crave,
The dreadful weapons they prepared,
And in the kitchen dug his grave.

12. The 'Five Pirates' from *The Illustrated Police News*, 20 February 1864. The 'Five Pirates' were executed on 23 February 1864 for their involvement in the mutiny on the Flowery Land.

Franz Muller and the world's first murder on a train

13a. Broadsheet recording the execution & confession of Franz Muller

THE EXECUTION AND CONFESSION OF FRANZ MULLER,
For the Murder of Mr. BRIGGS, November 14th, 1864.

At two o'clock on Saturday afternoon Sir George Grey returned an answer to the memorial presented to him, praying for a respite of the convict Muller, by the German Legal Protection Society. Previous to the delivery of his decision he had a long conversation with the Lord Chief Baron Pollock and Mr. Baron Martin, which terminated in his arriving at the conclusion that the memorial did not warrant his interfering with the verdict of the jury.

Immediately upon the receipt of the letter, Mr. Beard, with Alderman Wilson, proceeded to communicate to Muller the result of the efforts that had been made on his behalf. They were received by Mr. Jonas, the governor of Newgate, who conducted them to the condemned cell. They found the prisoner engaged in writing. He immediately rose, and extended his hand to Mr. Beard, who asked him how he was. The convict said, "I am very well." Mr. Jonas then informed the prisoner of the efforts that

Alderman and Sheriff Dakin, and the Under Sheriffs, Messrs. Davidson and De Jersey, arrived at the Sessions House, where they remained until summoned to the prison by the governor. About twenty minutes to eight they were informed that the condemned man would soon leave his cell. Upon receiving this information these officials left the Sessions House. A few minutes after this, the procession reached the door which opens into the chapel-yard. Here they awaited the arrival of the culprit.

THE EXECUTION.

While the officials were on their way from the Sessions House to the spot, Mr. Jonas had gone to the cell of the prisoner, and informed him that it was time for him to leave. The prisoner, who was deadly pale, trembled with emotion, but sought to bear the awful announcement with all the fortitude possible.

13b. Franz Muller

13c. 'Murder on the Railway Train' broadside

Murder in the Railway Train.

Listen to my song, and I will not detain you long,
And then I will tell you of what I've heard.
Of a murder that's been done, by some wicked one,
And the place where it all occurred;
Between Stepney and Bow they struck the fatal blow,
Murdered by some prigs was poor Mr Briggs
Whilst riding in a railway train.

Muller is accused, at present we cannot refuse
To believe that he is the very one,
But all his actions, you see, have been so very free,
Ever since the murder it was done;
From his home he never went, but such a happy time he spent,
He never looked troubled on the brain,
If he'd been the guilty man, he would have hid all he can,
From the murder in the railway train.

Muller he did state that he was going to emigrate
Long before this dreadful tragedy;
He often used to talk, about travelling to New York,
In the Victoria, that was going to sea.
Mr. Death, the jeweller, said, he was very much afraid,
He might not know the same man again,
When he heard of the reward, he started out abroad,
About the murder in the railway train.

If it's Muller, we can't deny, on the Cabman keep your eye,
Remember what he said the other day,
That Muller a ticket sold for money, which seems so very funny,
When he had no expenses for to pay.
They say his money he took, and his name entered on the book,

Long before this tragedy he came;
Like Muller's, the Cabman had a hat, and it may be his, perhaps
That was found in the railway train.

Would a murderer have forgot, to have destroyed the jeweller's box,
Or burnt up the sleeve of his coat,
Would he the chain ticket have sold, and himself exposed so bold,
And to all his friends a letter wrote,
Before Muller went away, why did not the cabman say,
And not give him so much start on the main
If the cabman knew—it's very wrong—to keep the secret up so long,
About the murder in the railway train.

When Muller does arrive, we shall not be much surprised,
To hear that that's him on the trial;
Give him time to repent, though he is not innocent,
To hear the evidence give no denial.
Muller's got the watch, you see, so it proves that he is guilty,
But like Townley don't prove that he's insane
For if it should be him, on the gallows let him swing,
For the murder on the railway train.

Now Muller's caught at last, tho' he's been so very fast,
And on him they found the watch and hat,
Tho' across the ocean he did roam, he had better stayed at home,
And hid himself in some little crack,
Tho' he pleads his innocence, but that is all nonsense,
For they'll hang him as sure as he's a man,
For he got up to his rigs, and murdered Mr. Briggs
While riding in a railway train.

London: Printed for the Vendors.

14a. The executed Fenians

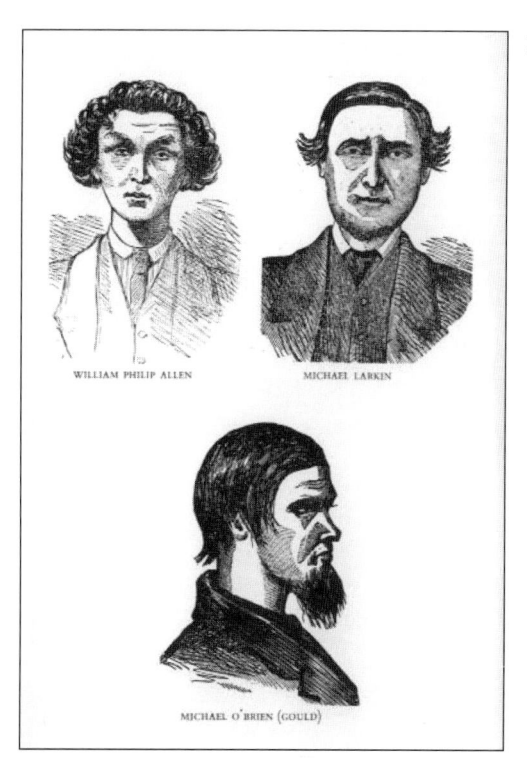

WILLIAM PHILIP ALLEN

MICHAEL LARKIN

MICHAEL O'BRIEN (GOULD)

14b. Drop Table

SCALE SHOWING THE STRIKING FORCE OF FALLING BODIES AT DIFFERENT DISTANCES.

Distance Falling in Feet Zero	8 Stone	9 Stone	10 Stone	11 Stone	12 Stone	13 Stone	14 Stone	15 Stone	16 Stone	17 Stone	18 Stone	19 Stone
	Cw. Qr. lb.	Cw. Qr. lb.	Cw. Qr. lb.	Cw. Qr. lb.	Cw. Qr. lb.	Cw. Qr. lb.	Cw. Qr. lb.	Cw. Qr. lb.	Cw. Qr. lb.	Cw. Qr. lb.	Cw. Qr. lb.	Cw. Qr. lb.
1 Ft.	8 0 0	9 0 0	10 0 0	11 0 0	12 0 0	13 0 0	14 0 0	15 0 0	16 0 0	17 0 0	18 0 0	19 0 0
2 ,,	11 1 15	12 2 23	14 0 14	15 2 4	16 3 22	18 1 12	19 3 2	21 0 21	22 2 11	24 0 1	25 1 19	26 3 9
3 ,,	13 3 16	15 2 15	17 1 14	19 0 12	20 3 11	22 2 9	24 1 8	26 0 7	27 3 5	29 2 4	31 1 2	33 0 1
4 ,,	16 0 0	18 0 0	20 0 0	22 0 0	24 0 0	26 0 0	28 0 0	30 0 0	32 0 0	34 0 0	36 0 0	40 0 0
5 ,,	17 2 11	19 3 5	22 0 0	24 0 22	26 1 16	28 2 11	30 3 5	33 0 0	35 0 22	37 0 16	39 2 11	41 3 15
6 ,,	19 2 11	22 0 5	24 2 0	26 3 22	29 1 16	31 3 11	34 1 5	36 3 0	39 0 22	41 2 16	44 0 11	46 2 5
7 ,,	21 0 22	23 3 11	26 2 0	29 0 16	31 3 5	34 1 22	37 0 11	39 3 0	42 1 16	45 0 5	47 2 22	50 1 11
8 ,,	22 2 22	25 2 4	28 1 14	31 0 23	34 0 5	36 3 15	39 2 25	42 2 7	45 1 16	48 0 26	51 0 8	53 3 18
9 ,,	24 0 11	27 0 12	30 0 14	33 0 23	36 0 16	39 0 18	42 0 19	45 0 21	48 0 22	51 0 23	54 0 25	57 0 26
10 ,,	25 1 5	28 1 23	31 2 14	34 3 4	37 3 22	41 0 12	44 1 2	47 1 21	50 2 11	53 3 1	56 3 19	60 0 9

This Drop table was devised by James Berry, executioner 1884-1892, who estimated that in order to break the victim's spinal cord and so bring about 'instant' death, the average person had to fall a distance such that his or her weight at the end of the descent was 24cwt (2,688lbs); e.g. a person weighing 11 stone (154 lbs) would be given a 5' drop, one weighing 15 stone (210lbs) would be given a 2½' drop, although the victim's age, physique and other similar factors would also have to be taken into consideration.

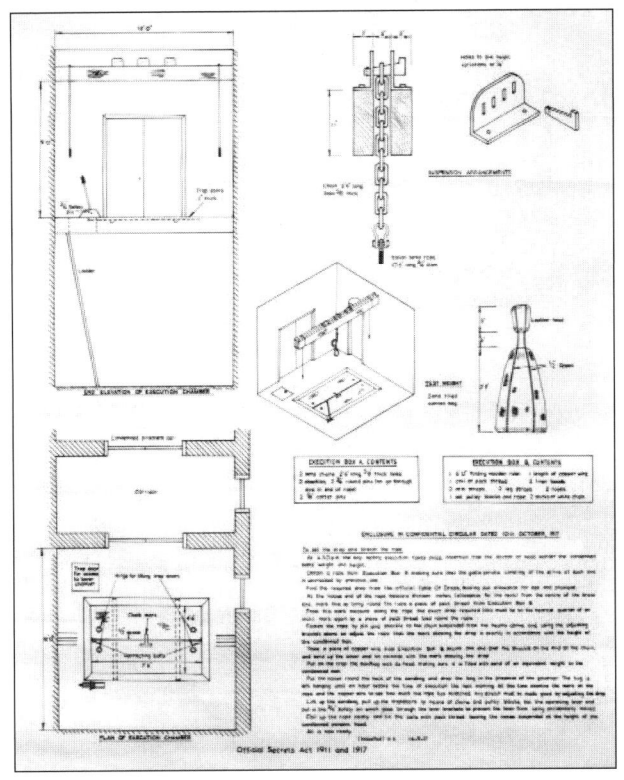

15a. 1917 Home Office Drop Diagram

15b. William Marwood – Hangman

16a. Muriel Brooke: Great grand-daughter of William Calcraft

16b. Thomas Henry Calcraft: Great grand-son of William Calcraft

the precincts of the prison, in a grave upwards of five feet deep, in the presence of the Governor and other officers of the gaol.'

And so for the last time, the crowds slowly drifted away from a public scaffold; the habitual gallows-watchers had perforce to take up a different and hopefully less bloodthirsty hobby. And the pamphlet poem-pedlars, whose final efforts to put their words into their victim's mouth may be read in Appendix 3, could exercise their literary talents in more innocuous ways – composing verses for birthday and Christmas cards, perhaps?!

CHAPTER TEN

CALCRAFT'S LAST EXECUTIONS

The *Capital Punishment Within Prison Law* came into force three days after Barrett's execution, although it was not passed without much controversy. Some opposed it because they advocated the total abolition of capital punishment; others on the grounds that this measure would allow clumsy or callous hangmen to continue to operate, tragic mishaps going unreported, hidden behind a screen of officialdom.

Strict rules were laid down regarding these private executions. They had to take place at 8 am on the first day after the intervention of three Sundays from the day on which the sentence was passed; the actual method of execution was to remain unchanged; a black flag was to be hoisted on an elevated and conspicuous part of the prison and remain there for one hour, and the bell of the prison or of a neighbouring church to be tolled for fifteen minutes before and after the execution. The sheriff was responsible for ensuring that the execution was carried out; the surgeon had to sign the death certificate, which was then to be exhibited for twenty-four hours near the principal entrance of the prison, and a coroner's inquest was to be held on the body.

To those who owned property overlooking the Newgate scaffold site and others who virtually had a season ticket for such events and would not miss a hanging for anything, either for the sadistic thrill of watching a man or a woman writhe at the end of a rope, or because it allowed them to pursue their chosen profession of picking pockets, selling pies, or hawking alleged 'deathbed' confessions among the spectators, the Act was a total disaster. Their protests, ignored by Parliament, echoed those voiced by the eminent Dr Samuel Johnson in 1783. Over the centuries prior to that particular year nearly all executions took place at Tyburn, near Marble Arch, but in order to do away with the macabre carnival whereby prisoners were conveyed in an almost ceremonial procession from Newgate prison to Tyburn through City streets lined with hundreds, if not thousands of jeering, cheering spectators (the gruesome origin of the saying 'Gone west'!), and because the fashionable part of the City was slowly spreading westwards into the Tyburn area, with the property developers impatient to move in, the venue was changed and criminals were hanged outside Newgate itself. At that time Dr. Johnson, a vehement supporter of visible deterrents, exclaimed "The age is running mad after innovation; all the business of the world is to be done in a new way; Tyburn itself is not safe from the fury of innovation!" When it was argued that the move was an improvement, he retorted "No, Sir, it is not an improvement; they object that the old method drew together a number of spectators. Sir, executions are intended to draw spectators. If they do not draw spectators, they don't answer their purpose. The old method was most satisfactory to all parties; the public was gratified by a procession, the criminal was supported by it. Why has all this to be swept away?"

Seventy-five years later, 'progress' had struck once more, the *Times* expressing its endorsement of the new Act; 'It is not right, perhaps, that a murderer's death should be surrounded by the pious and tender accessories which accompany the departure of a good man to a better world, but most assuredly the sight of public executions to those who have to witness them is as disgusting as it must be demoralising even to all the hordes of thieves and prostitutes it draws together. Yesterday the assembly was of its kind an orderly one, yet it was such as we feel grateful to think will, under the new law, never be drawn together again in England.'

To which sentiment William Calcraft no doubt uttered a heartfelt cry of agreement, while at the same time regretting that it had not come about earlier in his career. No longer the self-assured and capable man of forty years ago, now he was old, his self-confidence ebbing away, and he must have offered heartfelt thanks to whichever patron saint looks after executioners (St Emmeran, whose symbol is the ladder, needed originally to turn the victim off, and later to ascend the scaffold?), that never again would he have to face a sarcastically jocular or aggressively hostile crowd; no longer would he be the target of rotting fruit, dead cats or similarly revolting missiles; now, hidden by the mask of anonymity, he would be able to despatch political prisoners and criminal gang leaders without fear of menacing letters or personal attack by their vengeful colleagues.

The new Act now effective, Calcraft's next victim was Thomas Wells, an eighteen-year-old railway porter and carriage cleaner who had been found guilty of the murder of Mr Edward Adolphus Walsh, the station master at the Priory Railway Station, Dover. It was stated at the trial that after having been reproved by his superior for indiscipline and insolence, and threatened with dismissal, Wells had purchased fourpennyworth of gunpowder and twopennyworth of percussion caps and with them had loaded an old pistol used to scare birds from the station garden. He had then deliberately fired the weapon at the station master, killing him outright. What little defence raised was rejected and Wells was sentenced to death.

The young murderer had planned to marry later that month, but the only ceremony in which he actively participated took place on the scaffold within the walls of Maidstone Prison on 13 August 1868. William Calcraft, and his assistant George Smith, had carefully groomed him in readiness for the event, and provided a hempen ring to encircle his neck. The Ordinary read verses appropriate to the occasion and the congregation consisted of the Undersheriff, the Prison Governor, ten reporters – five from the City, five from the town – and the carpenter in charge of the scaffold, should any last minute repairs be needed. His services were not required.

Considering that an execution was taking place in the town that Thursday morning, the atmosphere was uncannily peaceful; no would-be onlookers massed at the prison gates demanding ringside seats, no demonstrators protested against capital punishment, even when the bell tolled and the black flag was hoisted, signifying that the grim event was taking place only a matter of yards from the busy highway.

To Calcraft, finding himself allowed to hood, noose and despatch his victim without catcall or insult, the whole proceedings must have seemed totally unreal. However while the new Act stipulated that henceforth the public should be excluded, it also stated that the method of execution should be unchanged, so although the crowd may indeed have been missing, alas, the short rope wasn't, and Wells took nearly four minutes to die.

One of the journalists present, with an eye for detail, painted a word-picture of the hangman, 'an old man, of low, stunted stature, with a pale, keen face and a long white beard; decently clad in somewhat faded black, and on his head a tall, shabby black hat, with a handsome gold watch-chain crossing his vest.' Another, in an article subsequently published in the *Morning Star*, stated 'The first private execution is over, and a criminal has been put to death without the traditional scaffold and crowd; it is right and proper that the citizens shall be freed from the odious accompaniment of an execution. However under the new arrangements new and ghastly elements are introduced; the want of ceremony, the little courtyard, the saw-pit, the rude instruments of strangulation, the handful of visitors; no, the English people cannot long tolerate the spectacle of criminals put to death in a private pit'. The courtyard and saw-pit alluded to in the article referred to the early arrangements for a prison execution; usually it took place in a shed situated in one of the exercise yards, a pit below a makeshift scaffold receiving the falling body.

And a London newspaper also commented on the historic occasion, albeit directing its more scathing comments at the much maligned hangman:

'The execution on Thursday last, the thirteenth of August (1868) marks the disappearance of William Calcraft from human life. He will henceforth be surrounded in the mystery of his terrible office, and the rising generation of criminals who take an interest in the matter will have to ask their seniors what type of man he was. To no man will this mystery be more welcome than Calcraft himself. He had shown on more than one occasion that his dread of facing a crowd is only inferior to the victim's dread of facing the gallows. At Manchester, where he had something more than the prospect of a public execution before him (possible violent retribution by the friends of the three Fenians he had to hang), he is said to have shown more signs of weakness than any man put to death. He shuffled about the prison yard and seemed loth to mount the gallows' steps, and the sweat fell from his face.

It is a great gain in every sense to have lost sight of him, for after all, he constituted perhaps the most unwelcome part of the spectacle of public executions. That more than prejudice – the very hatred of the crowd against him – was no doubt a most unjustifiable feeling, seeing that as a mere instrument of justice and of judgment, he was neither to be hated or judged, but it existed in such intensity that there was no prospect of it ever being lessened. The effect was extremely injurious, even to the poor kind of morality that public executions were supposed to prompt. The passive feeling of awe with which men might be disposed to look upon a criminal going to a rightful doom was changed to an active feeling of disgust and horror when they beheld a man by whom he was to be put to death, and there was too much reason to believe that they left the precincts of a prison with this feeling uppermost in their minds.'

But I don't suppose that Calcraft would have been unduly upset by such withering criticism; he would have been only too grateful for the opportunity henceforth to have a strictly official audience present while he went about his duties as Finisher of the Law.

The following month, on the 9 September to be precise, saw Alexander Mackay appear on the scaffold with Calcraft, again with his assistant, the velveteen-jacketed Stafford hangman, Smith of Dudley, their victim having been sentenced to death for the murder of a Mrs Grossmith. As usual the rope was short, a journalist reporting from the prison that 'signs of life were visible for a longer time after the bolt was drawn that we remember to have seen on a similar occasion'.

A drunken fight involving a girlfriend of one of the antagonists, the fight ending abruptly with the sudden thrust of a knife; these were the factors which resulted in the 'victor' standing in the dock at the Durham Assizes and hearing himself sentenced to death for murder.

It all started on 9 December 1868 when John Dolan had a night out with his friends in Sunderland. Having imbibed more than was good for him, he returned to the house owned by Catherine Keehan, in which he was a lodger. A fellow lodger, John Ward, had had a similarly convivial drinking session with friends and an altercation broke out in which Catherine was attacked. As the two men fought, Catherine called for the police, but by the time they arrived, Ward had been stabbed to death by his opponent. And on 23 March 1869 Dolan was on the drop at Durham Gaol – sharing it with one John McConville.

Like Dolan, McConville also had a partiality for strong liquor, also had an argument with another man – and also killed him, not in this instance, with a knife, but with a gun, firing it into the hostelry he had just left. The bullet struck Philip Trainer, the man with whom he had been violently disagreeing, the wound proving fatal. At his trial the evidence forthcoming from the other customers in the public house that night was sufficient to convince judge and jury alike. The foreman said "Guilty" and the Judge also made a statement, the last few words being "And may the Lord have mercy on your soul; take him down."

Dolan and McConville stood motionless side by side, pinioned and capped, matching nooses around their necks; a moment's silence broken only by the priest's final prayers – then both descended rapidly in concert as Calcraft released the bolt.

With executions now no longer taking place in public, there were no eyewitnesses' reports of the disruption of traffic caused by hordes of scaffold *aficionados*, no quotes of the derisive jibes hurled at the hangman, no vivid descriptions of the last dying moments of the felon, and so little regarding Calcraft's activities was published in the newspapers of the day, and it was not until September of the following year, 1869, that he once again received any great attention from the Press. Far from being the Finisher of the Law in this case, however; this time he was defending himself against the Law!

It seems that in 1867, while officiating at a hanging at Taunton in Devon, that of a farmer George Britten who had murdered his wife, he had stayed at an hotel but left without settling his bill, which amounted to about fourteen shillings. The landlord had subsequently spent the next two years attempting to get his money and finally received a letter from Calcraft in which he agreed to pay – eventually. Not content with this vague promise, the landlord took legal action, accusing Calcraft of fraud, and the case came to court. The hangman did not appear in person but wrote claiming in mitigation that, there having been but few hangings lately, his income had been sadly reduced. No doubt the judge took this into consideration, and ordered him to repay the debt within twenty-eight days. Whatever the verdict might have been, at least Calcraft did not run the risk of being transported to Australia; the last convict ship had sailed for that distant colony two years earlier!

The small group of officials gathered around the execution site within Newgate prison on 13 December 1869 witnessed the hanging of Frederick Hinson, the perpetrator of two brutal murders, found guilty 'of slaying his concubine Maria Death and her paramour William Boyd at Wood Green, London'. The unfortunately named young lady and her lover were avenged, Calcraft meting out the justice of the court – with agonising slowness.

But personal tragedy was to follow some months later, when Calcraft's wife Louisa died at the age of seventy-five. The couple had been married for forty-five years and the grief-stricken man found the death of the woman to whom he had been devoted, almost unbearable. He became morose and withdrawn, ceasing his social activities, and his tavern acquaintances saw him no more. However life had to go on and those of criminals terminated, and so he resumed his duties in prisons across the country.

On 1 August that year, 1870, the door of Newgate's condemned cell opened to allow Walter Millar to be escorted to the scaffold where Calcraft awaited, noose in hand. Millar had been sentenced to death for a double murder which had taken place in Chelsea, the Reverend Elias Huelin (or Llewellyn) and a woman named Anne Boss being savagely killed. In a vain attempt to cheat the gallows the murderer had tried to kill himself by smashing his head against the wall of his cell, but only suffered minor abrasions and, no doubt, a severe headache. Now, tied in a chair on the drop, the ever-obliging Calcraft granted him his wish – and drew the bolt.

A week later the hangman travelled to Aylesbury Gaol in Buckinghamshire where John Owen was scheduled to receive judicial attention. Millar's double murders had been shocking enough, but Owen's were truly horrific; the long-standing grievance he had been nursing had evidently warped his mind and turned him into a multiple killer, for he slew not only his employer Emmanuel Marshall but also Marshall's wife, her mother and sister; nor did he spare their three children, not ceasing the massacre until all seven lay dead. After that insensate slaughter, sanity had obviously deserted him, for not only did he ask for his coffin be brought to his cell so that he could sleep in it, but he threatened to punch Calcraft for not having the courtesy to visit him on the day prior to his execution! Such a blow from a near madman could have had Calcraft on the ropes; as it was, the only rope was the one the hangman dropped around Owen's neck, a knockout drop in more ways than one, avenging as it did the cruel death of seven innocent victims.

Calcraft's Last Executions 141

As already mentioned, the first private execution in England was that of Thomas Wells in 1868; now Calcraft was to enter the record books again by performing the same in Scotland when, on 4 October 1870, he hanged George Chalmers for murder. The battered body of John Miller, collector of the tolls exacted from those who travelled the lonely road between Crieff and Dunblane, Stirling, had been discovered, valuables stolen and, as clothes not belonging to Miller were found in the house, it was evident that the murderer had escaped wearing some of the dead man's garments. Investigations revealed that the likely suspect was George Chalmers, recently released from prison, but it was some months before he was eventually recognised and apprehended. At his trial at Perth on 7 September he disclaimed all knowledge of the heinous crime, a plea that hardly bore any credibility in view of the fact that, when arrested, he was still wearing the murdered man's clothes.

So Calcraft had to travel north once more, and on the scaffold erected in Perth's County Prison he closed his ears to the felon's plaintive protestations of innocence, closed his hand round the bolt, and brought his victim's life to a close as well.

Calcraft had barely returned to London when he was ordered to carry out another execution, one involving no travelling this time, it taking place in his home town. The murderer was a notorious baby farmer, Margaret Waters, who was one of a band of women posing as caring and dedicated foster parents willing to adopt babies, for payment of course. The promised care and dedication proved totally nonexistent, the women cruelly neglecting their charges even to the point of death, a fate which, in the case of a child born to Miss Jeannette Cowan, the daughter of the bandmaster of the Royal Irish Volunteers, was narrowly avoided.

For a description of the suffering inflicted on the baby, and the circumstances surrounding, both it and the suspicious deaths of other infants, we are again indebted to the popular and widely read periodical, the *Illustrated Police News* which, in Victorian times never failed to relate, in lurid detail, the horrific crimes of the day and the achievements of the police force in bringing those responsible to justice.

In this particular case the officer responsible was Sergeant Ralph who, in his testimony before the Lambeth magistrate, stated that 'About twenty minutes to one on 28 May (1870) I saw a four-wheeled cab draw up in front of No. 165 Camberwell Road, near New Church Road, the residence of Mrs Barton, a midwife. I saw an elderly woman get out of the cab, go into the house, and shortly afterwards return with a delicate looking young lady, who I thought had been recently confined (given birth). I followed the cab and saw the woman get out at Langhome Villas, Brixton. I ascertained that the young lady's name was Jeannette Tassie Cowen, and that she had recently been delivered of a male child at the Camberwell address. I made enquiries and ascertained that the child, being illegitimate, had been put out for adoption to a woman named Willis who advertised for infants, but no-one knew where she lived or what she was.

I saw an advertisement' the sergeant's testimony continued 'in Lloyd's of June 5th., signed by a Mrs Oliver, to adopt for £5 to cover every expense. I answered it and made an appointment to meet Mrs Oliver, which I kept at half past eight at Camberwell New Road, on the 12th. June. After seeing her, Mrs Oliver said she had been married fourteen years but had no family – this I have since ascertained to be false. She said her husband was a house decorator and lived at Herne Hill, about a mile away from Brixton, and that he was well-to-do, and if I entrusted my dear boy to her care, it would be well educated and put to her husband's trade. She seemed very anxious to get a boy and also for me to leave her. I traced her and found she resided at No. 4 Frederick Terrace, Brixton.

At 9 o'clock I went to the house and prisoner Oliver answered the door. I asked her to produce Miss Cowan's child. She said it was not there and that it had been put out to nurse. I went into the kitchen and found several infants, all huddled up together on a sofa. There were seven male and four female infants. They all lay with bottles by their sides. Mrs Waters said she was paid so much per week.

The local medical man, Dr. Pope, then gave evidence, stating that all the children were emaciated and very dirty, they all appeared to have been deprived of food and were in a sadly neglected condition. Evidence was given that Miss Cowan's child was remarkably large and healthy when born. Ann Rowland, a wet nurse, gave evidence showing the shocking condition of the infant of Miss Cowan when brought to her. All the infants with the exception of one, were conveyed in cabs to Lambeth Workhouse pending the remand,'

At her trial in October 1890, the prisoner in the dock was not only accused of maltreating Miss Cowan's baby, but also on more serious allegations that other infants given into her care had been deliberately allowed to die of neglect and starvation. It would seem from the report that the names Mrs Oliver and Mrs Willis were aliases, and it was Margaret Waters who, on the eleventh of that month, was entrusted into the care of William Calcraft in the execution shed of Horsemonger Lane Gaol where, no doubt, she suffered even more than any of those who had been entrusted to her.

Calcraft's hobby being angling, it is doubtful whether he took much notice of other sporting events of the day, among which were the foundation of the Rugby Football Union on 26 January 1871, and its first international match, Scotland beating England in Edinburgh, and the achievement by WG Grace, who scored 2,739 runs in the cricket season that year. But he would have noticed the Act introduced on 7 August, that date being the first ever Bank Holiday; no court sittings, no hangings!

More sporting milestones hit the headlines seven months later, when the first FA Cup Final took place, Wanderers beating the Royal Engineers; this was followed in November by the first international football match in the world, played at Partick, which resulted in a goalless draw between Scotland and England. There was probably little drunken brawling among the spectators, the Licensing Act having been passed on 31 July 1872, that legislation restricting both the drinking hours and the locations at which liquor could be sold.

It would seem that the measures introduced by the new law had little effect on those whose harsh way of life could only be ameliorated by frequent visits to the local public houses. That was certainly the case where labourer Charles Holmes was concerned. Married, with a severely disabled son, he took to drink and started to use violence against his wife. Fearing more brutality, she eventually took their child and sought refuge with friends, but Holmes came to the house and, under the pretext of wishing to give the boy some pocket money, attacked his wife with a razor, the fearsome wounds proving fatal.

He surrendered to the police without resistance, and at his trial, admitted his guilt. There were no grounds for an appeal to the Home Office to commute the death sentence, and on 12 August 1872 he joined Calcraft on the scaffold in Worcester Prison and paid the price demanded by the law. The payment took several minutes.

After most executions Calcraft was usually in no particular hurry to pack his straps and ropes away in his bag and leave the prison precincts, but after executing Holmes he wasted little time in hastily gathering his equipment together and making his way to the railway station, for on the following day, 13 August, he was due to perform a triple hanging at Maidstone, in Kent. A hundred and eighty miles separated the two towns, but that was as the crow flew, not as the steam train clanked along the rails; moreover he would probably have had to change at London, without even the chance to call in at his home in Hoxton, so it must have been a very travel-weary executioner who eventually reported to the governor in Maidstone Gaol in time to inspect the scaffold and prepare to hang his three victims.

Coincidentally all had military backgrounds, hardly surprising in view of the many Army and Navy establishments based in that part of the country. One of those condemned to death was Francis Bradford, a private who had been facing disciplinary action as a result of an adverse report submitted by a superior, Daniel Donahoe. Only too aware of the punishments then in force – they being singularly harsh in those Victorian times – he decided to take revenge on the man who had informed on him; taking his bayonet, the current model of which was nearly eighteen inches in length, he approached the bed where Donahue lay asleep and drove the weapon through his victim's body, killing him outright. Taken into custody by the military police and handed over to the civil authorities, he showed no regret for his action at his subsequent trial, and the death sentence was almost a formality.

One of the other two to join him on the scaffold was James Tooth, a Royal Marine stationed at Chatham Naval Base. At forty-two years of age he was older than Bradford, who was only nineteen, but like that young man he too had been found guilty of murdering a fellow serviceman. It transpired in court that he had been blamed and punished for the loss of a ring owned by one of the corporals, his accuser having been a Marine drummer boy, George Stock. Realising that such a black mark on his service records would jeopardise any future prospects of promotion, he spent his off-duty time drinking heavily in the canteen. The next morning, burning with resentment, he saw Stock leaving the church and proceeded to attack him with a knife, with which he cut the boy's throat.

A plea of insanity was put forward in his defence but was rejected out of hand, judge and jury having little to consider before the warders escorted the prisoner to the condemned cell, there to await execution day.

The third serviceman to be given his marching orders from this temporal plane by a judge was Thomas Moore, a veteran of the Crimean and Indian campaigns. He had been separated from his wife for some time, although they had met on occasions, without incident. But in May of that year they arranged to meet again, this time with disastrous results, for while out together he lost control and, seizing her round the throat, strangled her.

From the evidence given in court it appeared that during the heated argument they had undoubtedly had, Thomas Moore, in attempting to win her back, blamed one of her parents, either for breaking up their marriage or for vindictively preventing any reconciliation. His wife, out of loyalty to her family, refuted his allegations and thereby signed her own death warrant – an action duplicated later by the judge on the one that bore her husband's name.

On that day 13 August 1872, pinioned, hooded and noosed by the hangman and his assistant, George Smith of Dudley, the three men paraded on the drop; there was then no need for drill sergeant major Calcraft to give the order to "Fall in" – they did when he drew the bolt.

On 9 December 1872 Newgate scaffold again played host to Calcraft and a companion who, this time, was Augustus Elliot, sentenced to death for the murder of his girlfriend, but early in the next year the executioner had to take the train north again, to Durham, where a woman occupied the condemned cell in that city's gaol.

Mary Ann Cotton was no ordinary criminal, no run-of-the-mill, spur of the moment killer; her murderous instincts were alleged to have resulted in the deaths of fifteen, perhaps even twenty people, including four husbands and eight children, and she had gained the evil reputation of being the greatest mass murderer of all time.

By the age of forty she had married three times. Her first husband was a young miner named William Mowbray, by whom she had four children. All of them just 'happened' to die young, reportedly from gastric fever. William Mowbray also succumbed to illness, experiencing severe sickness and diarrhoea, and died in agony.

Mary, now seemingly grief-stricken at the loss of her husband and children, drew solace from her friends and cash from the insurance company. Realising that hospital work as a nurse would be the source, not only of supplies of the poison she needed, but of meeting further vulnerable and susceptible victims, she joined the staff of Sunderland Infirmary where, among others, she tended a patient named George Ward. So devoted were her ministrations that when he recovered, he proposed marriage, her subsequent promise 'in sickness and in health' only applying to fifty percent of the phrase, for within weeks he too shuffled off this mortal coil, but not before he had endowed all his worldly goods to her.

Not long afterwards, still in her widow's weeds, she met James Robinson, a widower with four children. They were married in May 1867, and by December of that year, unfortunate coincidences also overwhelmed that family, not only the two boys and two girls falling victim to gastric fever, but a later baby born to Mary and James joined its stepbrothers and sisters in the local cemetery. James himself had cause to thank his guardian angel and in a way, be grateful to his wife who, by selling some of his possessions, incensed him so much that he ordered her out of the house.

The fact that her husband was still alive did not deter her from starting an intimate association with her next prey, Frederick Cotton, a man who already had two young sons from a former marriage, and she bigamously married him. Being a prudent wife who had to take care of her future, naturally enough she took out three insurance policies, just in case. The number of children became three when she had a little boy by Frederick, and so the number of policies also increased in number.

Early in 1872 a James Nattrass entered the picture. This complicated matters, Frederick Cotton immediately becoming surplus to requirements – but not for long. Almost without warning he fell seriously ill, but by the time a doctor had arrived, he was past all medical aid. Frederick's ten-year-old son was not long in following his father to the grave, and Mary's child, Robert, never even reached puberty. Mary then decided that the £30, the sum in which James had been insured, was preferable to the man himself, and so another coffin received an occupant, another grave was dug.

She could have continued in this manner, unchecked and unsuspected, until her stock of arsenic, a poison little recognised or diagnosed at the time, ran out, but for some unaccountable reason, perhaps a rare, charitable thought, she spared the life of Charles Edward, the eight-year-old Cotton boy; instead she tried to hand him over to the workhouse. When told that such was not possible without the parents also being admitted, she retorted, "I could have married again but for the child. But there, he won't live long, he'll go the way of all the Cotton family." Nor did he. Dispensing with mercy, she dispensed arsenic instead, death again being certified as being caused by gastric fever. But news of the child's demise reached the ears of the workhouse master and, remembering the woman's ominous rejoinder, he notified the authorities of his suspicions. The child's body was exhumed and the amount of arsenic found within the viscera was unmistakeable. And when the corpses of her other victims were disinterred and their post mortems produced similar results, the game was up.

In March 1873 Mary Ann Cotton was charged at Durham with one murder, that of the young Charles Edward; so overwhelming was the evidence in that particular case that one charge was considered sufficient, and so it proved. Throughout the trial the woman in the dock remained composed and utterly self-assured; having born a charmed life so far, she probably saw no reason why it should not continue. She pleaded not guilty and coolly explained that the arsenic in her possession was used to kill bedbugs in the house, but when the judge pronounced her guilty and sentenced her to be hanged, she fainted in the dock and had to be carried down to the cells.

If she had thought that because she was pregnant – she had already taken a new lover, John Quick-Manning, a local customs officer – she would escape the gallows, she was sadly mistaken; there was, of course, no question of executing her while heavy with child, but once having given birth, the law would take its course. And so on 19 March she was deprived of her baby and arrangements were made for her to be deprived of her life in five days time.

The night before her execution she was heard by her warders to pray for salvation, a prayer which included James Robinson, the only one to escape her homicidal proclivities. Quick-Manning, the customs man, might also have congratulated himself on his lucky escape! Early the next morning, determined that the hangman should not find her dishevelled and distraught, she brushed her luxurious black hair until it shone. "Now I am ready", she exclaimed, as Calcraft entered the cell. Unresisting, she submitted to being pinioned and then led to the gallows within Durham Gaol.

Whatever reservations the executioner had felt in the past at having to hang a woman – and on occasion he had had some – he certainly did not experience any in this case. Feminine fashion at that time dictated that women wore dresses with long sleeves, plus a veil and gloves. Mary Ann Cotton's veil was the white cap Craft slipped over her head – nor did he omit the matching accessory, a hempen necklace. None of the watching officials saw him hesitate as he prepared his victim, then operated the bolt. They were, however, only too aware that, as usual, nearly three minutes elapsed before the twitching figure ceased rotating and finally hung deathly still.

Following removal from the scaffold, her body was taken back into the prison building where, in order to take a cast of her head for study by the West Hartlepool Phrenological Society, all her luxurious tresses were cut off close to her skull. It was later stated that, far from being kept as gruesome souvenirs, every severed strand of hair was deposited in the coffin with her body.

Such was the publicity surrounding the case that shock waves of disbelief and repugnance spread across the country when the prosecuting lawyer described the ghastly deaths of her other victims, and with the minimum of delay a wax model of her joined the company already occupying Mme Tussaud's Chamber of Horrors, the Museum publishing an updated catalogue which endorsed her execution as expiation 'for crimes for which no punishment in history could atone. The child she rocked on her knee today was poisoned tomorrow. Most of her murders were committed for petty gains; and she killed off husbands and children with the unconcern of a farm-girl killing poultry.'

In September 1872 a gamekeeper on an estate near Dundee was brutally murdered. Some time later his assailant, a man named Thomas Scobbie, was apprehended and on 8 April of the following year faced trial, the court being presided over by Lord Deas. The evidence was so overwhelming that the jury took only a matter of minutes before finding the prisoner guilty, though added a strong plea that mercy be shown. This rider was rejected by the Bench, Judge Lord Deas passing the death sentence, stipulating that it should take place on the twenty ninth of that month.

But those whose task it was to prepare the gallows, were wasting their time; the Sheriff need not have ordered his coachman in advance when to convey him to the prison; prison warders responsible for hoisting the black flag on the day, need never have bothered; journalists expecting to witness the hanging might as well have put aside their pencils and notebooks, and William Calcraft could have saved himself an interminably round trip by train, because the event never took place – and all because of an incredible administrative blunder! It seems that the clerk of the court, in recording the Judge's statement, employed the phrase 'on Tuesday, 29 April next to come.' And as the 'next to come' was not due to occur until five years hence, it was decided that the decision to hang Scobbie was null and void!

Calcraft, realising that in view of the reprieve his fee would be halved, must have experienced a certain amount of chagrin, but managed to conceal it admirably when interviewed by a reporter from the *Dundee Advertiser*, for the newspaper article described how 'the executioner had several conversations with gentlemen who happened to visit the gaol; he entered very minutely into his experiences, stating that he felt exceedingly pained when called upon to perform the functions of his office. It had, he said, afforded him much gratification to learn that the unfortunate prisoner whom he had come to hang, had been respited.'

The assumed date of the execution, and the identity of the man due to hang the murderer, had already been widely publicised, and when Calcraft arrived at the railway station to catch a train back to London, he was met by a throng of people eager to see the renowned hangman. He probably found it a welcome change from the hostility which usually greeted him on the scaffold, and actually responded good-humouredly to the reception, the *Advertiser* reporting that despite the crowds 'he did not however, manifest the slightest discomposure. He enquired of one or two bystanders what the people wanted to see, and was told that he was the object of their solicitation. Evidently anxious that all should have the fullest opportunity of inspecting him, after taking his seat in a second-class carriage, he rose to the window and kept his head out until the train had left the station.' A little hero-worship never hurt anyone, especially a hangman!

Any public admiration he may have had in the April of that year 1873 rapidly evaporated in the September, when he had to hang murderer James Connor at Kirkdale Prison, Liverpool. On the evening of 11 August 1873 Connor, a sturdily-built boilerman, had been drinking heavily in a pub in that city, and then decided to visit the nearby Music Hall. On leaving that place of entertainment he accosted a Mrs Mary Shears, who was walking down the street, and invited her to accompany him for a drink. Understandably she refused, whereupon he accused her of stealing his money.

The heated altercation continued for some minutes, and was interrupted by two passers-by, William Metcalfe and James Gaffrey, who sought to calm the situation. But Connor, in a drunken fury, attacked Gaffrey, drawing a knife and lashing out with it so violently that the blade entered the man's head just behind the ear, fatally wounding him. Connor then attempted to stab Metcalfe, and it was not until, after a considerable struggle, he was finally overpowered and taken into custody.

At his trial on 16 August he was charged with murder and attempted murder. His defence, that he had been provoked by the two men and in the fracas had only committed manslaughter, was rejected, the jury finding him guilty and Mr Justice Brett sentencing him to death, the execution to take place on 8 September 1873.

Calcraft's assistant on the scaffold that day was William Marwood, his eventual successor and, watching his No.1 in action, with things going wrong, he must have yearned to take over, to put into practice the more scientific and merciful ways of hanging a man which he was no doubt even then formulating in his mind.

Things did indeed go from bad to worse, and Calcraft found himself reliving the nightmare he last experienced back in 1829 when hanging young David Evans for murdering his sweetheart and the rope had snapped; This time he had capped and noosed Connor, then operated the drop – only to see the frayed end of the rope suddenly shoot upwards as his victim disappeared into the pit below – this rope had similarly snapped!

Frantically the hangman, accompanied by Marwood and the priest, Father Bont, scrambled down the steps and into the area beneath the scaffold platform, there to discover a dazed and shocked Connor who, with the shortened end of the rope still encircling his neck, raised his bound hands in supplication and, his voice muffled by the white cap covering his face, exclaimed pleadingly "I stood it bravely, didn't I? You will let me off, won't you? Let me off, do!"

But hanging meant hanging – to death. Calcraft had now been joined by prison warders, who proceeded to half-carry, half-drag the desperately protesting and still pinioned victim up on to the scaffold again. Meanwhile their colleagues had hastily obtained a new rope which Calcraft, thankful that only officials, rather than the general public, were witnessing this debacle, wasted no time in securing to the beam. With the warders supporting the victim on the drop, the hangman quickly removed the original noose from the man's neck, the rope having snapped before it had had time to tighten and, positioning the new one, stepped back off the trapdoors. Seconds later it became evident to all, Connor in particular, that there was nothing wrong whatsoever with the replacement item of equipment.

Although he would not be aware of it, the next three hangings were to be the last he performed before his compulsory retirement. On 5 January 1874 he executed Thomas Corrigan at Liverpool for murdering his mother; on 31 March, Thomas Chamberlain met a similar fate at Northampton for killing John Cox Newet. But it was on 25 May 1874 that he ended his career where he had started forty-five years earlier, at Newgate, wife-murderer James Godwin being his last victim. Nor had his technique altered during those long years, the *Times* reporting that 'Godwin died hard; his breast heaved convulsively, his hands were raised repeatedly to his throat. And these convulsions continued, not ceasing until some minutes had passed.'

Immediately after that execution William Calcraft was pensioned off by the Court of Aldermen with a pension equal to his former salary, twenty-five shillings per week. The hangman complained bitterly at his compulsory retirement, but the authorities rejected his plea to be allowed to continue working. Whether it was because of the approaching decrepitude of his advanced years, his callous, albeit unintentional method of despatching his victims, the emergence of a more humane attitude in society towards those who, evil as their deeds were, deserved a quicker death than one hitherto administered by their employee, or a combination of all those factors, their decision was final. After forty-five years the final instrument in the judicial system, the one who, regardless of his own opinions, impersonally executed the judgement of the courts, Calcraft had reached the end of the line; he had pinioned his last victim, tied his last slipknot, and descended the scaffold steps for the last time.

It is likely that, having earlier lost his wife and now his job, he simply lost heart, for he subsequently became even more of a recluse, dying in his home in Poole Street on the evening of Saturday 13 December 1879, in his eightieth year, leaving a daughter and two sons to carry on the family name. His death did not go unnoticed and unannounced, for over the next few days obituaries were published in the *Morning Advertiser*, the *Daily Telegraph*, the *Weekly Despatch*, the *Police News*, and the *Illustrated London News*, the obituary in the latter describing his resentment since being pensioned off; that he considered he had been unfairly treated by the authorities, and insisted to all who would listen, that he was still able to perform his duties on the scaffold.

William Calcraft was buried in the family grave in Abney Park Cemetery, off Stamford Hill Road, Stoke Newington, a mere four miles, as the crow flies, from where he made most of his public appearances – Newgate. Despite the castigation levelled at those of his profession, it should never be forgotten that he was a servant of the State, carrying out the task dictated by the courts of law, on behalf of us, the People. May he rest in peace.

Following his retirement, murderers and others condemned to death could, in a manner of speaking, look forward to dying easier and quicker, for the new No. 1 was William Marwood, the forerunner of a new generation of hangmen who realised that although their role was still that of meting out justice, it should be tempered with compassion and administered with speed and mercy. Marwood, a man of scientific aptitude, realised that the same length of rope for all victims was totally wrong; if too short it slowly strangled the victim; if too long the victim travelled too far and too fast, and was decapitated. He therefore theorised that instantaneous death could best be achieved by fracture of the spinal column, and that the length of rope, the drop, depended on the victim's age, body weight, muscular development and similar factors, a table showing the striking force, the body weight when the rope finally tautened, against the victim's weight, being eventually calculated and put into practice, with commendable results. But Marwood's life and work is another story!

APPENDIX ONE

CONFESSIONS OF BISHOP AND WILLIAMS

EXECUTED 5 DECEMBER 1831

John Bishop was born to his father's first wife and when his father died, leaving sufficient estate to provide for the last of his three wives, John promptly married his stepmother, so gaining control of her inheritance. His friend Thomas Williams became his brother-in-law by marrying one of his half-sisters, Rhoda, aged seventeen.

On the 4th December 1831, the day before they were hanged by William Calcraft, both murderers confessed to their crimes in the presence of the Under-Sheriff, as follows:

"I, John Bishop, do hereby declare and confess that I and Williams took the boy (Carlo Ferrari) to my house about half-past ten o'clock on the Thursday night the 3rd November, from the Bell, in Smithfield. He walked home with us. Williams promised to give him some work. Williams went with him from the Bell to the Old Bailey watering-house, whilst I went to the Fortune of War. Williams came from the Old Bailey watering-house to the Fortune of War for me, leaving the boy standing at the corner of the court by the watering-house at the Old Bailey. I went directly with Williams to the boy, and we walked then all three to Nova Scotia Gardens (where they lived – author), taking a pint of stout at a public house near Holloway Lane, Shoreditch, on our way, of which we gave the boy a part. We only stayed to drink it, and walked on to my house, where we arrived about eleven o'clock.

"My wife and children and Mrs Williams were not gone to bed, so we put him in the privy and I told him to wait for us. Williams went in and told them to go to bed, and I stayed in the garden. Williams came out directly, and we both walked out of the garden a little way, to give the family time getting to bed; we returned in about ten minutes or a quarter of an hour, and listened outside the window to ascertain whether the family had gone to bed. All was quiet and we then went to the boy in the privy and took him into the house; we lighted a candle and gave the boy some bread and cheese and, after he had eaten it, we gave him a cup full of rum, with about half a small phial of laudanum (tincture of opium) in it; I had bought the rum the same evening at the Three Tuns in Smithfield, and the laudanum also in small quantities at different shops. There was no water or other liquid put in the cup with the rum and laudanum. The boy drank the contents of the cup directly in two draughts and afterwards a little beer. In about two minutes he fell asleep on the chair in which he sat, and I removed him from the chair to the floor, and laid him on his side. We then went out and left him there.

"We had a quarter of gin and a pint of beer at the Feathers near Shoreditch Church and then went home again, having been away from the boy for about twenty minutes. We found him asleep as we had left him. We took him directly, asleep and insensible, into the garden, and tied a cord to his feet to enable us to pull him up by, and I then took him in my arms and let him slide from them headlong into the well in the garden, whilst Williams held the cord to prevent the body going altogether too low in the well. He was nearly wholly in the water in the well, his feet just above the surface. Williams fastened the other end of the cord around the palings to prevent the body getting beyond our reach. The boy struggled a little with his arms and legs in the water; the water bubbled for a minute.

"We waited until these symptoms were past and then went in, and afterwards I think we went out and walked down Shoreditch to occupy the time, and in about three-quarters of an hour we returned and took him out of the well, by pulling him by the cord attached to his feet. We undressed him in the paved yard (a surgeon would immediately realise that a clothed body had not been exhumed from a graveyard, but had been murdered – author), rolled his clothes up, and buried them where they were found by the witness. We carried the boy into the wash-house, laid him on the floor, and covered him with a bag.

We left him there and had some coffee in Old-Street Road, and then, a little before two in the morning of Friday, went back to my house.

"We immediately doubled the body up and put it into a box, which we corded so that nobody might open it to see what was in it, and then went out again and had some more coffee in the same place in Old-Street Road, where we stayed a little while, and then went home to bed, both in the same house and to our own beds as usual; we slept till about ten o'clock on Friday morning, when we got up, took breakfast together with the family, and then we went both of us to Smithfield to the Fortune of War – we had something to eat and drink there. In about half-an-hour May came in – I knew May, but had not seen him for about a fortnight before – he had some rum with me at the bar, Williams remaining in the taproom.'

"The condemned man then described the movements of himself and Williams during that day, in the course of which they were principally occupied in visiting public houses, though they called upon two lecturers on anatomy and offered them the body, but were refused.

"At the Fortune of War" the confession continued "we drank something again and then about six o'clock we all three went in the chariot (a type of horse-drawn cab – author) to Nova Scotia Gardens; we went into the wash-house, where I uncorded the trunk and showed May the body. He asked "How are the teeth?" I said I had not looked at them. Williams went and fetched a bradawl from the house and May took it and forced the teeth out; it is the constant practice to take the teeth out first, because if the body be lost (discovered and confiscated by the authorities), the teeth are saved. After the teeth were taken out, we put the body in a bag and took it to the chariot. May and I carried the body, and Williams got first into the coach and then assisted in pulling the body in."

The rest of this part of the confession is simply a record of 'having something to drink' and visiting more lecturers, who also refused to purchase the body. It concludes with an account of the apprehension of the men with the body in their possession. In addition to this confession of the murder of the boy, Bishop made a further statement:

"I declare that this statement is all true and that it contains all the facts so far as I can recollect. May knew nothing of the murder and I do not believe he suspected that I had got the body except in the usual way, and after the death of it. I always told him I got it from the ground and he never knew to the contrary until I confessed to Mr Williams, the clergyman, since the trial. I have known May as a body-snatcher for four or five years but I do not believe that he ever obtained a body except in the common course of men in that calling, by stealing it from the graves.

"I also confess that I and Williams were concerned with the murder of a female, whom I believe to have since been discovered as Fanny Pigburn, on or about 9 October last. I and Williams saw her sitting about eleven or twelve o'clock at night on the step of a door in Shoreditch, near the church. She had a child four or five years old on her lap. I asked her why she was sitting there. She said she had no home to go to, for her landlord had turned her out into the street. I told her that she might go home with us and sit by the fire all night. She said she would go with us and she walked with us to my house in Nova Scotia Gardens, carrying her child with her. When we got there we found the family abed, and we took the woman in and lighted the fire, by which we all sat down together. I went out for beer and we all took beer and rum – I had brought the rum from Smithfield in my pocket; the woman and her child lay down on some dirty linen on the floor, and I and Williams went to bed.

"About six o'clock the next morning, I and Williams told her to go away, and to meet us at the London Apprentice in Old-Street Road at one o'clock. This was before our families were up. She met us again at one o'clock at the London Apprentice, without her child. We gave her some halfpence and beer, and desired her to meet us again at ten o'clock at night at the same place. After this we bought rum and laudanum at different places, and at ten o'clock we met the woman again at the London Apprentice, she had no child with her.

"We drank three pints of beer between us there and stayed for about an hour, then went out. It rained heavily and we took shelter under a doorway in the Hackney Road for about an hour. We then walked to Nova Scotia Gardens, and Williams and I led her into No. 2, an empty house adjoining mine. We had no light. Williams stepped into the garden with the rum and laudanum, which I had handed to him; he there mixed them together in a half-pint bottle and came into the house to me and the woman, and gave her the bottle to drink. She drank the whole at two or three draughts; there was a quartern of rum and about half a phial of laudanum. She sat down on the step between two rooms in the house and went off to sleep in about ten minutes. She was falling back; I caught her to save her fall, and she laid back on the floor. Then Williams and I went to a public-house, got something to drink, and in about half an hour came back to the woman.

"We took her cloak off, tied a cord to her feet, carried her to the well in the garden and thrust her into it headlong; she struggled very little afterwards and the water bubbled a little at the top. We fastened the end to the palings to stop her going down beyond our reach, and left her and took a walk to Shoreditch and back, in about half an hour; we left the woman in the well for this length of time so that the rum and laudanum might run out of the body at the mouth (the murderers assuming that this would remove all traces of the poison from her body, the drug otherwise being discovered during dissection and so revealing that the victim had been murdered and not stolen from a grave – author).

"On our return we took her out of the well, cut her clothes off, put them down the privy of the empty house, carried the body into the wash-house of my own house, where we doubled it up and put it into a hair-box, which we corded and left there. We did not go to bed, but went to the house of Shields, a street porter, in Eagle Street, Red Lion Square, and called him up; this was between four and five o'clock in the morning (Shields had previously been employed as watchman and grave-digger in Moorfields Cemetery, his information regarding the location of the graves of the most recently buried corpses, and his subsequent assistance in the excavation and removal of the bodies proving invaluable to the Resurrection Men, as they were called – author).

"We went with Shields to a public-house near the Sessions-house, Clerkenwell, and had some gin, and from thence to my house, where we went in and stayed a little while, to wait the change-over of police (patrols). I told Shields he was to carry that trunk to St Thomas' Hospital. He asked if there was a woman in the house who could walk alongside of him, so that people might not take any notice. Williams called his wife up and asked her to walk with Shields and to carry the hatbox which he gave her to carry. There was nothing in it but it was tied up as if there were.

"We then put the box with the body on Shields' head and went to the hospital, Shields and Mrs Williams walking on one side of the street, and I and Williams on the other (so that they could flee if his wife and the porter were stopped and the box searched – author). At St Thomas' I saw Mr South's footman and sent him upstairs to Mr South (a surgeon) to ask him if he wanted a subject. The footman brought me word that his master wanted one but could not give an answer till the next day, as he had not had time to look at it. During this interview, Shields, Williams and his wife were waiting at a public-house. I then went alone to Mr Appleton at Mr. Grainger's Anatomical Theatre and agreed to sell it to him for eight guineas, and afterwards I fetched it from St Thomas' Hospital and took it to Mr Appleton, who paid me £5 then and the rest on the following Monday. After receiving the £5 I went to Shields and Williams and his wife at the public-house, when I paid Shields 10s for his trouble, and we then all went to the Flower Pot in Bishopsgate, where we had something to drink and then went home.

"I never saw the woman's child after the first time above mentioned. She said she had left the child with a person she had taken some of her things to, before the landlord took her goods. The woman murdered did not tell us her name; she said her age was thirty-five, I think, and that her husband, before he died, was a cabinet maker. She was thin, rather tall, and very much marked with the smallpox.

"I also confess the murder of a boy who told us his name was Cunningham. It was a fortnight after the murder of the woman. I and Williams found him sleeping about eleven or twelve o'clock at night on Friday 21 October, as I think, under the pigboards in the pig market at Smithfield. Williams woke him and asked him to come along with him, and the boy walked with Williams and me to my house in Nova Scotia Gardens.

"We took him into my house and gave him some warm beer sweetened with sugar, with rum and laudanum in it. He drank two or three cups full and then fell asleep in a little chair belonging to one of my children. We laid him on the floor and went out for a little while and got something to drink and then returned, carried the boy to the well, and threw him into it in the same way as we served the other boy and the woman. He died instantly in the well and we left him there a little while to give time for the mixture we had given him to run out of the body. We then took the body from the well, took off the clothes in the garden, and buried them there. The body we took into the wash-house and put it in the same box, and left it there until the next evening, when we got a porter to take it to St Bartholomew's Hospital, where I sold it to Mr Smith for eight guineas. This boy was about ten or eleven years old, said his mother lived in Kent Street, Haggerston, and that he had not been home for a twelvemonth or better.

"I solemnly declare that these were all the murders in which I have been concerned or that I know anything of; that I and Williams were alone concerned in these, and that no other person whatever knew anything about either of them, and that I do not know whether there are others who practice the same mode of obtaining bodies for sale. Until the transactions set forth, I never was concerned in obtaining a subject by the destruction of the living. I have followed the course of obtaining a livelihood as a body-snatcher for twelve years and have obtained and sold, I think, from 500 to 1000 bodies; but I do declare, before God, that they were all obtained after death, and that, without exception, I am ignorant of any murder for that or any other purpose."

Williams, whose proper name was Thomas Head, also confessed to rendering their victims unconscious by hocussing (adding a drug to liquor), and confirmed the confession given above as altogether true.

APPENDIX TWO

LAST STATEMENTS OF ALLEN, LARKIN & O'BRIEN

FENIANS, EXECUTED 23 NOVEMBER 1867

WILLIAM ALLEN: I wish to say a few words relative to the charge for which I am to die. In a few hours more, I will be going before my God. I state in the presence of that great God that I am not the man who shot Sergeant Brett. If that man's wife is alive, never let her think that I am the person who deprived her of her husband; and if his family is alive, never let them think that I am the man who deprived them of their father. I confess I have committed other sins against my God and I hope He will accept my death as the homage and adoration which I owe His Divine Majesty and in atonement for my past transgressions against Him.

There is not much use in dwelling on the subject much longer; for by this time I am sure it is plain that I am not the man who took away the life of Sergeant Brett. I state this to put juries on their guard for the future and to have them enquire into the characters of witnesses before they take away the lives of innocent men. But then I ought not to complain. Was not our Saviour sold for money and His life sworn away by false witnesses? With the help of the great God, I am only dying to a world of sorrow to arise to a world of joy. Before the judgment seat of God there will be no false witnesss tolerated, everyone must render an account of himself. I forgive all the enemies I have had in this world. May God forgive them; forgive them sweet Jesus, forgive them. I also ask pardon of all whom I have injured in any way.

In reference to the attack on the van, I confess I nobly aided in the rescue of the gallant Colonel Kelly and Captain Deasy. It is well known to the whole world what my poor country has to suffer and how her sons are exiles the world over; then tell me where is the Irishman who could look unmoved and see his countrymen taken prisoner and treated like murderers and robbers in British dungeons? May the Lord have mercy on our souls and deliver Ireland from her suffering! God save Ireland!

MICHAEL LARKIN: Men of the world – I, as a dying man going before my God, solemnly declare that I never fired a shot in all my life, much less on the day the attack was made on the van, nor did I ever put a hand on the van. The world will remember the widow's son's life that was sworn away, by which he leaves a wife and four children to mourn his loss. I am not dying for shooting Sergeant Brett, but for mentioning Colonel Kelly's and Deasy's names in the court. I am dying patriot for my God and my country, and Larkin will be remembered in time to come by the sons and daughters of Erin.

Farewell, dear Ireland, for I must leave you to die a martyr for your sake. Farwell, dear mother, wife and children, for I must leave you to die for poor Ireland's sake. Farewell, uncles, aunts and cousins, likewise, sons and daughters of Erin. I hope, in heaven we will meet another day. God be with you. Father in heaven, forgive those who have sworn my life away. I forgive them and the world.

MICHAEL O'BRIEN: I have only to make these few remarks. I did not use a revolver or any other firearm, or throw stones on the day Colonel Kelly and Captain Deasy were so gallantly released. I was not present when the van was attacked. I say this not by way of reproach or to give annoyance to any person, but I say it in the hope that witnesses may be more particular when identifying and that juries may look more closely to the character of the witnesses before they convict a person to send him before his God. I trust that those who swore to seeing me with a revolver or to throwing stones were nothing more than mistaken. I forgive them from my heart; likewise I forgive all those who have ever done me or intended to do me any injury.

I know I have been guilty of many sins against my God; in satisfaction for those sins, I have tried to do what little penance I could and have received the sacrament of the Church. I have humbly begged that He would accept my sufferings and death to be united to the sufferings and death of His innocent Son, through whom my suffering can be more acceptable. My Redeemer died a more shameful death, as far as men could make it, that I might receive pardon from Him and enjoy His glory in heaven. God grant that it may be so.

I earnestly beg my countrymen in America to heal their differences, to unite in God's name for the sake of Ireland and liberty. With reference to Colonel Kelly, I believe him to be a good, honourable man, unselfish and entirely devoted to the cause of Irish freedom.

APPENDIX THREE

BROADSHEETS OF CALCRAFT'S VICTIMS

Broadsheets, one-page pamphlets, were sold in their thousands, not only to those attending the executions of the more infamous criminals but also on the city streets. The vendors were known as 'patterers' because of their sales patter, vocally and loudly advertising their wares; 'running' patterers kept on the move, 'standing' patterers had their own pitch, usually on strategic street corners, where they held up poles bearing illustrations of the current production. Most of the pamphlets were printed in Seven Dials, a far from salubrious neighbourhood near Soho where seven streets led from a circular area, in the centre of which stood a tall column surmounted by a clock with, of course, seven dials. One printer was James Catnach (1792-1842), his press being situated at No. 2 Monmouth Court, and after his death his sister took over Catnach Press, competing for custom with a rival firm owned by one John Pitts.

The broadsheets themselves consisted of the felon's alleged 'last words' together with a crude woodcut of him or her in various surroundings, committing the crime, in the condemned cell, or on the gallows, these usually being reproduced from previous executions and bearing little or no resemblance to the criminal in question. They also included melodramatic accounts of the crime in the form of poems, some phrased to be sung to the tunes of popular songs by the waiting crowds ('Neckverses') while waiting for the executioner and his victim to appear on the scaffold (James Catnach reportedly employed a fiddler so that he would know how ballads would sound when set to music!) although had the victims themselves actually composed some of the following truly atrocious verses, no doubt dedicated versifiers would have found them guilty of committing crimes even more heinous than those of murder!

JAMES GREENACRE killed and dismembered Hannah Brown; he was hanged by William Calcraft 2 May 1837.

> You recollect about Christmas time,
> Both in country and in town,
> That the body of a female
> In Edgeware Road was found.
> Deprived of both her legs and head,
> As plainly might be seen,
> And ever since that time till now,
> A mystery has been.
>
> The legs were found near Brixton,
> How dreadful for to tell,
> And the head was found at Stepney,
> In the Regent's Canal.
> But the murderer could not be traced,
> In country or in town,
> For the base, inhuman murder
> Of Mrs. Hannah Brown.
>
> Of such a dreadful deed as this,
> We seldom ever hear,
> And may we never have again
> To hear such a sad affair.
> But Providence did so ordain
> It should be brought to light,
> And thus this awful Tragedy
> At length it was found out.
>
> When to High Street Office he did go,
> With people it was filled;
> And when he did confess the deed,
> Each breast with horror filled.
> He says he threw her from the chair,
> Which took away her life,

And the limbs cut from her body,
With a sharp and deadly knife.

And when he had the body torn,
Oh, where could the villain look?
From place to place he went about
And certain parts he took.
And when the whole he had dispos'd
(So Greenacre now does say),
Had he not so soon been taken
Abroad he meant to steer his way.

DANIEL GOOD killed and dismembered Jane Jones; he was hanged by William Calcraft 23 May 1842.

Of all the wild deeds upon Murder's black list,
Sure none is so barbarous and cruel as this,
Which in these few lines unto you I'll unfold,
The recital's enough to turn your blood cold.

In the great town of London, near Manchester Square,
Jane Jones kept a mangle in South Street we hear,
A gentleman's coachman oft visiting came,
A cold-blooded monster, Dan Good was his name.

As a single man unto her he made love,
And in course of time she pregnant did prove,
Then with false pretences he took her from home,
To murder his victim and the babe in her womb.

To his master's stables in Putney Park Lane,
They went, but she never returned again,
Prepare for your end then the monster did cry,
Your time it is come for this night you must die.

Then with a sharp hatchet her head he did cleave,
She begged for mercy, but none would he give,
Have mercy dear Daniel my wretched life spare
For the sake of your own child which you know I bear.

And when she was dead this sad deed to hide,
The limbs from her body he straight did divide,

Her bowels ript open and dripping with gore,
The child from the womb this black monster he tore.

He made a large fire in the harness room,
Her head, arms and legs in the fire did consume,
But e'er his intentions were fulfilled quite,
This dark deed by Providence was brought to light.

He soon was found guilty and sentenced to die,
The death of a murderer on the gallows high,
The blood of the murdered must not cry in vain,
And we hope that his like we shall ne'er see again.

In addition to the above poem, the following lyrics were composed for the benefit of the more musically minded spectators at Daniel Good's impending demise, to be sung to the tune of a popular song of the day, *The Gallant Poachers*; so any readers acquainted with the melody – altogether now:

Good people all, both young and old,
A dreadful tale I will unfold,
Will make your warm life blood run cold,
When you the same shall hear.
Of Good I'll tell, that wretch so fell,
Who a cruel deed has done,
As e'er was witness'd 'neath the sun.
But his career of crime is done,
His end is drawing near.

He helpless woman did betray,
His victim afterwards did slay,
To hide his guilt from open day,
The body hacked and hew'd,
No mercy show'd, for none he know'd,
From pity he, disdainful, turns,
Compunction and remorse he spurns,
The quivering limbs with fire he burns -
Thou monster, Daniel Good.

Her slender limbs he sawed and tore,
The entrails, reeking in their gore,
He gave the flames for to devour -

Oh, what a deed of blood!
Could no-one speed, and stop the deed?
Was there no-one to save thee nigh,
When thou for succour loud did cry?
No; no-one saw thy parting sigh,
But cruel Daniel Good.

A scaffold soon thy end will be,
And hissing thousands flock to see,
For none will cheer or pity thee,
Nor mourn the murderer's fate.
Youth and age will curse thy rage,
And ages yet unborn will tell,
And on thy crimes with anguish dwell,
And mourn thy cruel deed so fell,
Deserving scorn and hate!

JAMES BLOOMFIELD RUSH murdered his landlord and his landlord's son; he was hanged by William Calcraft on 21 April 1849; although Rush and his victims suffered, the 'patterers' certainly didn't, no fewer than two and a half million copies of this broadsheet being sold at the time!

THE SORROWFUL LAMENTATION OF JAMES BLOOMFIELD RUSH

now lying under Sentence of Death in Norwich Castle, for the horrid Murders at Stanfield Hall.

Kind Christians hear this doleful tale,
Whilst I for mercy cry,
And plead unto the Lord for me,
A wretch condemned to die.
'Twas horrid murder's dreadful crime -
That crime for which I'm tried,
It fires my brain with agony.
To think, by me they died.

The Father was by me shot dead,
And afterwards his Son,
My revenge it was not satisfied,
The dreadful crime's begun.
My murd'ring hand then did attempt

Still further to proceed,
And woman's innocence had no effect,
To deter me from the deed.

But Mercy here did step between,
Those victims for to shield;
The Maid and Mistress they were shot,
And wounded, but not kill'd.
At the Lent Assizes I was tried,
Such facts did then come out;
I was declared the murderer,
For there remained no doubt.

And for the space of six long days,
My trial it did last,
The sentence then of Death on me,
By the learned Judge was pass'd,
What agony my mind is in,
All in this dismal cell,
The horrors of my dreadful thoughts,
No mortal tongue can tell.

For mercy do I try to pray,
At the awful throne of God,
But mercy how can I expect,
Stained with my victims' blood.
Oh! give me death I loudly cry,
And ease my burning brains,
No answer in this lonely cell,
But the rattling of my chains.

Again I try to call on God,
Have mercy blessed Lord,
O may the cross of Jesus Christ
Wash out my deeds of blood,
I know that Christ my Saviour died
All on Mount Calvary;
To save the worst of sinners then,
A guilty wretch like me.

Now do I clasp my murd'ring hands,
With horror weep aloud;

I think I see each murdered form,
Wrapt'd in their deadly shroud.
Remorse now tears my troubled soul,
When I think on my guilt,
That through revenge alas! it was,
My victims' blood I spilt.

But soon alas! the time will come,
When I shall yield my breath,
And suffer for these crimes of blood,
An ignominious death.
No hopes on earth are now for me,
For crimes so black and foul;
My only hope must be in Christ,
For mercy on my soul.

JOHN GLEESON WILSON murdered a pregnant woman, her two children and the maid; he was hanged by William Calcraft 15 September 1849.

'Come all you feeling Christians and hearken unto me,
The like was not recorded in British history,
It is of four dreadful murders committed, I am told,
By one John Gleeson Wilson, for the sake of cursed gold.

On Wednesday the 28th. consternation did prevail,
In Leveson Street in Liverpool, where thousands did bewail,
The fate of this poor family, who we are left to deplore,
Snatched from a father's fond embrace, who never will see them more.

This monster in human shape did go there to dwell,
And that he went to plunder, to all it is known full well,
And when this callous villain saw their defenceless state,
He did resolve them all to kill, and rob them of the plate.

His bloody work he did commence all in the open day,
By striking at the children while their mother was away,
The servant girl did interfere, said he should not do so,
Then with a poker in his hand he gave her a severe blow.

Numberless times he did her strike till she could no longer stand,

The blood did flow profusely from her wounds, and did him brand,
Then the eldest boy of five years old, in supplication said
"Oh, master, spare our precious lives, don't serve us like the maid."

This darling child of five years old he brutally did kill,
Regardless of its tender years, its precious blood did spill,
The youngest child to the kitchen ran, to shun the awful knife,
This villain followed after, and took its precious life.

A surgeon thus describes the scene presented to his view,
A more appalling case than this he says he never knew,
Four human beings on the floor, all weltering in their gore,
The sight was sickening to behold on entering the door.

The mother's wound, three inches deep, upon her head and face,
And pools of blood as thick as mud, from all of them could trace,
None could identify the boy, his head was like a jelly;
This tragedy is worse by far than Greenacre or Kelly.

To the hospital in this sad state they quickly were conveyed,
The mother with her infant dear, and faithful servant maid,
Thousands did besiege the gates, their fate for to enquire
But in three days, from incise wounds, both of them did expire.

It will cause the captain many a pang to know their awful doom.
His loving wife and children, sent to an untimely tomb,
It will make his hair turn grey with grief, no skill their lives could save,
And he did go, borne down with woe, in sorrow to the grave.

But now he's taken for this deed, bound down in irons strong,
In Kirkdale Jail he now does lie, till his trial it comes on,
May God above receive the souls of those whom he has slain,
And may they all in heavenly bliss for ever with him reign.

ELIAS LUCAS & MARY READER were found guilty of poisoning his wife; both hanged by William Calcraft 14 April 1850.

> O God for mercy we do cry God's all-seeing eye doth watch
> Tomorrow we are doomed to die; The actions of the guilty wretch
> Our sins we own are very great, Wicked deeds he brings to light
> For which we meet a dreadful fate. Sure as day succeeds the night
>
> The crime of murder, all allow, For murder now condemn'd to die
> Is greater than any sin below, And end our days with infamy
> And by the law it is decreed A crime unequalled to be found
> On the gallows we shall bleed. If you search the world around.
>
> A deadly poison we confess A warning take now by our fate
> We put into our sister's mess, And shun the evils that await,
> Hoping when quiet in her grave A guilty passion which did tend
> More guilty intercourse to have. To bring us to this fatal end.

CAPTAIN HENRY ROGERS responsible for the death of seaman Andrew Rose; hanged by William Calcraft 12 September 1857, the following ballad being sung around the scaffold site;

> Andrew Rose, the British sailor
> Now to you his woes I'll name -
> 'Twas on the passage from Barbadoes
> Whilst on board of the "Martha Jane"
>
> (Chorus) Wasn't that most cruel usage,
> Without a friend to interpose?
> How they whipped and mangled, gagged and strangled
> The British sailor, Andrew Rose
>
> 'Twas on the quarter-deck they laid him,
> Gagged him with an iron bar;
> Wasn't that most cruel usage
> To put upon a British tar?

'Twas up aloft the captain sent him,
Naked beneath the burning sun,
Whilst the mate did follow after,
Lashing him till the blood did run

The captain gave him stuff to follow;
Stuff to you I will not name,
Whilst the crew got sick with horror,
While on board the "Martha Jane"

'Twas in a water-cask they put him;
Seven long days they kept him there,
When loud for mercy Rose did venture,
The captain swore no man should go there

For twenty days they did ill-use him,
When into Liverpool they arrived.
The judge he heard young Andrew's story;
"Captain Rogers, you must die"

Come all ye friends and near relations,
And all ye friends to interpose;
Never treat a British sailor
Like they did young Andrew Rose.

GEORGE SMITH murdered his father, Joseph; he was hanged by William Calcraft 16 August 1861. Such was the appalled reaction of Victorian society at the killing of a father by his son, that a veritable plethora of ballads was published, four of which, their spelling errors uncorrected, appear below.

**THE CONFESSION OF GEO. SMITH
TO THE GOVERNOR OF DERBY GAOL,
WHO IS TO BE EXECUTED
ON FRIDAY AUGUST 16th. 1861.**

You feeling Christian pray attend,
And listen unto me,
While unto you I will unfold
This dreadful tragedy.
Committed by a guilty one,
As you shall quickly hear,

Upon his father at Ilkeston,
Well known in Derbyshire.

Chorus – Oh, the dreadful deed was done.
A father murdered by his son.

I hope you will a warning take,
By what I now relate,
And think on my untimely end,
For wretched is my fate;
I might have lived in happiness,
As you shall quickly hear,
All with my aged father,
At Ilkeston, in Derbyshire.

Sure Satan must have tempted me,
Upon that fateful day,
My kind and tender Father,
To take his life away.
All with a deadly weapon,
It was my full intent,
I gave him not the shortest time,
On earth for to repent.
The jury found me guilty,
And I am condemned to die,
An awful death of public scorn,
Upon the gallows high.

The black cap being in readiness,
When I was tried and cast,
The learned judge with solemn voice,
The awful sentence passed;
You must prepare to meet your God,
We can no mercy show,
So pray for mercy from above,
For none is here below.

I dread to think upon the hour,
All on that fateful morn,
When I must ascend the scaffold high,
To die a death of scorn.
To the fateful spot, thousands will come,

That dreaded sight to see,
George Smith to end his days,
Upon the gallows tree.

I have brought disgrace upon myself,
My friends and family,
No one I'm sure will sympathize
Or soothe my misery.
I must prepare to meet my God,
I hear the solemn knell,
My time is come, I must away,
Farewell, a last farewell.

THE LAMENTATIONS OF GEORGE SMITH

Executed at Derby on Friday August 16,
FOR THE WILFUL MURDER OF HIS FATHER
At Ilkeston, on the night of May 1st, 1861.

You feeling Christians give attention,
While to you a tale I'll tell;
For the solemn hour has come
When I must say to all farewell.
For the horrid crime of murder,
I must die a death of scorn,
Upon Derby scaffold high!
Oh! would to God I'd ne'er been born!

Chorus – So young men all, I pray take warning,
Shun all evil company;
And think upon young George Smith,
Hung on Derby's gallows' tree.

At Ilkeston, in Derbyshire,
My father there he once did dwell,
And well known by old and young,
And by all, respected well.
'Till Satan must have tempted me
For to take his life away;
And through drink and company
Then I did my father slay.

Before I did the horrid deed,
To Nottingham I went straightway,
And bought a pistol and some shot,
Likewise some powder, as they say;
And I also bought some caps
For to do this horrid deed,
To think I should have been so cruel,
Oh! it makes my heart to bleed.

To my home I then did go,
And my mind on murder bent,
For to shoot my poor old father,
It was then my full intent;
But my resolution failed me -
When to get some drink I did repair,
After which I returned again,
And shot my father in his chair.

It was upon the day of trial,
So harden'd at the bar I stood,
But the jury found me guilty
For spilling of my father's blood.
Then the judge he sentenced me
For to die a public show,
And look for mercy from above,
For they'd show none here below.

Now the hour is approaching,
When to this world I bid adieu,
Also friends and kind relations,
Likewise sister and brothers too;
And I hope that no one ever,
After I am dead and gone,
Will cast reflection on my brothers,
For the deed that I have done.

See what thousands are approaching,
To see a wretched culprit die,
At the age of twenty years,
Upon Derby scaffold high.
Now the solemn bell is tolling;
I must leave this wicked world;

Tho' on the tree I die for murder,
May God receive my guilty soul.

Then will no one pity poor George Smith?
No one for him shed a tear?
Farewell friends and kind relations,
Farewell friends of Derbyshire.

THE SORROWFUL LAMENTATIONS ON GEORGE SMITH NOW LYING UNDER SENTANCE OF DEATH AT DERBY GAOL

In the condemned cell of Derby Goal,
George Smith he now does lie;
His sad career is nearly o'er,
And he will shortly die.
His guilt is heavy on his soul,
Death comes too soon for him,
His life blood warms his sinking heart,
But still he is a dying man.

Chorus – In Derby goal he now does lie,
George Smith he is condemned to die.

When he looks back to childhood's day
The tears start in his eye;
When happy in a mother's love,
The time past swiftly by,
But he forsook the righteous path,
And took the ways of crime,
A shameful death will be his end,
In manhood's health and prime.

They said that he so harden'd was,
As he stood on his trial,
But well you know the heart can bleed,
Tho' the face may wear a smile.
If you want to know what misery is?
The stoutest heart will try;

Go seek it in the condemned cell,
Of him condemned to die.

To see his brothers Henry
And Edward standing by,
Praying o'er their murdered father,
Tears falling from each eye:
Would almost pierce a heart of steel,
To see how they did weep,
O'er their mangled murdered father,
Who in death's cold arms did sleep.

Chorus – His own dear father he did slay,
At Ilkeston, on the first of May.

Within the cell in dreary night,
Sad visions often rise,
The frowning gallows seem to stand
Before his aching eyes,
But his hands he has stained with blood,
That he has caused to flow,
Our God, we hope, will cleanse him yet,
As pure as spotless snow.

Oh! children be dutiful,
Unto your parents kind,
The good advice they give to you
Always bear it in your mind.
Their is one above that watches you,
Throughout the night and day,
Then think upon the wretched son,
Who did his father slay.

All you who go to see him die,
Oh! pray be warned in time,
For one false step will bring you down,
To the lowest depths of crime.
Always lead a sober life,
And walk in virtue's way,
Then you will not fear to meet your death,
Let it come whene'er it may.

A COPY OF VERSES ON THE MURDER OF JOSEPH SMITH BY HIS OWN SON, AT ILKESTON, MAY 2, 1861.

A dreadful deed of murder to you I will unfold,
'Tis a tale as sad and horrid as ever yet was told;
At Ilkeston, in Derbyshire, alas it is too true -
A wretched son the deed has done – his own dear father slew.

Chorus – His own dear father he did slay,
On Wednesday eve, the first of May.

George Smith, a sad and wretched man, his father's blood did spill,
On that fatal spot he did fire the shot that did his father kill.
It is supposed he meant to rob his parent of his wealth
And when the deed was done, he said his father killed himself.

His wedding day was drawing near – he did premeditate
That his father and himself should meet with an untimely fate -
The fatal murderous weapon he grasped in his hand,
And fired on his father dear, as we can understand

To see his brothers Henry, and Edwin standing by,
Praying o'er their murdered father, tears falling from each eye,
Would almost pierce a heart of steel to see how they did weep,
O'er their mangled, murder'd father, who in death's cold arms did sleep.

Their brother George to murder him with Satan had engaged -
The son who shot his father is but twenty years of age;
Now lying in a gaol, and pond'ring o'er the deed he done -
Reflecting on the murder of a father by his son.

Oh, list you tender parents and all your sons likewise!
This cannot fail to draw a tear from every human eye.
Whatever could posses him such a dreadful deed to do;
When on Wednesday night, the first of May, his own kind father slew.

He now his trial does await, approaching is the time,
His dear unhappy parent was aged forty-nine -
Murder'd in the prime of life, oh, awful tragedy,
By one whom he fondly cherished and dandled on his knee.

The dear and younger children when they their father saw,
The agony they did endure, they on their knees did fall,
While tears fell from their weping eyes in torrents on the floor,
Crying "Our dearest father on earth we'll see no more.

Oh, children be dutiful unto your parents kind,
The good advice they give you bear always in your mind.
There is one above who watches you throughout the night
and day -
Then think upon the wretched youth who did his father slay.

Chorus – At Ilkeston they were known well,
Where they many happy years did dwell.

RICHARD THORLEY murdered Elizabeth Morrow; he was hanged by William Calcraft 11 April 1862. Unusually it seeks almost to reproach the victim and make excuses for her murderer!

REFLECTIONS
upon the untimely end of
ELIZA MORROW
and the awful fate of
RICHARD THORLEY

Richard Thorley was hanged at Derby, Friday, 11 April 1862, for the Wilful Murder of Eliza Morrow on Thursday, 13 February 1862, to whom he was paying his addresses, but which she had latterly desired to be discontinued.

Young men and maidens! list, I pray
To what I'm going to preach;
And when you've heard me, do not say,
"Stern facts can never teach."

Poor Richard Thorley's dead, and gone
Into another world;

Then let not vengeful thoughts upon
His mis-spent life be hurl'd.

Much good he had within his mind,
For all its rough outside
To wife and mother truly kind,
As to his destin'd bride.

And though his faults were very great,
There's some excuse for all,
Which formed his manhood's fatal state,
And brought his dreadful fall.

No father's arm, of lawful power,
Control'd his ripening age,
Till habits, formed from hour to hour,
Should make his manhood sage.

Thoughtless and gay, he joined the ring,
Round mirth and ribald laughter,
With those, who to the wild waves fling,
All thoughts of an hereafter.

And one he woo'd in honest heart,
And lov'd but to his sorrow,
Smil'd as she barb'd the poison'd dart -
Poor lost Eliza Morrow.

How little could her silly pride
Foresee so sad an end,
Or sure she would have gently tried
That erring soul to mend.

Better than taunt or cruel jeer,
Had been that purpose, wise -
Love might have chang'd his mad career,
But now, a felon dies!

O! Woman! let not vain desires
Your tender bosoms stir,
For ah! these dark infernal fires
Have made a murderer.

Be to your nature nobly true,
In feeling and behaviour
Till God in you, shall form anew,
Man's help-meet, guide and saviour.

FRANZ MULLER murdered Thomas Briggs, the first such crime on a railway train; he was hanged by William Calcraft on 14 November 1864.

Within a dark and dreary dungeon
In grief and anguish now I lie
For a base and dreadful murder,
In youth and vigour I must die.
Far from home and far from kindred,
In grief and sorrow I deplore,
Unhappy man, on a foreign land,
I die at the age of twenty-four.

When I had done that dreadful murder
I sailed across the raging main;
Justice followed poor Franz Muller,
For the murder in the railway train.

That fatal night I was determined,
Poor Thomas Briggs to rob and slay,
And in that fatal railway carriage,
That night, I took his life away.
His crimson gore did stain the carriage,
I threw him from the same, alack!
I on the railway left him bleeding,
I robbed him of his watch and hat.

When I poor Thomas Briggs did murder,
I went across the briny sea,
And I was fully then determined,
To reach New York, in America.
My guilty soul was pierced with anguish,
When the stormy winds did roar,
And justice ready was to seize me,
Before I reached Columbia's shore.

Poor Brigg's goods were found upon me,

Sufficient evidence you see,
To bring me to the bar of Newgate,
And hang me on the fatal tree;
Oh! was there ever such excitement,
Or will there ever be again,
As there has been with poor Franz Muller
For the murder in the railway train.

My noble council pleaded for me,
And done their best my life to save,
A British jury found me guilty,
I must lie in a murderer's grave;
Numbers thought they'd not convict me,
When at the bar they did me try,
Oh! God above, look down, in pity,
My fate is sealed, and I must die!

Oh, I must die a malefactor,
In front of Newgate's dismal door,
In the midst of health and vigour,
Aged only twenty-four.
I never thought the law would take me,
When I sailed o'er the raging main,
All my courage did forsake me -
A murderer in the railway train.

Swift the moments are approaching,
On the gallows I must die,
The cruel hangman stands before me,
On the wretched tree so high,
I am full of grief and anguish,
Full of sorrow, care and pain -
A warning taken by poor Franz Muller,
The murderer in the railway train.

JAMES LONGHURST murdered seven-year-old Jane Sax; he was hanged by William Calcraft 16 April 1867.

Good people all I pray draw near
And my sad history you soon shall hear
And when the same I do relate,
I trust you will a warning take.

At Horsemonger-lane on the scaffold high,
For a cruel murder I was doomed to die,
James Longhurst, it is my name,
I've brought myself to grief and shame,
Through the dreadful deed that I had done,
At Churchill-field near Guildford town.

It was last June, the twenty-eighth,
I did this deed as I now state,
An innocent child I did there slay,
And with a knife took her life away.

Poor Jane Sax, on that fatal day-
A child scarce seven years of age;
In Churchill-field I her did meet,
And shamefully did her illtreat.

Then coward-like I drew my knife,
To rob this helpless child of life;
I stabbed her in the throat – her blood did pour -
Then left her weltering in her gore.

Then I was taken for this cruel deed,
And sent for trial as you may read,
At Kingston assizes, tried and cast,
Oh, would I could recall the past.

She cried for help, did poor little Jane,
David Edsor to her assistance came,
Whilst I, a guilty wretch did stand,
And licked her blood from off my hand.

The judge said, James Longhurst you are guilty found,
You will go from here to London town,
And there you'll die a death of shame,
And meet your fate at Horsemonger-lane.

While I lay in my prison cell,
My state of mind, no tongue can tell,
I could not rest by day or night,
Poor Jane was always in my sight.

My tender parents came to visit me,
My heart was breaking their grief to see,
Tears from their eyes did in torrents fall,
While for mercy to my God did call.

I hope that none will them upbraid,
While I am in my silent grave,
Farewell to all – the bell doth toll,
Have mercy, God, on my sinful soul.'

MICHAEL BARRETT a Fenian found guilty of causing an explosion that resulted in many deaths and casualties; he was hanged by William Calcraft 26 May 1868, the last execution carried out in public.

Throughout the kingdom, among high and low
A great excitement has long been caused,
Of a dreadful crime – horrible to tell,
The fatal explosion at Clerkenwell.

Out of the seven they for crime did try,
One Michael Barratt is condemned to die.

Patrick Mullany was a witness made,
A military tailor he was by trade
To save himself, he evidence gave,
Which he his neck has saved.

The dreadful affair was at Clerkenwell,
In a neighbourhood were poor folks did dwell,
Caused great destruction – it many killed;
Houses fell – some wounded – and much blood was spilled.

The informers swore, and others beside,
When the prisoners, all at the bar was tried;
That by Michael Barratt the deed was done,
And from the spot did to Scotland run.

He was taken in Glasgow and to London brought,
He says of the crime he never thought,
He would not be guilty of such a deed,
But he was convicted as we may read.

When before a jury he had been tried,
That he was guilty he strongly denied;
And to the judge he aloud did say,
They had wrongfully taken his life away.

But Barrett's pleading was all in vain,
He could no mercy at all obtain,
The judge said, taken back you must be,
And from thence be hanged up to the tree.

Now Michael Barratt is doomed to die,
For the crime of murder on a tree so high;
He says Mullany caused his downfall,
May God have mercy upon his soul.

The jury said, when they did retire,
That Michael Barratt did the powder fire;
Convinced they were that he did the work,
To rescue two prisoners, Casey and Burke.

Though Michael Barratt is condemned to die,
The dreadful deed he strongly does deny,
There is One above who all secrets know,
He can tell whether Barratt is guilty or no.

The witnesses were examined strict,
By their evidence they did him convict,
And for wilful murder he is doomed to die,
In front of Newgate on the gallows high.

We hope all men will a warning take,
And long remember poor Barratt's fate;
We find it difficult throughout the land,
For man to even trust his fellow-man.

A dreadful tale we'll have long to tell,
The fatal explosion at Clerkenwell.

APPENDIX FOUR

OTHER EXECUTIONERS AND THEIR IDIOSYNCRASIES

Calcraft, with his short drop method, was not unique in having personal eccentricities and failures; as more fully described in my *Lords of the Scaffold*, reprinted by the present publishers in 2001, executioners, despite their profession, were as human and as vulnerable to Fate as the rest of us. For instance;

English executioner John Thrift was so soft-hearted that he wept as he wielded the axe while decapitating Scottish Lords in 1747, which hardly improved his aim.

William Marvell was later convicted for theft, two of his sons were hanged and a third transported to the colonies.

Edward Barlow, caught stealing a horse, was sentenced to be hanged, but the sentence was commuted to ten years in prison, living 'over the shop' as it were – being allowed out to perform hangings and floggings.

French executioner Gabriel Sanson, a member of the famous dynasty of French executioners, neglected to look where he was putting his feet, slipped on the blood-soaked boards of the guillotine scaffold, fell off the platform and broke his neck.

Henri-Clement Sanson lost his job when, an execution being unexpectedly due to take place, it was found that he had got into debt and had pawned the guillotine.

When young, Charles-Henri Sanson had been a secret admirer of Mme Du Barry – yet during the French Revolution he had to restrain her frantic struggles on the scaffold and then guillotine her.

German executioner Friedrich had a profitable sideline making counterfeit coins; alas he was caught and burned alive for the crime.

Another compatriot, hangman Hans, plotted against the authorities and was beheaded by his own assistant.

Meister Valtin was so inaccurate that three strokes of the execution sword were necessary to behead the poor woman strapped in the chair.

Mary, Queen of Scots, was not decapitated until Simon Bull had delivered two blows of the axe, then had to sever a little gristle with his knife.

Jack Ketch struck James, Duke of Monmouth two blows with the axe and would have given up had he not been threatened by the crowd; a further three blows were then required to complete the beheading.

Hangman Ned Dennis, sentenced to death for joining a riot in the City, pleaded that his son be allowed to succeed him as executioner, until it was pointed out that in that case a son would have to hang his own father! Dennis was later reprieved due to the backlog of executions.

James Berry hanged Robert Goodale on 30 November 1885; unlike Calcraft, he gave too *long* a drop; on going down into the pit afterwards, the executioner was faced with a ghastly sight, the head having been completely severed, and lying some distance away from the torso.

So although dying by slow strangulation on Calcraft's short rope, perhaps his victims could nevertheless count themselves lucky!

SELECT BIBLIOGRAPHY

ABBOTT, G. *Book of Executions* (Headline 1994)

ABBOTT, G. *Lords of the Scaffold* (Headline 1991, Dobby 2001)

ABBOTT, G. *Rack, Rope and Red-Hot Pincers* (Headline 1993, Dobby 2002)

ANDREWS, W. *Bygone Punishments* (Philip Allan 1899)

ANDREWS, W. *Old Time Punishments* (Andrews & Co. 1890)

ANON. *Doings in London* (Hodgson, 1828)

ANON. *The Life and Recollections of William Calcraft, The Hangman* (London 1880)

BALL, J.M. *The Sack-'em-Up Men* (Oliver & Boyd 1928)

BAILEY, J.B. *Diary of a Resurrectionist* (Swan Sonnenschein 1896)

BARRINGTON, S. *Broadsheets, Ballads and Epitaphs* (Harrison, 1904)

BERRY, J. *My Experiences as an Executioner* (Percy Lund, 1892)

BLEAKLEY, J. *Hangmen of England* (Chapman & Hall, 1929)

CARMENT, J. *Glimpses of the Olden Times* (Jackson 1893)

DAVEY, R. *Pageant of London* (Methuen 1906)

DUFF, C. *A Handbook on Hanging* (Melrose 1938)

EDEN HOOPER *History of Newgate and the Old Bailey* (1909)

GORDON, C. *The Old Bailey & Newgate* (Fisher Unwin 1902)

HOOPER, W. *History of Newgate & the Old Bailey* (1909)

JOHNSON, T. *A Gossiping Book about Lancaster Castle* (1893)

JONES, T.A. *Without my Wig* (Brython Press 1939)

MACGREGOR, G. *The History of Burke and Hare* (Morison 1884)

Select Bibliography 189

MACKAY, J. *History of the Burgh of Canongate* (Anderson/ Ferrier 1900)

MARKS, A. *Tyburn Tree, its History & Annals* (Brown, Langham,1908)

MAYHEW/BINNEY *The Criminal Prisons of London* (Griffin, Bohn 1862)

MILLER, T. *Sketches of London* (Nat. Illus. Library 1852)

OGDEN, S. *Death by the Rope* (Brendon, 1901)

PETTIFER, E.W. *Punishments of Former Days* (1939)

SCOTT, G.R. *The History of Capital Punishment* (Torchstream 1950)

SWAIN, J. *Pleasures of the Torture Chamber* (Douglas 1931)

THORNBURY, R. *Old & New London* (Cassell, Petter & Galpin, 1874-93)

TIMBS, J. *Romance of London* (Warne, 1865)

TOD, T.M. *The Scots Black Kalendar* (Munro & Scott 1938)

TURNER, C.H. *The Inhumanists* (Ousley Ltd. 1932)

WILLIAMSON, M.G. *Edinburgh* (Methuen, 1906)

Chronicles of Crime (Camden, Pelham, 1887)

Newgate Calendar & Criminal Recorder (Miles & Co. 1891)

Neckverse and Worse (Anon. 1903)

Tyburn Gallows (London County Council 1909)

The Illustrated Police News series

Mme Tussaud's Exhibition Guide (1936)

The Hangman's Record 1601-1909

The Penny Magazine Series (1836)

INDEX

Albert, Prince 36
Alexandra, Princess of Denmark 74
Allen, William O'Meara 122, 123, 124, 160, 161, 162
Anderson, Robert - see Evans, Evan
Appleton, Mr. 158
Appleton, Rev. 99
Armstrong, hangman 122, 123
Ashburner, John 75
Atkinson, Mrs. 95, 97

Ballantyne, Serjeant-at-Law 82
Bannister, Rev. 58
Barlow, Edward, hangman 186
Barnes, Phoebe 58, 59
Barrett, Michael 128 *et seq.*, 184, 185
Barton, James 117, 118
Barton, Mrs. 142
Bell, Joseph 116, 117
Bell, Sarah 125
Berry, James, hangman 187
Bishop, John 20 *et seq.*, 153 *et seq.*
Blackwood, Helen 63, 64
Blanco (pirate) 102, 103, 104
Blantyre, Lady 47
Bodier, Louis 120
Booth, John 78
Bont, Father 150
Boss, Anne 140
Bousfield, William 69, 70, 120
Bowler, T &W 57

Bow Street Police Station 20
Bowling, Thomas 97, 98, 99
Boyd, Alexander 63
Boyd, William 139
Bradford, Francis 144
Brett, Sergeant 122, 160, 161
Briggs, Thomas 106.130, 181, 182
Britten, George 139
Brown, Andrew 115, 116
Brown, Elizabeth Martha 71, 72
Brown, Hannah 29, 30, 164, 165
Brunel, Isambard Kingdom 38
Brunt, John Thomas 2
Bull, Simon, hangman 187
Burke, Mary Ann 110
Burke, Richard O'Sullivan 128
Burke, Stephen 109, 110
Burke, William 19, 20, 21
Butcher, Lydia Susannah 36
Buton, Anne 26

Calcraft, Louise 4 *passim.*
Calcraft, Muriel 54
Calcraft, Sarah 52, 53, 54
Calcraft, Thomas 54
Cantwell, Canon 123
Capital Punishment Within Prison Law 134
Cappel, Dr. Louis 108
Camell, Sarah 96, 97
Carr, Daniel 98
Carver, Rev. 33
Cassidy, James 83
Catnach, James 163
Chalmers, George 141

Index 191

Chamberlain, Thomas 151
Charles, Luke 100, 101
Charles, Mary 189
Cheshire, Thomas, hangman 1 et seq.
Chestney, Eliza 43
Christie, George 62
Connor, James 150, 151
Cook, Edward 26
Cook, Thomas 88
Corrigan, Thomas 151
Cotton, Charles Edward 147
Cotton, Frederick 146
Cotton, Mary Ann 145 et seq.
Couvoisier, François Benjamin 33 et seq.
Coventry, Lord 34
Cowan, Jeannette Tassie 141, 142
Cumming, William 66, 67
Cunningham, Alexander 67
Cunningham (boy) 158
Cunningham, Janet 67

Davis, Rev. 108
Davison, William 3
Deas, Lord Justice 73, 79, 90, 148
Deasy, Captain 122, 124, 161
Death, Maria 139
Death, Robert 107
Dennis, Ned, hangman 187
Dickens, Charles 35, 48, 49, 50, 51
Dixon, Mr. 94, 97
Dolan, John 138, 139
Donahoe, Daniel 144
Dunn, Julia 100, 101
Durrano (pirate) 102, 103, 104

Elizabeth 1, Queen 54
Elliot, Augustus 145
Elliotson, Dr. 38
Emmeran, Saint 135
Emms, Walter Thomas 82, 83

Emsley, Mary 82, 83
Evans, David 17, 18, 150
Evans, Evan (aka Robert), hangman 71
Eyre, Emma 83

Faherty, Michael 126, 127
Fauntleroy, Henry 2
Ferrari, Carlo 20, 153 et seq.
Ferrers, Earl 12
FitzClarence, Lord Adolphus 34
Ford, Ellen 100, 101
Foxton (aka Foxen, Foxon), James, hangman 1 et seq.
Friedrich, hangman 187

Gadd, Father 123, 124, 127
Gaffrey, James 150
Gardiner, William 36
Gay, William 29
George IV 18
Girdwood, Mr. 13
Godwin, James 151
Good, Daniel 36 et seq., 165, 166, 167
Goodale, Robert 187
Grace, WG 143
Greenacre, James 29 et seq., 164
Greenwood, James 8, 9
Greig, John 115
Grime, James 117, 118
Grime, Thomas 117, 118
Grossmith, Mrs. 138

Hanmer, Mary 126
Hannah, Ann 90
Hans, hangman 187
Hansom, Joseph Aloysius 28
Hardman, Edward 74 et seq.
Hardman, Ellen 74, 75
Hardy, Thomas 72
Hare, William 19, 20, 21
Hart, Sarah 39, 40
Hartley, Benjamin 98, 99

Hearson, George 19
Heenan, John 81
Henrichson, Mrs. 45
Henrichson, Henry George 45
Henrichson, John Alfred 45
Hibner, Esther 16, 17, 69, 120
Hill, Rowland 22
Hill, William 20
Hinson, Frederick 139
Holden, William 74
Holloway, John 24, 25
Holmes, Charles 143, 144
Hope, Lord 74
Horsemonger Lane Gaol 6 passim
Huelin, Elias - see Llewellyn
Hughes, Thomas Alvarez 14, 15
Hunt, William 44
Huskisson, William 19
Hussey, Rev. James 130

Ilkeston Parricide, see Smith, George
Ings, James 2

James, Duke of Monmouth 187
Jermy, Isaac 43
Jermy, Jermy 43
Johnson, Dr. Samuel 134, 135
Jones, Henry 42
Jones, Jane 36, 37, 165, 166, 167
Jump, William 92

Keehan, Catherine 138
Kelly, Captain 122, 124, 161, 162
Ketch, Jack, hangman 187
Kidden, Frances 124
Knackers Act 7

Lancaster Castle 64
Larkin, Philip 122, 123, 124, 160, 161, 162

Leone (pirate) 102, 103, 104
Leslie, William 18
Littledale, Mr. Justice 21
Llewellyn, Rev. Elias 140
Longhurst, James 119, 120, 182, 183, 184
Lopez (pirate) 102, 103, 104
Lucas, Elias 55, 56, 57, 170
Lucas, Susan 55, 56
Lunnay, Patrick 83

Mackay, Alexander 138
Manning, Frederick 46 *et seq.*
Manning, Maria 46 *et seq.*
Marshall, Emmanuel 140
Marvell, William 186
Marwood, William 150, 151
Mary, Queen of Scots 187
Mason, Mary Ann 67, 68
Mason, Mr. 79, 80
Matthews, Mr. 107
Mawer, Peter 94, 97
Maxwell, Margaret 61
Maxwell, Thomas 73, 74
May, James 20 *et seq.*, 155 *et seq.*
Maynard, Thomas 18
M'Cloud, Mary 111, 112
McConville, John 138, 139
McEwan, Alexander 116
M'Farlane, Hans Smith 63, 64
M'Lean, Peter 73, 74
McPhail, Duncan 97, 98, 99
Meadows, Joseph 67, 68
Mellor, Evan 91
Metcalfe, William 150
Mill, Andrew 62
Millar, Walter 140
Miller, John 141
Mills, Thomas 20
Montgomery, Agnes 79
Moore, Thomas 145
Morrow, Eliza 86, 87, 179, 180
Mowbray, William 145
Mullany, Patrick 128

Muller, Franz 107, 108, 109, 130, 181, 182
Mullins, James 82, 83
Murdoch, John, hangman 46
Murray, David 14

Natrass, James 146
Nelson, Admiral Lord Horatio 39
Newet, John Cox 151
Newgate Prison 3 *passim*
Newitt, William 18
Northampton County Gaol 12
North Prison, Glasgow 63
Norwich Prison 43

Oates, Agnes 120
O'Brien (*aka* Gould), Michael 122, 123, 124, 160, 161, 162
O'Connor, Patrick 46, 47, 50
Old Bailey Central Criminal Court 7 *passim*
Oliver, Mrs. 142, 143
Orridge, Mr. 57
Owen, John 140

Paget, Lord 34
Palmer, Dr. William 71
Palmer, Samuel 36
Parr, Mary 45
Partridge, Mr. 20
Pedder, Richard 64, 65, 66
Peddie, hangman 73
Peel, Sir Robert 17
Perry, Stephen 42
Pigburn, Fanny 156, 157, 158
Pitts, John 163
Plow, Rev. 125
Pope, Dr. 142
Prince of Wales 74
Pritchard, Dr. Edward William 111 *et seq.*
Pritchard, Mary Jane(Minnie) 111, 112

Quick, Father 123
Quick-Manning, John 147

Ralph, Police Sergeant 141
Reader, Mary 56, 57, 171
Reid (*aka* Timney), Mary 90, 91
Reilly, John (*aka* 'Sodger') 99, 100
Rice, Peter 122
Robb, James 46
Roberts, Rev. 57
Robinson, James 146, 147
Rogers, Henry 77, 78, 171, 172
Rose, Andrew 77, 78
Rose, Thomas 37
Ross, Barbara 62
Ross, Eliza 25 *et seq.*
Ross, Ned. 26, 27
Rowland, Ann 142
Rush, James Bloomfield 43, 167, 168, 169
Russell, Lord William. 33

Sandford, Emily 43, 44
Sanson, Charles-Henri 186
Sanson, Gabriel 186
Sanson, Henri-Clement 186
Sax, Jane 119, 182, 183, 184
Sayers, Tom 81
Scanlan, Michael 61, 62
Scanlan, Peter 61, 62
Scobbie, Thomas 148, 149
Scott, Samuel 35
Shakespeare, William 26
Shears, Mary 150
Shiel, Quelaz 36
Shields, porter 157, 158
Shillibeer, George 17
Sim, Mr. 84, 85
Smith, George 83 *et seq.*, 172 *et seq.*
Smith, George (of Dudley), hangman 71, 136, 138, 145
Smith, Jane 125

Smith, Joseph 83, 84, 172 *et seq.*
Smith, Mary 46
Soames, Mrs. 94, 95, 97
South, Mr. 158
South Prison, Glasgow 100
Stanford, Stephen 18
Stock, George 144
Stone, Mr. 24
Streeter, Mary 80, 81
Sussex, HRH Duke of 21, 36
Swan, Joseph 83

Tawell, John 40, 41
Taylor, Jane 112
Taylor, Martha 91, 92
Taylor, William Robert 91, 92, 93
Thackeray, William Makepeace 13, 34, 35
Thistlewood, Arthur 2
Thomas, Sarah Harriett 42, 69
Thompson, John (*aka* Peter Walker) 79, 80
Thompson, William 118
Thorley, Richard 86, 87, 88, 179, 180
Thrift, John, hangman 186
Thurtell, James 12
Tidd, Richard 3
Tindal, Chief Justice 21
Tooth, James 144
Tower of London 3 *passim*
Trainer, Philip 138
Treason Act 7
Turner, Anthony 58, 59, 60
Tussaud, Mme. 8 *passim*

Usnea 24

Vagrancy Act 7
Valtin, hangman 187
Vaughan, Mr. Baron 21
Vernon Street Prison, Derby 84, 87
Vessey, Detective Sergeant 87
Victoria, Queen 32 *passim*

Walne, Ann 97, 98
Walsh, Catherine 26, 27
Walsh, Station Master 136
Ward, George 92, 93
Ward, George (murdered by Cotton) 146
Ward, John 138
Waters, Margaret 141, 142, 143
Watts (pirate) 102, 103, 104
Weatherill, Miles 125, 126, 127
Wells, Thomas 136, 141
Whidburn, Dr. 94, 95
Whipping of Female Offenders Abolition Act 7
Whiteley, William 97
Wiggins, John 120, 121
Willes, Mr. Justice 84
William IV 18, 32, 102
Williams (*aka* Head), Thomas 20 *et seq.*, 153 *et seq.*
Williams, hangman 20
Williams, John 62, 63
Williams, Rhoda 153 *et seq.*
Wilson, Catherine 93 *et seq.*
Wilson, John Gleeson 45, 169, 170
Woods, George 97, 98, 99

Youngman, William Godfrey 80, 81